4/16
15

327.73 G

THE UNQUIET FRONTIER

THE UNQUIET FRONTIER

Rising Rivals, Vulnerable Allies,
and the Crisis of American Power

JAKUB J. GRYGIEL
A. WESS MITCHELL

PRINCETON UNIVERSITY PRESS
PRINCETON AND OXFORD

Copyright © 2016 by Princeton University Press
Published by Princeton University Press, 41 William Street, Princeton,
New Jersey 08540
In the United Kingdom: Princeton University Press, 6 Oxford Street,
Woodstock, Oxfordshire OX20 1TW
press.princeton.edu
Jacket image courtesy of Shutterstock / Typeface by Lost Type
All Rights Reserved
ISBN 978-0-691-16375-8
Library of Congress Control Number 2015954474
British Library Cataloging-in-Publication Data is available
This book has been composed in Sabon Next LT & ScalaSansOT
Printed on acid-free paper. ∞
Printed in the United States of America
1 3 5 7 9 10 8 6 4 2

FOR
PRIYA
AND
ELIZABETH

CONTENTS

ILLUSTRATIONS

ACKNOWLEDGMENTS

In the many months since we began the research that led to this book we have formed debts too extensive to repay here. We are especially grateful to Nadia Schadlow for her encouragement, ideas, and support, as well as to her colleagues at the Smith Richardson Foundation, Marin Strmecki and Allan Song, for providing the grants to the Center for European Policy Analysis (CEPA) where this project was conceived, researched, and written. We are indebted to CEPA chairman Larry Hirsch for his friendship and tireless commitment to deepening U.S. strategic thinking to navigate a more dangerous world. School of Advanced International Studies (SAIS) colleagues Charles Doran and Eliot Cohen heard various iterations of arguments presented here and offered support and comments. SAIS deans Vali Nasr and John Harrington also made possible a sabbatical for Jakub that helped when we made our final writing push.

This book would not have come into being without Adam Garfinkle's agreement to publish an early version of the argument as an article in *The American Interest*. We're also grateful to *The National Interest* for publishing a subsequent article in which many of the recommendations in this book were first aired. We received critical appraisals and suggestions from Aaron Friedberg and Colin Dueck that helped to sharpen key parts of our argument. We are grateful to our colleagues at CEPA, especially Peter Doran and Ilona Teleki, for creating a supportive intellectual environment for creative thinking about Central and Eastern European and global geopolitics, as well as to Milda Boyce at CEPA and Starr Lee at SAIS-JHU for seamless administration, planning, and trips.

A small army of CEPA research assistants fielded an array of unquenchable inquiries. We're grateful to Leah Scheunemann for her enthusiasm and efficiency in tracking down everything from Asian defense expenditures to arcane trivia on interwar diplomacy. Jennifer Hill collected much of the data on which our main security sections were built, and Octavian Manea provided help with international military comparisons. Victoria Siegelman, Michal Harmata, Stephanie Peng, Koen Maaskant, and Virginijus Sinkevičius helped with notes and charts, and Alexander Bellah sharpened our understanding of Chinese military thinking. This book would not have seen the light of day without the support of Eric Crahan and the team at Princeton University Press, Ben Pokross and Ali Parrington. Anita O'Brien helped with the copyediting and Maria DenBoer compiled the index. Finally, we would like to thank the numerous officials in allied capitals in East Asia and Central and Eastern Europe as well as colleagues in Washington for providing the sobering insights on the disarranged state of global geopolitics that gave us the understanding and urgency to write this book.

NOTE TO READERS

Two things have changed since we began writing this book. First, the pace of the geopolitical dynamics that we set out to describe has accelerated. Rising powers have become more aggressive, U.S. allies have become more nervous, and the United States has found itself confronted with crises in multiple regional theaters. Second, the risk of war between revisionist powers and the United States and its allies has become more real. The ingredients for a military confrontation between great powers—an event that has not occurred since the 1940s and that has been virtually unthinkable for the past twenty-five years—now exist in the western Pacific and in Central and Eastern Europe, and the conditions for a major regional war are present in the Persian Gulf. From the vantage point of 2015, the probing behavior on the part of America's rivals as well as the coping responses of frontline allies that are described in this book have become less theoretical or futuristic. Our argument is becoming a reality, and the speed and seriousness of events support our thesis. While this is reassuring for us as authors, it is worrisome for U.S. policy makers concerned with ensuring national security.

THE UNQUIET FRONTIER

CHAPTER 1

INTRODUCTION: AMERICAN POWER AT THE GLOBAL FRONTIER

It is by the combined efforts of the weak, to resist the reign of force and constant wrong, that in the rapid change but slow progress of four hundred years, liberty has been preserved and finally understood.
—Lord Acton

What is the value of allies at the outer frontier of American power? Since the end of the Second World War, the United States has maintained a network of alliances with vulnerable states situated near the strategic crossroads, choke points, and arteries of the world's major regions. In East Asia, Washington has built formal and informal security relationships with island and coastal states dotting the Asian mainland: South Korea, Taiwan, Singapore, Thailand, the Philippines, as well as midsized offshore powers Japan and Australia. In the Middle East, it has maintained a special relationship with democratic ally Israel and security links with moderate Arab states Kuwait, Qatar, Bahrain, Saudi Arabia, and United Arab Emirates (UAE). And in East-Central Europe, in the period since the Cold War, the United States has formed alliances with the group of mostly small, post-communist states—Estonia, Latvia, Lithuania, Poland, Czech Republic, Slovakia, Hungary, Romania, and Bulgaria—that line the Baltic-to-Black-Sea corridor between Germany and Russia.

Figure 1.1. U.S. frontier allies worldwide.

Despite their obvious geographic and political dissimilarities, these three regional clusters of U.S. allies share a number of important strategic characteristics (see figure 1.1). All are composed of small and midsized powers (most have between five and fifty million inhabitants and small landmass). Most are democracies and free market economies deeply invested in the Bretton Woods global economic and institutional framework. All, to a greater extent than other U.S. allies, occupy strategically important global real estate along three of the world's most contested geopolitical fault lines. Most sit near a maritime choke point or critical land corridor: the Asian littoral routes (South China Sea, North China Sea, Sea of Japan, Straits of Taiwan, Straits of Malacca); the Persian Gulf and eastern Mediterranean;

and the Baltic and Black Seas and space connecting them that underpins the stability of the western Eurasian littoral.

Perhaps most important from a twenty-first-century U.S. strategic perspective, all these allies are located in close proximity to larger, historically predatory powers—China, Iran, and Russia, respectively—that are international competitors to the United States and within whose respective spheres of influence they would likely fall, should they lose some or all of their strategic independence. None of these states is militarily powerful; with the important exceptions of Japan and Israel, they lack a realistic prospect for military self-sufficiency in any protracted crisis. As a result, all look to the United States, either explicitly or implicitly, to act as the ultimate guarantor of their national independence and security provider of last resort.

The view has begun to take root in the United States that these sprawling alliances are a liability—either because of the costs that they impose through the necessity of maintaining a large military and overseas bases or because of the perils of entrapment in conflicts involving faraway disputes. Maintaining extensive, expensive, and binding relationships with exposed and militarily weak states located near large rivals, we are told, will cause more problems than they are worth in the geopolitics of the twenty-first century. Citing nineteenth-century Britain's alleged aloofness to foreign states, domestic critics of alliances counsel Washington to spurn continental commitments to small and needy allies. Echoing Prussian chancellor Otto von Bismarck, these critics warn that the United States must avoid intervening in conflicts that aren't "worth the bones of a single Pomeranian grenadier," whether that conflict be in Estonia or in the South China Sea.

But these views are wrong—and dangerous. For the past sixty years U.S. foreign policy has pursued exactly the opposite course, and for good reason. The United States has deliberately cultivated bilateral security linkages with small, otherwise defenseless states strewn across the world's most hotly contested regions, militarily building them up and even providing overt guarantees to them. In fact, it has often seemed to value these states precisely *because of* their dangerous locations. During the Cold War America's overriding imperative of containing the Soviet Union lent geopolitical value to relationships with even the weakest allies, which in turn utilized U.S. support to strengthen regional bulwarks against the spread of communist influence. In the unipolar landscape that followed, the United States surprised many foreign policy analysts by not only *not* dismantling this globe-circling alliance network (as would be expected of a great power after winning a major war) but actually expanding it through the recruitment of new allies from among the former communist zone of Central and Eastern Europe (CEE). In both structural environments, allies have been the "glue" of the U.S.-led global order: in the Cold War by containing the Soviet Union and in the post–Cold War period by sustaining the benefits of stability and prosperity that the Cold War victory helped to create.

These alliances have not been cheap for America to maintain, in either financial or strategic terms. To a greater extent than in relationships with large, wealthy, insulated states like Britain, Germany, or Australia, American patronage of frontier states like Poland, Israel, and Taiwan entails potential strategic costs, insofar as such states lie at the outer reaches of American power and require recurrent demonstrations of physical support vis-à-vis would-be aggressors. To underwrite the independence and security of these states, the United States has for decades made available a wide array of support that includes both "normal" alliance mechanisms—formal or informal security guarantees, military basing, coverage under the U.S. nuclear umbrella—as well as other special forms of support targeted to the needs of these states, such as military funding, troop exercises, forward naval deployments, technology transfers, access to special U.S. weapons, and various forms of economic, political, and military aid. In the diplomatic realm, Washington has paid a kind of "sponsorship premium" for these states, providing backing and support in the regional disputes in which many inevitably find themselves embroiled. The more exposed the ally, the higher this sponsorship premium is.

Not surprisingly, critics of an active U.S. foreign policy have often complained about the expense and risk required for maintaining these alliances.[1] But despite this criticism, America's commitment to these states has remained steady for the better part of seventy years, making it one of the most consistent tenets of modern U.S. foreign policy. And in both strategic and economic terms, it would be hard to argue that the United States has not gotten a good return on this investment. By exerting a strong, benign presence in formerly unstable regions, U.S. patronage of alliances in East Asia, the Middle East, and East-Central Europe has helped to contain and deter the ambitions of large rivals, suppress regional conflicts, keep crucial trade routes open, and promote democracy and rule of law in historic conflict zones. In East Asia, the U.S. presence facilitated pathways of financial investment that contributed to the creation of some of the world's most dynamic economies and major engines of global growth while guarding the sea-lanes through which the majority of U.S.-bound energy supplies and consumer goods pass. In East-Central Europe, U.S. efforts to propel NATO and European Union (EU) expansion effectively eliminated the geopolitical vacuum that had helped to generate the conditions for three global wars in the twentieth century—two hot and one cold. And in the Middle East, U.S. engagement has helped to contain regional cycles of instability and prevent their spillover into global energy markets and the American homeland. In both the bipolar and unipolar international settings, allies have been indispensable to maintaining the global order that has allowed for the peace and prosperity of the "American" century.

Part of the reason U.S. patronage of states in these regions has been so successful is that U.S. allies and potential challengers have understood that it is unlikely to change suddenly, in large part because of how deeply encoded in contemporary American strategic thinking has been the support of small allies. Since the turn of the twentieth century the United States has invested its strategic resources in a combination of naval power and, after two world wars, "defense in depth" through a presence in the Eurasian littorals—what the mid-twentieth-century American strategist Nicholas Spykman called the global "rimland" (see figure 1.2). This pattern of forward engagement is not only the basis for American investment in allies located in the three hinge-point regions, it is a central tenet of U.S. foreign policy. Building on this foundation, America, though primarily a maritime power like Britain, has avoided the island dilemma of being perceived as fickle, retiring, and unreliable—in short, of becoming a second "perfidious Albion."

Figure 1.2. Spykman's rimlands.
Source: Mark R. Polelle, *Raising Cartographic Consciousness: The Social and Foreign Policy Vision of Geopolitics in the Twentieth Century* (Lanham, MD: Lexington Books, 1999), 118.

But there are signs that America may be beginning to rethink its approach to alliances. In recent years U.S. policy makers' view of the relative costs and benefits of maintaining far-flung small-ally networks has begun to shift. The change is partly fueled by adjustments in global geopolitics and the "rise" or resurgence of revisionist states, many of which claim to have historic spheres of influence that overlap with the regions where America's alliance obligations are highest and its strategic reach most constrained. Another driver has been the changing U.S. economic landscape and constraints on the U.S. defense budget, which call into question whether the United States will continue to maintain the force structures that have made its geographically widespread alliances possible to begin with. Finally, and perhaps most important, Washington appears to be deprioritizing many of its longest-standing relationships with traditional allies in pursuit of grand bargains with large-power rivals, if necessary over the heads of its allies.

The net effect of these changes in the geopolitical, economic, and political realms has been to challenge the central paradigm on which the United States has based its strategy for managing global alliances since the Second World War. What value do alliances hold for America in the twenty-first century? Do the benefits of alliances that led the United States to accumulate them during bipolarity and unipolarity still apply under conditions of contested primacy? How does a great power that has accumulated extensive small-power security commitments maintain them when the geopolitical landscape becomes more competitive? What do geopolitically vulnerable allies like Israel, Poland, or Taiwan have to offer America amid the rise of large powers? Is it still worth paying the economic and strategic costs to provide for their security? If so, how should the United States rank the importance of the weapons, bases, and funding that sustain these alliances alongside other national security priorities in an era of constricted budgets? Would the United States be better off reducing its commitments to these states and maintaining a freer hand in global politics, as critics claim?

These are the kinds of questions that are likely to confront American diplomats and strategists with growing frequency—and urgency—in the years ahead, as the shift from the post–Cold War global order accelerates. Such questions are not new in the history of international politics, but they are relatively unfamiliar to the U.S. policy establishment, which has arguably not had to reexamine the fundamentals of American grand strategy in many decades. In recent years Washington has been slow to study the geopolitical changes that are under way in the world and respond to them in a strategic way. Increasingly the U.S. foreign policy agenda seems to be driven by a combination of crisis management—Iran, Syria, North Korea—and a political agenda that takes the basic contours of the U.S.-led international system for granted and focuses on achieving laudable but unrealistic and outright silly goals, such as global nuclear disarmament. Both approaches tend to magnify the apparent advantages of partnering with large powers on ad hoc issues as the preferred template for U.S. foreign policy over the near term while deferring for a later day bigger questions about how to sustain U.S. leadership in the international order.

But American grand strategy cannot remain on autopilot forever—geopolitics is forcing its way onto the agenda. Rivals and allies of the United States alike perceive that changes are afoot in America's capabilities and comportment as a great power and are responding purposefully to the opportunities and threats that these changes present. This is partly driven by the hypothesis of American "decline." In many of the world's capitals, it is taken as an article of faith that the United States is slipping from its decades-long position of global preeminence and that the long-standing U.S.-led international system will eventually give way to a multipolar global power configuration. It is also driven by the perception that, declining or not, the United States is simply not interested in maintaining the stability of frontier regions—that the alliances it inherited from previous eras will be a net liability in an age of more fluid geopolitical competition.

U.S. retrenchment from these regions creates a permissive environment for rising or reassertive powers. All three of America's primary regional rivals—China, Iran, and Russia—possess prospective spheres of influence that overlap with America's exposed strategic appendages in their respective regions. Should China manage to co-opt or coerce the foreign policies of the small littoral states surrounding it, Beijing would be able to alleviate pressures on its lengthy maritime energy routes, shift strategic attention to the second island chain, and focus more on landward expansion. Similarly, should Russia, for all its economic backwardness, manage to reinsert its influence into the belt of small states along its western frontier, Moscow could consolidate its commanding position in European energy security, regain access to warm-water ports, and stymie NATO and EU influence east of Germany. Should Iran manage to gain greater influence among its small Arab neighbors, particularly those along the Persian Gulf coastline, it would be able to enhance its ability to disrupt international oil supplies.

In all three cases, America's rivals stand to gain in potentially significant ways from U.S. retrenchment. But these powers face a dilemma. While they may sense that changes are under way in the international system and even imagine enlarged opportunities to revise the status quo, they don't want to incur the potentially high costs of a direct confrontation with the United States. Sensing an opportunity, they want to revise the regional order, but they are uncertain about the amount of geopolitical leeway they have and therefore the degree of license they can take in safely challenging the status quo. From the standpoint of these revisionist powers, the United States may be in retreat, by choice or necessity, but it is unclear by how much. And this makes it risky to pick a direct fight. Even in the era of sequestration, America retains many hegemonic capabilities and characteristics—including the forward-deployed system of alliances and security commitments that America continues to maintain in their own neighborhoods—that present real obstacles to aspirant powers.

Rising powers therefore have an incentive to look for *low-cost* revision—marginal gains that offer the highest possible geopolitical payoff at the lowest possible strategic price. That means not moving more aggressively or earlier than power realities will allow. And that, in turn, requires getting an accurate read of global power relationships. How deep is the top state's power reservoir? How spendable are its power assets? How determined is it to use them to stay on top? And how committed is it to defending stated interests on issues and areas that conflict with the riser? Would-be powers need to understand the likely answers to these questions *before* they act.

Historically, rising powers faced with this dilemma have found creative ways to gauge how far they can go in a fluid international system before encountering determined resistance of the leading power. One way would-be revisionists have done so historically is to employ a strategy of what might be called "probing"—that is, using low-intensity tests of the leading power on the outer limits of its strategic position. The purpose is both to assess the hegemon's willingness and ability to defend the status quo and to accomplish gradual territorial or reputational gains at the expense of the leading power if possible. These probes are conducted not where the hegemon is strong but at the outer limits of its power position, where its commitments are established (and potentially extensive) but require the greatest exertion to maintain. Here, at the periphery, the costs of probing are more manageable than those of confronting the hegemon directly, which could generate a strong response by the leader.

Probing, though not widely studied, is the natural strategy for many revisionist powers. This was the technique a rising imperial

Germany used in the late nineteenth and early twentieth centuries as it concocted low-intensity diplomatic crises to test British resolve and alliances in various regions. There is growing evidence to suggest that the rising and resurgent powers of the twenty-first century are using this same strategy. The Russo-Georgia War (2008), the Hormuz Straits crisis (2012), the Senkaku Islands dispute (2013), the Ukrainian War (2014–present), the Baltic Sea air and naval tensions (2015), and the Spratly Islands confrontations (2015) are all examples of an increasingly frequent category of strategic behavior by revisionist powers to assess U.S. strength and level of commitment to defending the global security order. Although the exact nature of the tools involved in these crises may differ, the basic principle is the same: to avoid high-stakes challenges to America itself while conducting low-intensity reconnoitering of remote positions on the U.S. strategic map.

U.S. allies find themselves on the receiving end of these probes. Owing to their exposed geography, allies in frontier regions like Central Europe, littoral East Asia, and the Persian Gulf are some of the most security-conscious states in the world. Leaders there analyze local and global power shifts for signs of changing threat possibilities. Their first instinct is to look to America for reassurance, in keeping with the long-standing assumption of U.S. strategic support that has been the fail-safe centerpiece of their foreign policies for decades. But faced with the combination of mounting pressure from rising neighbors and growing indications of decreased political support from Washington, these states have begun to reexamine the full range of coping mechanisms available to states in their exposed positions. For the first time in decades they are contemplating new strategic menu cards in the quest for backups to, alternatives to, or possibly even eventual replacements for their decades-long security links with Washington. Like small states at previous moments of uncertainty in the history of international relations, they are exploring a variety of options, from military self-help and regional security groupings to so-called Finlandization and even bandwagoning with the nearby rising power.

Though still in its early phases, this emerging trend of allied reassessment and repositioning holds profound implications for long-term U.S. national security interests. Together the cycles of revisionist probing and allied anxiety could fundamentally alter the security dynamics of global geopolitics, undermining factors of stability that have provided for the peace and prosperity of the world's most strategically vital regions, to the benefit of the United States and the world, since the Second World War. Such stability has not been the norm for most of these regions' histories. While a continuation of current trends would not necessarily bring an overnight deterioration in global stability (though that is certainly possible), it would impose steep costs on U.S. interests and values down the road, bringing reactivated regional security dilemmas that could ultimately drive up the costs of U.S. diplomacy; a more fragile global alliance system, fueling the need for U.S. reassurance in multiple places and stretching U.S. attention and resources; less support for U.S. missions, as allies that are worried about their own security devote less energy or will to help the United States in international missions; and, most dangerously, emboldened revisionist powers, fueled by the sense of uncertainty in frontier regions to accelerate probes of the allied periphery in hopes of low-cost gains.

This is not a world the United States should want to see emerge. Yet in many ways it is a world that current U.S. policy is helping to create.

✻ ✻ ✻

In 2010 we began to write about the emerging changes that are under way in America's allied frontier in a series of opinion pieces and analytical briefs for the Center for European Policy Analysis. In a spring 2011 article for *The American Interest* magazine, we described the growing tendency toward allied insecurity, revisionist probing, and the linkages between these dynamics as nascent phenomena, capable of being addressed if dealt with creatively and aggressively by U.S. policy. We continued developing this line of thinking, including elaborations of the methods of our rivals and possible counterstrategies for the United States and its allies, in subsequent articles for *The American Interest* and *The National Interest*. When we first wrote about these issues our arguments were novel and somewhat controversial. In the period since, as signs of the growing global disorder have increased, other scholars have embraced our thesis.[2] To further test our assumptions, we conducted two years of additional research, visiting the capitals of key U.S. allies in East-Central Europe and East Asia and talking with U.S. and allied diplomats and military officers.

What we found was alarming. The dynamics of allied insecurity and rival probing in frontier regions are intensifying. The American alliance network is in a state of advanced crisis. Many long-standing U.S. allies believe that the United States, for reasons of either decline or disinterest, is in the process of pulling back from decades-long commitments and inaugurating a multiregional diplomatic and military retrenchment. In the three years since our first article was published, a steady succession of U.S. actions—cancellations of regionally deployed U.S. weapons systems, reductions in forward-deployed U.S. combat units, lessening of U.S. diplomatic support for traditional allies, participation in tacit bilateral bargaining with large authoritarian states, a much-touted but under-resourced Asian "pivot"—have seemed to confirm their suspicions.

Defenders of current U.S. foreign policy dispute that any one of these decisions has harmed American credibility. But it is the aggregate effect of the decisions, across regions and alongside U.S. defense budget reductions, that has convinced many U.S. allies that a downward shift in the strategic, political, and material foundations of American power is now under way. These allies see signs of advanced decay in the U.S. extended deterrence that undergirds the stability of their regions. America's rivals have taken note of these things too. Leaders in Beijing, Moscow, and Tehran are increasingly cocky: they perceive the opening of a more permissive environment, are convinced of the justness of their revisionist ambitions, and believe in the inevitability of an eventual American retrenchment from the regions that matter most to them. For these players, even a seemingly decrepit Russia, confidence in their own power potential is at an all-time high at exactly a moment when the confidence of their small neighbors (and maybe even of America itself) in U.S. power and credibility is at an all-time low. Perhaps as a result, over the past year U.S. opponents have steadily ratcheted up their probes, which in some cases—such as Russia in Ukraine—have turned violent and in other cases—such as China in the South China Sea—are coming perilously close to military confrontation.

We are at a dangerous moment in global geopolitics. The international system that the United States has built and maintained for the past several decades is still in place, but it is very fragile. For the first time in the post–Cold War era, the continuation of this system can no longer be taken for granted; virtually every element in its foundation is increasingly in question. If current trends hold, the U.S.-led global alliance network could unravel in coming years through a combination of external pressure from opportunistic powers convinced that America is in decline, internal pressures of allies that are unconvinced America will still support them in a crisis, and the failure of U.S. statecraft to prove both views wrong. Such an unraveling could undo in a few years what it took America three generations to build.

Should such an unraveling occur, it would have far-reaching negative consequences for U.S. national security, the American economy, and the wider world as we have known it for more than half a century. Unfortunately, U.S. leaders do not appear to be fully aware of this unfolding reality or the extent of its implications for the United States. This void in U.S. strategic thinking reflects a lack of understanding not only about the perceptions of America's allies and the intentions of its rivals but also about how U.S. moves are interpreted competitively. Moreover, it reflects a general memory loss about why the United States is involved in the world's strategic crossroad regions to begin with and the benefits we derive from maintaining a robust presence in these places. Most of all, it reflects a crisis of confidence in our own ideals and power potential at a moment in world history when a diminished American global role could fuel negative (and avoidable) geopolitical adjustments worldwide. This void in both strategy and confidence must be filled if America is to thrive and prosper in this emerging new world.

The purpose of this book is to make the strategic case for America's frontier alliances—why they matter, how we are losing them, and what America needs to do to preserve them for a new era. We argue that, far from a hindrance, America's global networks of frontline allies are essential elements in its success and prosperity as a great power. If anything, the changes that are under way in the international system, particularly the emergence of more assertive rival powers to contest U.S. leadership, have enhanced the strategic value of these alliances to the United States in the twenty-first century.

In chapter 2 we track the deterioration that has occurred in the foundations of America's relations with many of its longest-standing allies over the past few years, both through a weakening of the political bonds with Washington and through diplomatic and military probes at the hands of U.S. rivals.

In chapter 3 we examine the nature of revisionist probing and the form that it takes in various regions. Drawing on historical examples of imperial Germany's use of low-intensity colonial crises to challenge Britain and its allies in the early twentieth century, we argue that rising powers are employing similar techniques in the global periphery to test America's resolve in the twenty-first century.

In chapter 4 we examine how U.S. allies are responding to the combination of probes and America's deprioritization of alliances by reconsidering their "menu cards" of options for surviving geopolitical change. Using historical examples such as Central and Eastern European states during the interwar period of the 1930s, we argue that U.S. allies, to an extent largely overlooked in Washington, are now considering a wide range of coping mechanisms to prepare for the possibility of U.S. retrenchment and examine the effects that their strategic choices could have over time.

In chapter 5 we assess the benefits of frontier alliances for the United States both historically and today. Referring to earlier work of strategists such as Sir Harold Mackinder, Nicholas Spykman, and Walter Lippmann, we argue that, for the United States as a maritime power of global reach, using forward-deployed alliances in the rimlands of Eurasia is a cost-effective tool for managing the international system that is preferable to the strategic alternatives now being presented for U.S. foreign policy.

In chapter 6 we conclude by reviewing the options at America's disposal for reversing the erosion of its frontier alliances and countering the probes of its rivals to ensure stability in the early decades of the twenty-first century. We offer recommendations for how the United States can revitalize its credibility and capabilities of itself and its allies in the world's most critical regions.

CHAPTER 2

AMERICA'S
DEPRIORITIZATION
OF ALLIES

Assist your allies as you promised and do not sacrifice friends and kindred to their bitterest enemies, and drive the rest of us in despair to some other alliance.

— Corinthians' speech at Sparta,
Thucydides,
The Peloponnesian War

No world order that elevates one nation or group of people over another will succeed. . . . The traditional divisions between nations . . . make no sense in an interconnected world; nor do alignments of nations rooted in the cleavages of a long-gone Cold War.

— President Barack Obama,
United Nations General Assembly,
September 23, 2009

Great-power rivalries are first and foremost contests for allies. Since the beginning of international relations, to upstage an opponent, polities vied for the military and diplomatic support of others. Strategic loneliness has always been deemed dangerous in a self-help world. To have allies is no guarantee of victory, but to engage in strategic rivalry alone can be a deadly disadvantage. As Thucydides recounts, before their direct clash Athens and Sparta were jockeying to show support to their allies and to attract to their side new ones in search of strategic advantage. The contest for states located at the frontier between the competing great powers was particularly heated because it is there that conflicts take shape.

In recent years the United States has been tempted to ignore the historic need for strong alliances, especially those with the most exposed states at the periphery of our power. Washington often seems to think of great-power rivalries as dyadic affairs, with the other states as dispensable accessories rather than as the strategic prizes. This is nothing new. For millennia states have viewed fixed commitments of friendship with other states as a mixed blessing, to be accumulated or discarded as changes in the external environment dictate. Not surprisingly, leaders have tended to see alliances, particularly those involving binding treaty obligations, as beneficial in times of war but of questionable value in seasons of peace. This has been especially the case for maritime great powers, whose relative geographic insulation makes the strategic imperative of maintaining alliances seem less pressing and their costs more onerous, until the emergence of a threat renders them essential—by which point willing and capable allies are often hard to find. Hence Great Britain famously allowed its various continental alliances during the European dynastic struggles of the eighteenth century to lapse, only to hastily cobble together new coalitions for each new conflict—a pattern that held constant in British foreign policy, with few interruptions, until the early twentieth century.

It is certainly not the case that the United States is somehow ill suited for alliances. On the contrary, the democratic nature of the United States, combined with geographic separation from the world, give it structural advantages in establishing and maintaining alliances; there is no better friend, no worse enemy, than the United States. But in our policies there is often an underlying strand of doubt about the necessity and importance of allies, and at times, like the present day, this doubt becomes more prominent.

On closer examination, there are deeply rooted sources of the American temptation to deprioritize alliances. Geography, technology, and ideology tempt us to think that we do not need allies to compete effectively in global geopolitics. In addition, in recent years domestic political pressures have emerged that generate doubts about U.S.

overseas commitments. The Obama administration's rhetoric and actions—partly a reflection of these pressures—have been perceived, correctly in our view, as downgrading the importance of allies.

THE THREE TEMPTATIONS

America's deprioritization of alliances antedates the Obama administration. In fact, there is a recurrent American temptation to avoid alliances, rooted in the sense of safety that stems from geographic distance, technological superiority, and ideological conviction. These factors give the United States the luxury of strategic choice, a blessing that distinguishes it from small and midsized powers for whom territorial security is often the only concern and goal. The United States can choose, or so it is argued, between widely different foreign policy objectives, ranging from humanitarian interventions to preventive wars in distant lands. Moreover, this strategic luxury seems to carry also a spectrum of choices of how to pursue these objectives, from backing our allies with "boots on the ground" to "coming home" militarily and diplomatically. The luxury of choice is, however, also a curse because it introduces doubt about the reliability of the United States as an ally; the wider the spectrum of possible strategic options, the greater the perception of untrustworthiness. The same reasons that tempt the United States to disengage from distant allies generate in U.S. allies the suspicion of a weaker American commitment.

At various moments in history different mixes of these three broad drivers, namely, geography, technology, and ideology, enter the grand strategy debate, pushing the argument of alliance deprioritization. The outcome is that the strategic necessity of transoceanic commitments is discounted and the costs of keeping the most vulnerable frontier allies secure are deemed higher than the potential benefits.

Geography

The most enduring source of temptation is geography. A uniquely fortunate geographic condition of the North American continent,

abundant in natural resources and lacking the competitive political environment of Europe and Asia, sets the United States apart
from other great powers. The safety of the oceanic moats separating
North America from Eurasia provided the young American republic
with some respite from European tribulations in the late eighteenth
century.[1] In the more than two centuries since then, the oceans protected the United States from hostile states for whom the projection
of power across the Atlantic waters was too costly or simply unfeasible. Finally, the hot and cold wars of the twentieth century were
fought in Eurasia and on the Atlantic and Pacific oceans, not on American shores, a clear benefit of the quasi-insularity of the United States.

The geopolitical insularity of the North American continent,
therefore, seems to allow the possibility of a hemispheric defense
with few or no out-of-continent commitments. As has been argued,
the United States enjoys "free security" behind the vastness of its
two oceans and need not be involved in guaranteeing the safety of
Eurasian states.[2] The result is a preference for some variant of isolationism, usually advocating no long-term military presence abroad
combined with sporadic, limited, and quick interventions to restore
an equilibrium of power in Eurasia. Some go so far as to argue that
U.S. intervention in the Second World War was unnecessary because the Western Hemisphere would have been sufficient to sustain
American economic and military power. As a current critic writes,
"Continental-sized powers are nearly impossible to defeat, especially
when they are an ocean away from their would-be conquerors. The
United States would have been able to defend itself, if not indefi-
nitely, then at least for a long time."[3] In brief, geography is used to
justify opposition to a continued and deep U.S. involvement abroad.

This geography-driven temptation is not unique to the United
States but is common among maritime and, even more so, island nations. It is tempting to see one's own security as limited to the immediate homeland while considering distant allies as at best unnecessary and at worst burdensome. The traditional British reluctance to
accept a "continental commitment," preferring to rely on the safety
provided by the English Channel and the Royal Navy, is a classic case.
A certain geographic arrogance in large measure drove this unwillingness to do more than try to choke the enemies on the European

mainland by a naval blockade and perhaps at times harass them with limited military interventions. "Ruling the waves," it was deemed, would have sufficed to protect the British islands and guarantee citizens' well-being. As naval strategist Julian Corbett would argue in the early twentieth century, an island power could rely only on its geography, its naval forces, and perhaps a "disposable force" to harass continental rivals.[4]

A similar logic characterized another, more ancient, maritime power: Athens. At the outset of their war with Sparta, the Athenians were tempted to focus on their city and their surrounding fields, under direct assault from the Spartan land forces. Pericles was forced to remind his fellow citizens that their strength was in the alliance system, not in the fields the Spartans put to waste below the city's walls, and as long as they maintained this vast diplomatic architecture they could have withstood the recurrent assaults of the Peloponnesians. The homeland was made more secure by protecting the allies than by operating a defensive line to keep Spartans out of Athens's olive groves. But, like the British approach, the Periclean strategy was also keen to avoid a "Peloponnesian commitment" that would have established a foothold on the land around Sparta.[5] Again, the temptation was to weather the war beyond the safety of the maritime realm. But without continental allies, Athens could never defeat Spartan land power, and its only hope was that the Spartan leaders would simply tire of the annual expeditions to Attica. This hope proved to be unrealistic and ultimately contributed to the Athenian defeat.

This Anglo-Athenian geographic temptation to avoid a deep continental involvement is present in the United States too. But while there are good reasons to rejoice at the geographic blessings of the United States, it is a mistake to base its security on the geological particularities of North America. First, the history of the United States is not one of geopolitical detachment. The United States developed not outside of the European balance of power but because of it. From the early days of the republic, American leaders have been keenly aware that internal European squabbles should be used to our advantage, not ignored as too distant and thus strategically irrelevant. France can be played against Great Britain; British naval superiority can be borrowed to evict other European powers from the hemisphere;

the decline of Spanish power can be an opportunity to expand. The blessing is not geology but a history of competing, weakening, or sympathetic transoceanic powers.

Second, oceans are "not barriers but highways."[6] Surely, distance hinders projections of power, and bodies of water in particular are effective barriers. As Robert Jervis observes, if all states were islands, the world would have been much more stable. The "United States, and to a lesser extent Great Britain, have partly been able to escape from the state of nature because their geographical positions approximated this ideal."[7] But oceans are not uncrossable, and technological developments, such as airpower and intercontinental ballistic missiles, combined with growing ease and frequency of mobility of goods and people, make hemispheric security a dangerous illusion. To indulge in the temptation of geopolitical insularity is to court disaster.

Technology

The geographic argument against the need for allies goes hand in hand, therefore, with a certain technological conceit. In its basic formulation, it is a faith in the power of the navy to protect islands in general, and the United States in particular. Naval superiority allows a power to exercise control over the sea approaches to its homeland, keeping its enemies at bay and perhaps choking them in the long run. Geopolitical insularity can be thus perfected through the protection supplied by a powerful navy.

The temptation to be independent from allies through technology is not limited to maritime powers. Some states are tempted to think that they can erect a defensive barrier built on technology. In the 1930s, for example, France built sophisticated static defenses along its eastern frontier—the Maginot Line—with this idea in mind. In the most extreme case, this line of thinking can lead to overreliance on one's own nuclear weapons as a means of guaranteeing survival and independence from allies. The ultimate deterrent is deemed to provide freedom from alliances. It is a temptation of geopolitical self-sufficiency based on technological superiority.

In the case of the United States, the faith in the ability of naval power to guarantee security has always been strong. Even in the darkest moments of World War II, several politicians clearly articulated and supported this faith. The U.S. Senate Committee on Naval Affairs, for instance, reported in May 1940 that the "armies of Europe and Asia do not menace us. . . . Our geographical situation considered together with that of our potential enemies reveals at once that we can depend primarily upon a navy for our security and that we should adopt a predominantly naval policy as the keystone of our national defense." The report continued by arguing that the United States "need not form military alliances to maintain a balance of power; we need not maintain large land military establishments as in Europe or Asia to insure safety for our country. We need only a navy."[8] The navy would have sufficed to quarantine the North American continent from the tribulations on the Eurasian landmass.

Yet toward the end of World War II some American strategists saw the limitations of a static defense based only on naval power. The presence of an expanding hegemon in Eurasia, threatening geopolitical pluralism there, was now clearly seen as a danger to American security that demanded more than simply controlling the Pacific and Atlantic sea routes. In 1943 Walter Lippmann already argued that the "immense coast line of the two Americas cannot be defended by standing guard on the beaches and by maintaining the coastal defenses, or even by a navy based upon the Americas and, therefore, compelled to let the enemy decide where and when he would strike." Because of this geopolitical situation, Lippmann continued, "the strategic defenses of the United States are not at the three-mile limit in American waters, but extend across both oceans and to all the trans-oceanic lands from which an attack by sea or by air can be launched."[9] Several analysts, including Bernard Brodie, observed that the presence of "strong allies who were contiguous with our enemies has been an incalculable benefit to us. It has enabled us to hit our enemies hard, and to do so on their own thresholds rather than on ours."[10] The defense of the United States had to be established well beyond its immediate borders and had to rely on the ability to "project American power quickly and effectively against any potential adversary."[11] From a strictly military standpoint, this required planning a vast system of bases to control ocean and air routes (including polar routes and in the Mediterranean and North Africa).[12] Their purpose was both to enhance strategic deterrence and to provide logistical support for power projection.[13]

In the end, U.S. foreign policy reflected Nicholas Spykman's view that it would "be cheaper in the long run to remain a working member of the European power zone than to withdraw for short intermissions to our insular domain only to be forced to apply later the whole of our national strength to redress a balance that might have needed but a slight weight at the beginning."[14] As Colin Gray observes, it is "in the U.S. interest to balance power in, rather than with, Eurasia."[15] The security of the United States is not in the oceans separating it from the world, nor in the navy, air force, or missile defense capabilities, but in the balance of power in Eurasia. That balance will not occur by itself and requires American participation in the constant jockeying of Eurasian powers.

The allure of a technological defensive moat is recurrent. Airpower was the means by which this moat was to be constructed in Spykman's time and remains a fixation of isolationist-minded strategists today. A current incarnation of this argument is present in the tempting vision of a United States protected by a ballistic missile defense and cheap and far-reaching drones. Regardless of the strategic and tactical merits of these technologies, the risk is that they will be seen as alternatives to alliances. If we think that our security can be guaranteed merely by controlling the oceanic and air approaches to the North American continent, then overseas allies are expendable. If through technology we can protect the U.S. homeland from overseas threats, establishing a self-sufficient "fortress America," commitments to distant allies may be considered expendable.

An extreme version of the technological temptation is based on nuclear capabilities and can be seen in the strategic predilections of the French Fifth Republic. It is the French technological temptation to be ally-independent. France's quest to acquire nuclear weapons was driven in part by the search for greater prestige and thus a more powerful voice in the Western alliance, not subordinate to others.[16]

But in part, and perhaps more important, it was the result of a perception that alliances in the nuclear age were less credible: a state, such as the United States, would not come to the aid of its ally, say France, were it to risk nuclear annihilation in exchange. As French strategist Pierre Gallois articulated, the risk of supporting one's own allies outweighed any potential benefits in a war under the nuclear shadow, making the effectiveness of extended deterrence doubtful. As a result, Charles de Gaulle claimed that "nobody in the world, in particular nobody in America, can say whether, where, how, to what extent the U.S. nuclear arms would be used to defend Europe."[17] The perceived decline of extended deterrence therefore led to faith in an independent force de frappe, which would have solved the security conundrum, substituting for "obsolete alliances."[18] It was a nuclear isolationism of sorts, and it had its proponents on both sides of the Atlantic.[19] In an article critical of the Gaullist nuclear temptation, Albert Wohlstetter put it thus: "The possibility of withdrawal is offered as bait by those Europeans and Americans who want us to give our allies bombs and, hopefully, the ability to shift for themselves."[20]

The French temptation is not limited to a particular set of individuals with ideals of national grandeur. Hints of that view are present also among some American thinkers who are eager to see the United States less involved in continental affairs of Eurasia. One way to achieve that, according to political scientist John Mearsheimer, is by encouraging a managed nuclear proliferation. This would build international stability as states become gradually capable of massive retaliation in their mutual interactions.[21] Rationality, even when it did not exist beforehand, would be instilled by the mere possession of nuclear weapons. States become security monads, fully independent of others, untouchable, and thus in no need of external security protectors. Neither Mearsheimer nor Kenneth Waltz, nor other advocates of nuclear proliferation, go as far as to argue that the United States will need no allies, but their logic leans in that direction. In the moment U.S. allies turn nuclear, preferably with a second-strike capability, their security becomes autochthonous, and the expensive extended deterrent provided by the United States is no longer necessary. The spread of nuclear weapons is seen as a way to diminish

American commitments abroad. In this worldview, Ukraine would have been safer had it kept Soviet nuclear weapons, which would have served as the only credible deterrent against a Russian attack.[22] This is another version of that temptation to provide security, and in this case even international stability, through technological means rather than alliances.

The "French nuclear temptation" is an interesting academic exercise, which thankfully no American policy maker has yet adopted and translated into policy. The dangers of nuclear proliferation are immense, ranging from the risk of a "valley of vulnerability" when states have only first-strike capabilities, to the difficulties associated with the maintenance and control of the weapons. Not only it is unlikely that a nuclear Ukraine would have been able to use and maintain Soviet weapons, but also a nuclear deterrent is not a panacea against low-intensity, limited wars.

More broadly, technology does not obviate the need for allies. For instance, both a navy and drones still require resources and overseas bases. Without the former even a large power is rendered isolated and strategically lonely and cannot compete effectively. As Halford Mackinder observed, from "the early history of Britain herself it is evident that mere insularity gives no indefeasible title to marine sovereignty."[23] Technological superiority is not a given and needs to be developed and maintained. Competition for naval (or, in general, technological) superiority, as shown by the Anglo-German case at the turn of the twentieth century or as insinuated by China-U.S. antagonism, is a recurrent fact of history, and waging it requires more than the isolated resources of a power. Moreover, naval power and airpower have serious limitations if deprived of overseas bases. Bases are still needed for logistical support, straits and channels continue to be choke points, and, more broadly, allies can augment one's own power. Technology changes the geographic requirements but not the necessity of allies. Technology, in brief, can never be a substitute for allies.

Moreover, the ability to keep the enemy off our shores can frustrate but not defeat a hostile power. It is akin to a wall, and walls are poor offensive tools. As Spykman observed about sea power, it "cannot invade a country, storm a fortress, or occupy territory; it can bombard a coast, but the effect is seldom conclusive."[24] Technological superiority enhances the stopping power of the geographic location of the United States but cannot prevent the rise, or achieve the defeat, of a rival.

Ideology

The final driver of alliance deprioritization in American grand strategy is ideology. It has deep roots that go back to the intellectual debates of the American founding and results in the two coexisting, yet somewhat contradictory, views of liberalism and isolationism. As historian Felix Gilbert put it, "isolationism existed in a sphere of timelessness; internationalism existed in the future."[25] By "internationalism," he meant the view that cooperative rather than competitive behavior of states characterizes the international arena. By contrast, the isolationist view counsels "abstention from power competition or, more specifically speaking, from the Balance of Power"[26] to avoid arms races and wars, deemed to be dangerous practices unique to Europe and leading to the rise of a menacing centralized state. Despite their differences, these views converge in the hope and expectation that the United States could avoid deep foreign involvement because the world is seen as either self-balancing or harmonious. Both are "escapist" because they are grounded in impossible assumptions about present or future international relations.[27] Finally, both are based on a unique "historical accident" when "Asia was dormant, Europe divided, and Britain's command of the sea unchallenged" that allowed Americans to conduct a foreign policy without considering the means necessary for it.[28] In other words, the temptation to see international relations as characterized by cooperation or automatic equilibrium coincided with a particular historical period that nurtured and strengthened this belief, firmly embedding it in American strategic thinking.

The liberal perspective posits that there exists a harmony of interests among all states, and consequently cooperation is likely to arise. States engage in cooperative behavior; they are partners seeking solutions to common problems, not rivals competing for resources or allies binding themselves in search of security against another power. The reason now is that threats are globalized and thus can be addressed only together, in a cooperative posture. As Secretary of State Hillary Clinton said in 2010, U.S. foreign policy ought to build "a new global architecture that could help nations come together as partners to solve shared problems."[29] Similarly, President Obama expressed his belief that "more than at any point in human history—the interests of nations and peoples are shared."[30] Even discounting these statements for the usual diplomatic rhetoric, they are striking in the description of a world that is harmonious in its nature and requires only some sort of institutional solution to be translated into practice.

The rhetorical symptom of this view is the use of the term "partners," which encompasses rivals and friends alike, rather than "allies." It is an enticing view, promising an international equilibrium arising naturally from the common awareness of global interdependence and calling for a limited need of American intervention. For many the greatest danger to this global order is U.S. "hyperactivity," defined as military interventions (à la Iraq in 2003) but also the constant provision of security to Eurasian allies, both damaging to the delicate mechanism of cooperation. U.S. allies' demands for strong security assurance are seen as a nuisance, vestiges of a long-gone past. The world is seen as entering a new era in which the traditional concerns and policy no longer apply. As Secretary of State Clinton argued, "Our approach to foreign policy must reflect the world as it is, not as it used to be. It does not make sense to adapt a 19th century concert of powers, or a 20th century balance of power strategy."[31]

The second vision of the world, seen as self-balancing, is based on a different assumption but reaches a similar conclusion. According to this worldview, the world is not harmonious, but states balance against the most proximate and threatening power.[32] International stability is the outcome of constant balancing acts by states, capable and willing to understand their national interest and to act on it. The natural reaction of any state when threatened is to counter the menace and increase its security through the tools at its disposal, including diplomatic deals and military buildup. Balancing may not prevent wars, but those are part of the reestablishment of an equilibrium, which sooner or later will reappear.

Eurasia, in particular, is seen as endowed with a geopolitical configuration conducive to a continent-wide equilibrium. Historically the
attempts of coastal or peripheral powers to extend control over the
lands deep inside the continent were exceedingly costly and short-
lived. Napoleon tried and failed; so did Nazi Germany as well as
imperial Japan. Similarly, the outward projections of force by continental powers, such as Russia, was challenging and never succeeded
in establishing a lasting hegemony. In brief, the sheer difficulty of establishing a continent-wide hegemony has maintained a rough balance of power. Moreover, the geographic closeness of Eurasian powers has enhanced states' alertness to changes of equilibrium and
created clear incentives to respond to them. It follows from this nar-
rative that American interventions in the Eurasian balance of power
are unnecessary from a purely realpolitik rationale. Few, of course,
regret the U.S. waging of war against Nazi Germany, but for some
the obligation was exclusively a moral one and not based on American security needs.[33]

The vision of the world as regulated by regional balancing has
clear prescriptions for U.S. foreign policy. Eurasia not only does not
need but also does not benefit from American intervention. In this
view, the presence of American power on that continental mass alters
its natural internal balancing strategies. Instead of balancing against
each other, some states start balancing against the United States, and
those who do not do so free ride.[34] The United States is a foreign object of sorts in Eurasia. Its introduction there generates more problems than solutions.

In brief, American overseas commitments are detrimental according to the argument of a self-balancing world, while they are not
needed for the liberal vision. The resulting strategic preference shared
by both is one that foresees a minimal involvement of the United
States outside of its hemisphere. The United States ought to participate alongside all the other world powers in the global cooperative
efforts, exercising influence as a persuasive leader to solve the various
threats to all (e.g., climate change, nuclear proliferation). It should
certainly avoid twentieth-century-type military interventions, which
are seen as dangerous adventurism. Whether one calls this strategy "offshore balancing," "restraint," or "liberal institutionalism,"

the strategic outcome is remarkably similar: the United States ought to decrease its military interventions and overseas presence, thereby increasing its security. It is where various strains of strategic thought, having started from often diametrically opposed assumptions, meet in agreement. It is where, in the United States, the isolationist wing of Republican persuasion meets the retrenchment advocates from the Democratic camp.[35]

DEPRIORITIZATION OF ALLIES TODAY

So far, the idea of an American hemispheric defense or strategic disengagement has been only a temptation, driven by the persistent presence of the three factors described above. At times it has appeared more prominent because of a greater desire to focus on domestic affairs or the scarring impact of a war. The 1920s, for instance, are often considered as an ideal-type period in which the United States had an isolationist posture as exemplified by the Senate rejection of the League of Nations and a preference for economic rather than political or military engagement in the world.[36] That "isolationist consensus" ended only when it became clear that the rise of a hostile, authoritarian hegemon in Europe would threaten American security.[37] In other words, the alluring promise of strategic insularity is shattered only by the dramatic realization that there are enemies bent on and capable of attacking the United States and its way of life. Whenever the perception of such a threat diminishes, because either the political nature of rivals is deemed irrelevant (the liberal view) or their strategic capabilities are seen as inadequate to reach the American continent and affect U.S. welfare (the isolationist claim), there is a renewed tendency to see American overseas commitments as excessive and even counterproductive. The result is not isolationism, which in its perfect form never took place, but a period of doubts about the value of U.S. forward presence in Eurasia.

The United States is going through one of these periods. It has not "retrenched," nor has it abandoned its allies. But the temptation to ignore the world is more prominent, and consequently doubts about the continued benefits of U.S. overseas commitments are rising.

These tendencies are most evident in a multifaceted deprioritization of alliances. Allies, in brief, are perceived as a fiscal and strategic burden and, more broadly, as a remnant of the past, in this case the Cold War.

There are multiple reasons for the current deprioritization of alliances. As was evident during the presidential elections of 2008 and 2012, there is a general fatigue with the wars in Iraq and now Afghanistan, resulting in an understandable reluctance to advocate and support American military interventions and presence abroad. In the Chicago Council on Global Affairs poll in 2012, close to 40 percent of respondents were in favor of the United States "staying out of world affairs."[38] This is still a minority, but with the exception of a decrease in 2002, likely due to the 9/11 attacks, the percentage of those advocating disengagement from the world has steadily risen over the past two decades. Furthermore, noninterventionism often goes hand in hand with a wider disinclination to maintain a forward military posture, seen as unnecessarily provocative and expensive. In the same poll, the American public was split on the question of whether the United States ought to have long-term bases in Japan and Germany, with a clear majority in favor of continued military presence only in South Korea because of the North Korean nuclear threat.[39]

The economic slowdown since 2008 and the long-term fiscal imbalances in the United States are also contributing to the diminishing desire for overseas obligations. It is a disinterest in allies, and in the world in general, that stems out of a perception of our own weakness. There is a clear political preference for domestic expenditures that cuts across party lines. Both George W. Bush and Barack Obama during their electoral campaigns in 2000 and 2008, respectively, advocated the need to focus on domestic issues. Famously, in a presidential debate with Al Gore, Bush criticized his opponent for favoring the use of U.S. military forces for nation building—prolonged efforts to reconstruct war-torn countries.[40] Bush did not advocate withdrawal from the world or abandoning allies, but he certainly gave voice to a deep popular discontent with using American forces and resources in distant lands. Similarly, in a speech in 2012, President Obama proclaimed that "the nation we need to be rebuilding is the United States of America."[41] In brief, as in the interwar period, economic conditions pressure politicians to focus on domestic rather than international affairs, and only dramatic events such as the 9/11 terrorist attacks alter this inward-looking tendency. The biggest threat to American security comes from within.[42]

The political unwillingness of some U.S. allies, particularly in Europe, to increase their own spending on defense exacerbates the problem. As an academic proponent of ending alliances argues, it is "time for America to stop being a nanny state and for our wards, now among the richest, most advanced places on earth, to fend for themselves."[43] America's leading libertarian foreign-policy intellectuals have long voiced variants of this view, but they have rarely acquired relevance in U.S. policy and have been largely on the margins of the national-security debate. Within the past decade these views have entered more and more into the political mainstream, as budgetary constraints and fatigue from the wars in Iraq and Afghanistan have helped to create a political constituency to support incorporating them into U.S. foreign policy.

The growth in popularity of these views can be explained by the fact that, though strategically myopic, they are politically appealing. American politicians cannot sell to their constituencies the necessity of spending money on the security of allies when those allies do not pull their own weight. This is a problem in particular in Europe, where defense spending has been anemic for decades (see chapter 4). It is no surprise, therefore, that in recent years several U.S. cabinet members have expressed frustration with the level of defense spending in Europe. Two U.S. secretaries of defense, Robert Gates and Leon Panetta, were particularly outspoken. Toward the end of his tenure in June 2011, Gates bluntly warned European allies that "there will be dwindling appetite and patience in the U.S. Congress—and in the American body politic writ large—to expend increasingly precious funds on behalf of nations that are apparently unwilling to devote the necessary resources or make the necessary changes to be serious and capable partners in their own defense."[44] Panetta echoed similar worries in the succeeding months.[45]

The military superiority of the United States has an additional impact on the American perception of alliances. The "capabilities gap" has affected all joint military operations since the Kosovo campaign, including the wars in Iraq, Afghanistan, and Libya. Limited power projection capabilities, small forces, and legal limitations on use of force that hamper many U.S. allies (Germany and Japan in particular) generate the opinion that United States is better off "going it alone," and allies are often sought out only as a diplomatic cover. They are seen as a publicity photo opportunity, not as an operational asset. This is not an altogether unjustified sentiment as the main standard of alliances is, as Arnold Wolfers put it, "whether the allies can offer something worthwhile in terms of military assistance."[46] But the danger is that the operational concerns about U.S. allies overflow to the grand strategic level, pushing the view that alliances are an unnecessary burden. While U.S. criticism of allies in the previous paragraph stems from domestic fiscal worries and resentment at paying more than they do, here the criticism is that the United States is unmatched in its own capabilities and allies slow us down. Both views end up questioning the value of alliances.

Hence the deprioritization of alliances is not an exclusive domain of those who fret about the decline of the United States. In fact, there is a disinterest in allies and in the world in general that stems out of a perception of U.S. strength and self-sufficiency. The belief is that, for instance, discoveries of new energy deposits, combined with the continued blessings of other natural resources (food, water), give an incomparable advantage to the United States. In the long run, the argument goes, the United States will reverse its economic slide. In part, the end of the declinist trend may be simply relative, caused by demographic, social, environmental, and economic problems facing other world power centers more than the United States. China will get old before it is wealthy; Russia will grow increasingly corrupt, destitute, and sick; Iran will be torn by social conflicts and will face a deadly regional instability; and Europe, the favorite exemplar of the post-American world, is a cauldron of centrifugal forces caused by deep economic problems.[47]

The "shale gas" revolution will only strengthen the superior position of the United States by making it less dependent on foreign supplies of energy, thus reducing American strategic vulnerability to the political vagaries of the Middle East, Russia, and Venezuela.[48] A Citibank report even suggested that, assuming the continuation of current consumption and production trends, the United States could be relying exclusively on North American oil by 2020.[49] The most immediate outcome is "that the United States will no longer have any direct interest in ensuring supply flows out of the Gulf."[50] Naturally, such a development worries U.S. allies, such as Japan, which depend heavily on energy supplies from the Middle East and are concerned that an energy-independent United States could someday cease to provide security to sea-lanes.[51]

In brief, in this view, the United States will be secure and powerful irrespective of whether the rest of the world is prosperous or a decaying mess because the North American continent will provide the resources necessary for self-sufficiency. What stems from this is the belief that the United States can afford to be less engaged in the world. The idea of hemispheric defense is grounded in the possibility of maintaining security and prosperity without overseas commitments in Eurasia.

What is the evidence that these long- and short-term trends are resulting in a deprioritization of allies? Naturally, no U.S. administration will claim publicly that alliances are no longer needed. And the pure isolationist or offshore balancing position is, after all, an academic pursuit that has never been fully implemented and, with few exceptions that are mostly limited to naval circles, has no policy traction.[52] International pressures, strategic surprises, and political prudence keep in check the "come home, America" temptations of the right and left of the U.S. political spectrum.

Yet over the past few years Washington's rhetoric and actions have been at best ambivalent and at worst dismissive of many of America's staunchest allies. While this behavior does not amount to a full-fledged abandonment of allies, it certainly suggests a lower priority assigned to them—in particular to those that are most exposed to the menace of revisionist powers.

An important driver behind the Obama administration's deprioritization of alliances is the desire to focus attention and resources on domestic programs. The president, for instance, has been "reluctant to build relationships with foreign leaders," saving his time for the promotion of his domestic policies.[53] But the traditional temptations of trusting in a self-stabilizing world and seeking security through technology are influential in shaping the foreign policy approach that ought to allow the implementation of more inward-looking policies. These tendencies manifest themselves not as an open downgrading of the strategic relationships with key allies, much less as a formal renunciation of alliances themselves, but rather as greater reliance on certain mechanisms—big-power bargaining, international harmony, or technology—that deal with the sources of conflict for which alliances are intended as a solution.

Seeking a Great-Power Settlement

The first temptation is the assumption that U.S. rivals are essentially defensive in nature and a negotiated settlement of our conflict of interest is possible. The view is that the three main powers, China, Russia, and Iran, that have been increasingly assertive in their respective regions can be persuaded to channel their aspirations in more positive, peaceful ways and ultimately can be responsible regional actors instilling stability in their neighborhoods. To achieve this, it is necessary to manage through "accommodation" the challenges such powers pose.[54] The term "accommodation" carries politically risky connotations of "appeasement," and therefore other phrases have been used to describe the search for a grand bargain with U.S. rivals, such as "reset" or "responsible stakeholder." The term "strategic reassurance," for example, has been used to describe the Obama administration's policy, in the period prior to the Asia "pivot," of avoiding confrontation with Beijing and accommodating China's regional ascent.[55]

The underlying idea of all these concepts is that rival powers have some legitimate interests in their immediately adjacent regions, and Washington should be prepared to acknowledge them even if it entails giving ground on traditional American interests or values. By doing so the rivals would be satisfied, and some of the aggressiveness that has been directed against the United States and our core interests would abate. And, at a minimum, there could be a quid pro quo where the acceptance of some of their claims would be repaid by their support in other regions or on other issues. In practice this translated into a marked "great-power preference," predicated on the belief that our rival powers—Russia, China, Iran—would become less antagonistic were the United States to accommodate some of their perceived interests.

The purpose is to assuage U.S. enemies' fears, accommodate their regional interests, and engage in what is hoped will be a win-win cooperative relationship. The benefits would be twofold. First, the rival power, now a "partner," would help in some other area, whether with logistical aid in the Afghanistan War (in the case of Russia) or in mitigating North Korean behavior (in the case of China). If the world is a puzzle that demands cooperation rather than a chessboard where competition rules, such partnerships are not just desirable but feasible and lasting; it is a win-win situation. As Hillary Clinton stated, the United States "will lead by inducing greater cooperation among a greater number of actors and reducing competition, tilting the balance away from a multi-polar world and toward a multi-partner world."[56]

The second benefit would be a lowering of tensions in the international landscape. This would allow Washington to redirect resources away from foreign commitments toward domestic programs, the primary driver of the Obama doctrine. In fact, even after the initial approach of engaging rivals as "partners" clearly failed because none of them mitigated their behavior—and, particularly in the case of China, they became more aggressive—the Obama administration firmly stood by the idea that the world did not need continued high-level U.S. involvement. As the *Economist* put it, the White House pursues "a macro-policy of engagement that shuns the micromanagement of intervention."[57]

Regardless of the detailed substance of these approaches, the fundamental vision is heavily tinted by the view that these strategic competitors either have very limited, defensive interests that can be accommodated or have concerns that are in syntony with ours, or perhaps both. In any case, the outcome of this view is that the United States ought to pursue a preferential option for a great-power agreement that would accommodate them. But these assumptions are highly dubious, and the resulting policy stems more from a certain ideological rigidity than from prudence. Conflicts of interests between the United States and the mentioned powers are real.

Russian imperial aspirations, Iranian nuclear ambitions, and Chinese maritime claims create a zero-sum relationship with the United States, and certainly with American allies most proximate to those powers. Even if we may think that the world is no longer characterized by nineteenth-century balance-of-power logic, our rivals do not. Pursuing a cooperative, win-win strategy with a rival who has a zero-sum perspective is like inviting a grizzly bear to a backyard barbeque.

The "great bargain" approach is rarely in the interests of the smaller states in the respective regions. Some scholars distinguish between benign and coercive great-power agreement or concert. The former allows for the inputs of small states in the region in question, seen as key actors in the maintenance of local stability; their sovereignty and interests need to be taken into consideration by the great powers seeking an overarching agreement that would abate, if not end, their regional contest, and they need to be persuaded to accept the new order. The latter is an imposition of the great-power agreement, achieved without much consultation with the smaller powers.[58] In reality, when a great power seeks to accommodate another, there is little room for the inclusion of the interests of small states, as they are often the ones least interested in accepting the expansion of the local revisionist great power. These small states are on the path of that revision, making them strong supporters of the status quo, not of an accepted and negotiated enlargement of the revisionist's sphere of influence. Accommodation or appeasement is a strategy of great powers, not of small ones.

What this means is that there is a necessary, if perhaps unwanted, trade-off. By seeking a bargain with a rival, a great power weakens its own allies. And the more aggressively a great power pursues this accommodation, the more tenuous are its credibility with and influence over its allies. The reason is simple: states seek an alliance with a great power with the expectation that it will protect them against a nearby revisionist. They are deeply vested in the maintenance of the existing regional order, in which a mix of security guarantees and an absence of a revanchist power have guaranteed their independence and autonomy. When a regional potentate turns revisionist, nearby states expect greater support from their security guarantor and ally. A posture of accommodation by the latter then inevitably leads to ally alienation and nervousness. A great power cannot seek to accommodate a rival and retain the same level of alliance solidarity.

The temptation to seek a great-power agreement in the attempt to reduce costs of geopolitical rivalry has shaped U.S. policies toward the three main competitors in recent years. But it has been particularly visible in U.S. relations with Russia, receiving even the special moniker of "reset."[59] In essence, the reset meant that Washington blunted its criticism of human rights violations in Russia and deemphasized support for democracy in the post-Soviet space and U.S. security guarantees to NATO's easternmost members, hoping in return to receive Moscow's support in the Middle East and Afghanistan. The fact that Russia provided little cooperation in those regions and, as in the case of Iran and Syria, has actively opposed American interests appeared to have done little to discourage the Obama administration from continuing a posture of accommodation. The September 2009 cancellation of the ballistic missile defense accords that foresaw the building of the so-called third site in Poland and the Czech Republic was perceived as a friendly gesture to Putin's regime, a vocal opponent of a lasting U.S. presence in the territories of these Central European countries. The importance of both the ground-based interceptors (GBI) to be deployed in Poland and the midcourse-tracking radar to be placed in the Czech Republic transcended their mere technological usefulness. They would have meant a long-term presence of U.S. military personnel in these NATO countries, a source of security reassurance to them and deterrence to a revisionist Russia. As then Polish foreign minister Radek Sikorski put it a year earlier, "Everyone agrees that countries that have U.S. soldiers on their territory do not get invaded."[60] Unsurprisingly, Putin welcomed the cancellation of the third BMD site.

The overall result has been to weaken the bonds of the U.S. alliance in the region. As former Czech government official Aleksandr Vondra said, the "risk of [Obama's] approach to foreign policy lies in the U.S. reliance upon their traditional rivals rather than their longtime partners or allies." This cannot but undermine the trust and hence the strength of the alliance because allies will begin to doubt the usefulness of the security arrangement. Allies can no longer be taken "for granted if rivals get the carrot while the allies are just assigned the new tasks."[61]

Similarly, the Obama administration has persistently sought a grand reconciliation with Iran.[62] Driven by the desire to erase decades of enmity since the Iranian Revolution, the White House has pursued a dual-track approach. First, it has opposed in principle the development of Iranian nuclear weapons, seeking a diplomatic agreement that would be acceptable to Tehran. Second, it has de facto withdrawn from the regional contest that pitted it against Iran, in particular in Syria. Over the course of its tenure, the administration has engaged in several vocal openings toward the Iranian regime. For instance, in a high-publicity episode, Obama and Iran's president Hassan Rouhani exchanged letters, followed by a phone call.[63] One of the purposes was to convey to Tehran that Washington was eager to resolve disagreements about nuclear capacity and allow Iran to "demonstrate that its nuclear program is for exclusively peaceful purposes."[64] Similarly, Secretary of State John Kerry wrote in a message to the Iranian people that "we are strongly committed to resolving the differences between Iran and the United States, and continuing to work toward a new day in our relationship."[65]

Even discounting for excessive diplomatic rhetoric, Washington's posture has been one of openly seeking an accommodation with Iran in the hope that Tehran would turn into a status quo power—perhaps one that is capable of taking greater responsibility for the stability of its region. As President Obama stated in an interview with the *New Yorker*, "If we were able to get Iran to operate in a responsible fashion—not funding terrorist organizations, not trying to stir up sectarian discontent in other countries, and not developing a nuclear weapon—you could see an equilibrium developing between Sunni, or predominantly Sunni, Gulf states and Iran in which there's competition, perhaps suspicion, but not an active or proxy warfare."[66] The underlying argument seems to be that a grand bargain based on a historic reconciliation and a negotiated settlement of the conflict of interests would drastically alter the behavior of Iran. Again, the assumption is that the rival is defensive in nature, and U.S. policies are the principal cause of its overly aggressive conduct.

But the trade-off between great-power accommodation and alliance unity is inescapable. Washington's desire to accommodate Iran in the expectation that its energies can be channeled toward regional responsibility rather than revisionism worries traditional U.S. allies in the Middle East. As Saudi analysts recently warned, the "U.S.-Iranian dialogue will come at the expense of the Syrian and Lebanese people, and give Iran a renewed mandate to meddle in regional affairs."[67] The perception is that when the United States seeks a diplomatic settlement with a rival such as Iran, it will have to concede to it some interests, leaving the most vulnerable in the region at the mercy of the regional revisionist.[68] But the fear among other states in the region is more than simply a reinvigorated Iran. It is a fear that the United States is no longer competing, preferring to withdraw from the regional contest and seek the historical grand bargain with Iran. Many U.S. allies interpreted the unwillingness to react in any meaningful way to the collapse of Syria as a willful concession to Iran. As Iran expert Ray Takeyh writes, the "United States cannot reclaim its allies' confidence without being an active player in the Syria saga. . . . As long as the United States exempts itself from this conflict, its other pledges ring hollow to a skeptical Arab audience."[69] The trust of allies is commensurate with America's willingness to be a strategic actor in their region.

Technological Superiority

The other contemporary driver of alliance deprioritization is technology. It is a problem that transcends the particular American administration in power, and it may be a long-term trend that will make the credibility of an alliance with the United States more difficult in the future. The problem is not in the technological superiority of American power, which has made coalition warfare more difficult and has led some, like former secretary of defense Donald Rumsfeld, to be less than enthusiastic about war fighting with allies. Rather, it is a broader temptation to approach security threats through technological solutions alone rather than by combining them with political involvement, including alliances.

Drones have occupied front-page attention in recent years, but the technological temptation is broader. Since World War II, for instance, there has been a lingering hope that airpower alone could suffice to coerce the enemy.[70] If this could be achieved, the United States could avoid costly invasions and messy political involvements. A similar hope is that the threat of hostile missiles striking American soil could be decreased, if perhaps not outright defeated in the future, through some version of missile defense. In none of these cases has the technological reality made possible the hoped-for outcome, but the temptation remains and is often translated into policies.

Precision strikes from a safe distance, with minimal or, in the case of drones, no risk to American lives, are tactically appealing, and the United States should do all it can to maintain supremacy in this area. However, there is also the danger that American strategy becomes driven by its capabilities rather than the other way around.[71] In particular, this Promethean attitude may encourage a detachment from the political competition on the ground. The argument is that the United States does not need to participate in the political jostling on the ground in the region, whether it is Libya or Iraq or Pakistan, because it can keep the security conditions under check from a distance. A targeted strike, or in the future a defensive wall against a missile strike, may suffice to limit the effects of a menace arising in faraway regions without the need of sustained American presence. The war in Libya that ousted Muammar Gaddafi was a test run of such a view. Despite the resulting political chaos in Tripoli, the allure of one-off strikes allowed by American power projection and precision-strike capabilities continues to shape U.S. policies, most recently in the limited bombing campaign to hinder ISIS advances in Iraq. It is an approach that favors using American technological supremacy in place of political participation and military presence.

The effects are, however, problematic. The outcomes may be tactically dazzling: Gaddafi is dead or ISIS military columns may have been destroyed. But strategically the United States is turning in a purposeless military tool with limited political influence in the targeted regions. Moreover, for the argument of this book, U.S. allies worry that this approach leads to an either-or American strategy: either Washington uses military means or it is disengaged and absent. As

Nadia Schadlow points out, the "space in between" remains empty, leaving American allies alone in the regional competitive environment.[72] Surely there are many reasons why this is the case, but the attraction of technological solutions to security and political problems is a crucial one.

The Fear of Abandonment

The clearest outcome of this posture that seeks great-power accommodation and puts a premium on technological solution has been that U.S. allies are nervous while rivals are emboldened. Alliances are fragile associations, and their existence is contingent on multiple factors, ranging from the political will of the parties that makes the alliance possible to the larger geopolitical environment that makes it necessary. They therefore require constant maintenance, mitigating the fear that the alliance will not increase the security of its signatories.

Historically, the greatest fear of the weaker allies is that of abandonment, which in its broadest connotation means that not all involved actors consider credible the security guarantees offered to a state. The clearest form of abandonment is when one side reneges on the security commitments to the other party, like in the case of France and Great Britain negotiating with Nazi Germany in 1938 over their ally Czechoslovakia. But abandonment can take other, less conspicuous forms, driven in part by the fear of entrapment that the less dependent and more powerful ally may have. The stronger ally, in fact, wants to avoid being dragged into a local conflict instigated by its smaller ally, a conflict in which it has few immediate interests at stake.[73] To do so, it is tempting to ignore, or even undermine, the most immediate security concerns of the weaker, more dependent ally. The goal is to sidestep a war or tensions deemed unnecessary and distracting from more important objectives. The weak fear abandonment; the strong fear entrapment.[74]

A distant maritime power, such as the United States, is particularly susceptible to this entrapment anxiety. Geographic distance removes the perception of immediacy of the threat and puts a premium on global stability, often at the expense of local allies' interests. Such an approach was visible in U.S. foreign policy toward East Asia in the early Cold War, when the objective was not just to contain China but also to restrain U.S. allies from engaging in "little wars" that had the potential of escalating into great-power confrontation with China and the Soviet Union.[75] It is also possible to observe similar U.S. behavior in the Middle East, East Asia, and Central Europe in recent years. Washington seems preoccupied more with the possibility that some of its frontline, small, and exposed allies would engage in an overly aggressive foreign policy than with the persistent rhetorical aggressiveness and geopolitical expansion of the rival powers. In the Middle East, Washington often seems more worried about a potential Israeli attack on Iranian nuclear facilities than about Tehran's policies.[76] Israel, on the other hand, fears a nuclear Iran and frets at any sign of U.S. neglect. Similarly, in East Asia, the United States is always preoccupied with an overly assertive ally, such as Japan in the South China Sea disputes that could draw American forces into a local conflict, insignificant to Washington while vital to Tokyo. And in Central Europe, states such as Poland express their disappointment in the uselessness of the United States as an ally, while Washington worries about an anti-Russian Poland spoiling Moscow's promises of geopolitical cooperation.

The challenge is that the answer to entrapment fears often is a reluctance to support firmly the smaller ally and a posture of accommodation toward the common rival. This generates ally nervousness. As Glenn Snyder puts it, "The most undesirable side effect of conciliating the adversary is that it entails the risk of abandonment by the ally. His fear that one is contemplating realignment may induce him, not to try to discourage this by becoming more accommodative, as suggested above, but to realign preemptively or at least move closer to the opponent."[77] An attitude that deprioritizes allies forces those states to reconsider their foreign policy preferences. As we will discuss in the next chapter, such behavior on the part of the United States also emboldens our rivals.

CHAPTER 3

REVISIONIST POWERS' PROBING BEHAVIOR

The Morocco Question welds England and France together and must therefore be "liquidated." I tell you this confidentially, it is somewhat for show. We cannot yield too much.

—German chancellor
Bethmann-Hollweg, 1911

As U.S. power declines, Washington needs to rely on its allies in order to reach its goal of containing China's development. But whether it will get involved or use military intervention once there is a territorial dispute involving China and its neighbors, that is another issue.

—Major General Zhu Chenghu,
People's Liberation Army, 2014

America's deprioritization of allies creates opportunities for revisionist powers. Such transition is recurrent in geopolitics; international relations are always characterized by uncertainty. Policy makers have to navigate a landscape that is often difficult to delineate, full of strategic actors whose purposes are often obscure and whose power is difficult to assess. Intentions are notoriously hard to divine, in part because rival states obfuscate them but in part because often the states themselves do not have a clear and consistent perception of what they want to achieve. Uncertainty arises also out of a more quantifiable source of knowledge, an assessment of hard power, which is imperfect and results in widely different estimates. It is sufficient to recall the challenges of assessing Soviet power throughout the Cold War.

Moments characterized by alleged large shifts in relative power present particularly acute problems of assessing power and intentions, adding an additional layer of ambiguity and uncertainty. Rumors of change put in doubt the relatively well-known, or at least familiar, geopolitical situation. All parties involved are unsure about their position relative to the others, the extent of their political sway, and the match between their commitments and their power. The established great powers may have a crisis of confidence, while emboldened rising states are uncertain how far their influence extends as well as how solid and credible is the power reach of their weakening rival. Revisionist powers now openly but cautiously question what was the grudgingly accepted geopolitical status quo.

Rising powers are thus curious but careful. They are interested in pushing the existing boundaries of their influence but do not know how far they can do so without meeting a firm opposition of the other power. In the current case, U.S. rivals—China, Russia, and Iran—appear keen to assert their influence and establish what they deem their rightful position in their respective regions and in the world but are also eager to avoid a direct confrontation with the United States. Uncertain about their own power relative to the United States, they test the hypothesis of a growing American economic and military fragility and decaying political reach. To figure out the new map of power, and possibly to redraw it at low cost, revisionist powers engage in probing.

In this chapter we examine this behavior—the probing by revisionist powers. We define probing as a low-intensity and low-risk test aimed at gauging the opposing state's power and will to maintain security and influence over a region. It is a set of actions that studiously avoids a direct military confrontation with the leading power by targeting the outer limits of its commitments and interests. There, along the outer rim of its influence, the hegemon is at the furthest of its commitments and power projection. The perception, or rather the suspicion, of its decline is most consequential along these frontiers of power because the revisionist state senses opportunities in its own neighborhood and searches for confirmation of the rival's weakness.

Probing is an opportunistic behavior. It occurs when the revisionist states detect a permissive international situation, namely, when they think that the existing great power is retreating. It is still a behavior that is characterized by self-doubt and uncertainty, although if unanswered it results in the confirmation of the belief in the rival's decline and may lead to ever more assertive challenges to the international order and expansions of influence by the geopolitical challenger.

Over the past few years, and with greater frequency and brazenness, regional powers opposed to the United States have been engaging in probing. Russia, Iran, and China in their respective regions have been working under the hypothesis that the United States is retreating, out of choice, fatigue, or weakness, or all three combined. The American retrenchment is more pronounced in the Middle East, with the ending of U.S. combat presence in Iraq and the drawdown in Afghanistan as well as the unwillingness to intervene in Syria, leaving a vacuum for Iranian influence. But there is an equally pervasive perception of American withdrawal or decline in the other two key regions, Europe and Asia. In Europe, the perception is that Washington is redirecting its strategic focus and resources toward Asia and has limited willpower to back its extended deterrent, giving Moscow a window of opportunity to redraw the map in Europe's eastern "borderlands." And in Asia, a rising and confident China looks at a United States hobbled by financial crises, fiscal imbalances, and a decade-long military overstretch in the Middle East. The reasons are different, but the broad perception is similar: the revisionist states sense an opening left by a distracted and weakening United States. And they probe along the periphery of American influence, from Ukraine to the South China Sea through the Persian Gulf.

ORIGINS OF PROBING BEHAVIOR

Probing stems out of a tentative belief that the existing geopolitical order is amenable to change, and it seeks to confirm this suspicion. A perceived geopolitical change remains only that, perceived, until facts on the ground confirm it. An assessment of a state's power is merely an estimate of how that state may fare in a clash with others. As such, it informs a set of expectations for the future, and it may or may not reflect reality. Often there is little agreement among powers as well as within those powers as to which assessment of power is correct.[1] Today, for instance, questions about the continued resilience of American power abound both abroad and in the United States, and there are analysts on both sides of the argument.[2] Regardless of where one stands on the issue of American relative decline or retrenchment, the mere existence of such a debate is a source of concern because it points to an absence of clarity on the geopolitical scene. The various strategic actors no longer know where they stand on the international pecking order and are confused as to how far their own influence can reach and what the responses of their rivals may be.[3] These are periods of a tense peace but also of great uncertainty about the nature of the security environment. As a scholar put it, it is the "fog of peace" that makes strategic planning more difficult because it is unclear who the enemy is, how much power a potential rival may have, and where the boundaries of political influence are.[4] As history indicates, often such an uncertain strategic environment degenerates into war, which is a "dispute about the measurement of power."[5]

The outcome of a war is the violent clarification of such confusion. It settles the dispute about the assessment of power. A victory or defeat in war, followed by changes in boundaries, military bases, or political affiliations of governments, is one way to prove or disprove a perceived alteration in relative power. As British historian A.J.P. Taylor observed, the "test of a Great Power is ... the test of strength for war."[6] After its defeat in the 1853–1856 Crimean War, Russia was clearly militarily inferior to European states (even though the victorious powers, Britain, France, Turkey, and later Austria, also encountered serious difficulties in projecting power to the Black Sea theater) and consciously chose to retreat, reform, and rebuild its foundations of power, known as a policy of *recueillement*, in order to maintain its status as a European great power.[7] There is no clearer confirmation of a state's decline than a loss in a direct confrontation with a rising power; there is equally no better proof that the perception of relative decline was incorrect when the aspirant revisionist state is soundly defeated. In the immediate aftermath of a war it is therefore easier to assess one's own power relative to that of the other players. War lifts the "fog of peace."

But war is rarely pursued simply to clarify one's own uncertain standing relative to the other strategic actors. To engage in war, the ultimate test of power, is exceedingly dangerous, and no leader wants to enter into a violent conflict simply as a way of assessing the power of its own state relative to the target. Wars are realms of luck and unknowns as much as of more calculable kinetic clashes, and consequently the outcomes do not always align with the expectations preceding them.[8] In fact, the losing party in a conflict has often entered that war having overestimated its own capability relative to the rival. Many in Europe, for instance, expected in summer 1914 to be "home for Christmas," only to remain in the bloody trenches for several years. Given this inherent uncertainty, the risk of being proven wrong for both the perceived rising and declining powers is high, and great powers in history seem to stumble into wars rather than consciously pursue them as tests of strength. The risks of war are incalculable and thus extremely high.

A less risky way of assessing a changing equilibrium of power is through probing. This is a form of strategic behavior meant to test existing perceptions of power relations, seeking at the same time to draw the presumably new boundaries of influence. The rising or revisionist state, in particular, is strongly motivated to test the will of its seemingly declining rival power. It has the aspiration, mitigated by the fear of the rival great power, to alter the existing geopolitical map. Such states, unhappy with the existing international order, which they perceive perhaps as imposed on them and certainly as increasingly not reflective of their own rising aspirations and power, have the most to gain from probing. If this behavior confirms the perception that the existing great power is on the wane and that the map drawn by it is no longer supported by its strength and will, the revisionist state may be able to reassert lost influence over its neighborhood and revise a previous settlement. At the same time, such a state has also a strong incentive to avoid a direct clash with its main antagonist lest the perception of its relative weakening turns out not to match reality. A strategy of direct confrontation is risky because its success is predicated on the relative weakness of the targeted power, the existing hegemon, and this is exactly what is unknown. If the probing power becomes convinced that its hypothesis of its own superiority (and of the relative decline of the rival) is true, then a direct clash may occur. But until that confirmation, a safer, less risky course of action is to engage in a probing behavior, akin to testing the water before jumping in. Probes target the frontier of the rival power's influence, where its interests are less pronounced, its power is at its farthest projection, and its political clout at its weakest. At these outer edges the response of the great power is expected to be most restrained, while the gains of the probing state are most likely to occur.

The purpose of probing, therefore, is to gauge the resolve of the targeted powers. We will return to this later, but here it is important to note that a probing action is also a way of showing the renewed or freshly acquired capabilities and aspirations that otherwise would remain latent and without tangible effects. One cannot revise an established order by keeping one's own intentions and capabilities hidden. Showing a new military platform, often in a carefully choreographed event, is one way of signaling growing power. The 1907–1909 voyage of the American "Great White Fleet," meant to showcase the emergent global naval strength of the United States, was one such episode. The round-the-globe cruise was not targeted at a specific power and did not aim to extend American influence over a particular state or region. Rather, it was a broad assertion of American capabilities and global reach, and the other powers, Great Britain in particular, certainly received it as a sign that the United States was a power to be reckoned with.

But probing is more than showing off. It is not simply an action of strutting on the world stage with newly acquired military gadgets and political confidence but a precisely targeted action with clear objectives. Through probing, a revisionist state aims at changing the existing geopolitical order where it thinks it can, namely, at the farthest points of the ruling great power's influence. Probing, therefore, is not just mere signaling of displeasure with the rules of the international order and the map of power; it aims to revise the order gradually and carefully, starting from the outer layers of the rival great power's influence.

FEATURES OF PROBING

The purpose of probing is threefold. First, a probing state aims to check whether the rumors of its rival's weakening are true. A probe is a test, meant to elicit a response from the targeted power. Second, the revisionist state that engages in probing behavior wants to avoid a direct military clash with the existing great power. The risks of being wrong about the rival's resolve and capability are simply too big. Third, the state's objective is to achieve, if possible, low-cost revision of the existing regional order.

These purposes can be seen in the features that characterize a probe and distinguish it from other types of behavior, ranging from full-out aggression to commercial pressures and diplomatic démarches.

First, probes are *low intensity*, vigilantly avoiding a direct war with the main rival power. They are below the horizon of direct military confrontation. The revisionist state has no interest in starting an all-out military conflict with the rival great power, perhaps declining but still more than a match. The level of violence used, therefore, is low, and probes are limited projections of power in areas of less pronounced interest to the rival. A probing power engages in a lot of self-restraint; it intentionally elects to keep the use of force at a minimum. It can but chooses not to escalate. A probe is a calculated gamble, not a foolish thrashing around.

The desire to avoid a war with the existing hegemon often leads the revisionist to project power under cover of civilian or paramilitary forces, part of a larger trend of "civilianization" of conflict.[9] By using unmarked units to harass a U.S. protégé, a state is able to deny authorship of provocative actions and thereby avoid a more violent and direct war while at the same time chipping away at the rival's influence and wealth. The possibility of denying that an aggression has occurred drives costs of revisionism lower. For instance, the sixteenth-century privateer Sir Francis Drake acted on behalf of Queen Elizabeth I, raiding Spanish shipping but never in an official capacity. The queen went so far as to tell a Spanish ambassador that "Drake was a private adventurer, and that she had nothing to object to his alleged execution." She was careful in not provoking Spain too much but eager to "singe the King of Spain's beard."[10]

A similar approach can be seen around the world today. The initial Russian push into Crimea in 2014 was done anonymously with unmarked special forces, dubbed by Ukrainians as the "little green men," a clear example of a long-standing Russian practice of tactical deception and disguise (*maskirovka*).[11] It was an indication that Moscow was unsure whether Ukrainian forces would react, and, in the event of a determined opposition, it maintained the option of either escalating with larger conventional forces or halting operations and denying. Moscow seemed to be more careful in masking the identity of its forces in eastern Ukraine, where the local opposition was more assertive and the Western displeasure with Russian aggression more pronounced. The greater the risk of a strong response from the actors targeted, the more carefully tailored, dissimulated, and low-intensity is the probe. The use of unmarked troops and paramilitary forces allows Russia to claim that no aggression has occurred, and thus no military response from Ukraine or from the West is warranted.

China has been testing the limits of the influence of the United States and its allies in the South China Sea using an array of civilian-looking vessels. Its fishing fleet, combined with a fishery-enforcement fleet, is integrated into its military institutions and plays an active role in expanding China's maritime reach. As Lyle Goldstein observes, this is part of a "strategy of 'defeating harshness with kindness' (*yi rou ke gang*)" whereby China deploys "unarmed fishing vessels or fisheries enforcement vessels to confront foreign vessels operating in its EEZ and claimed waters."[12] This low-intensity push tests the frontier of American influence in a way that makes a U.S. response difficult.[13] A foray by a Chinese naval vessel into contested waters can be countered with the might of the United States and its ally's navy; a probe by fishing vessels manned by Chinese fishermen does not warrant the involvement of the U.S. Seventh Fleet. This is risky behavior, but it also indicates a desire by China to avoid a war with the other regional powers as well as with the United States.[14]

If it is openly a military attack, a probe is conducted with a strong and perhaps warranted belief that the rival power will not intervene because it is distracted elsewhere and because it deems the targeted region to be of little immediate interest. This was the case of the Russian war with Georgia in 2008, when Moscow felt emboldened by NATO ambivalence to extending its membership process to Tbilisi and by the American strategic distraction by the wars in Afghanistan and Iraq (where a small Georgian contingent was deployed). The Russian gamble was based on the expectation of no meaningful Western, and American in particular, response. The objective was to chip away at the unwelcome Western influence in Russia's neighborhood but without spurring an equally unwelcome Western military reply—to "singe America's beard," as it were.

Second, a revisionist state engages in probing because it sees it as a *low-risk but high-reward* behavior. The low risk stems in part from the first feature, the carefully tailored level of aggressiveness that is expected not to elicit a full-out military response by the rival. It is also related to the third feature, explained below, namely, the fact that the immediate target of probing is geographically and political peripheral to the interests of the rival great power, and consequently contributes to the low likelihood of a forceful military response. But on top of being pursued as a low-risk action, a probe can yield high strategic rewards. Most often the revisionist power seems to direct probing behavior to its immediate vicinity, hoping to expand its influence over neighboring and thus more controllable regions.[15] It is there that it has the greatest chances of extending its own political shadow successfully. Probes are rarely long-distance projections of power because incursions deep into the rival's sphere of influence are more liable to be met with more assertive responses as well as being less likely to establish durable control by the probing state. The farther the revisionist state engages in probing behavior, the more high risk and low reward it is, and vice versa. Hence the more likely locations for probing behavior are in the near neighborhood of the revisionist power.

Furthermore, probes focus on strategically important regions, either resource rich or located along lines of communication, or both. Elizabethan England, for example, conducted raiding probes of Spain's vulnerable transatlantic arteries bringing gold from the New World—not its stronger positions in the Mediterranean. Imperial Germany's probes of the Anglo-French alliance targeted Morocco, located near the strategically important choke point of Gibraltar but beyond easy reach of the main British fleet. Today China's probes of U.S. allies in Asia often target oil and gas fields in the South China Sea. In all these cases, since the goal of probing is to test the power and commitment of a rival state, it has to be directed at regions where the rival's influence is present but not preponderant. It is unlikely that regions of no geostrategic value or with few resources have much of a presence of the rival great power, and as such they are not prime material for probing. A state may still have imperial aspirations in such regions, but not every extension of power is a probe. Probing is not simply grabbing new areas of influence but first and foremost to test the will of the rival. There may be, of course, the bonus that if the probe is successful, it may result in the addition of strategically important regions.

The third feature of probing is that it is *peripheral or indirect*. The target of the probe is the periphery or the frontier of the tested power where the rival's presence is at its farthest reach, its interests are less pronounced, and thus its response is expected to be muted. Fearful of a militarily assertive response, the state that is probing is careful not to target areas that are clearly considered of primary and existential interests, such as the rival's homeland or its immediate neighbors. Hence the visits of Russian or Iranian naval vessels to Venezuelan ports are less a probe per se than an act of grandstanding, since all sides know that the United States could quickly bring overwhelming force to bear in the event of a crisis. These are temporary publicity stunts rather than a calculated attempt to test the hegemon's commitment to maintaining the status quo.

Probes test for perceived weaknesses, not strengths, and it is on the outer boundaries of the existing great power that its influence is likely to appear the most fragile. The revisionist power is interested in probing the power and influence of its rival in places where that influence is at its weakest, overstretched, and uncertain. During the Peloponnesian War the Spartan general Brasidas adopted such a peripheral strategy, but only a decade into the conflict. The initial Spartan approach of annual invasion of Attica, Athens's immediate neighborhood, failed to inflict sufficient damage to end the war. It was only with Brasidas, sent north with a small force of helots (minimizing thus the risk to Spartan manpower), that Sparta changed its strategy to one similar to probing, by persuading or forcing distant Athenian allies in Thrace to switch sides. And many did reconsider their allegiance to Athens, because, as Thucydides observes, there did not seem to be much risk given the distance from Athens and their belief that this empire was on the wane.[16] Striking the rival's periphery, and its allies, not only was cheaper than assaulting it directly but also forced it to devote a lot of resources to reasserting the lost influence.

Global powers in particular have a "periphery or frontier problem" that invites probing. A lengthy frontier, distant from the homeland and thus from key logistical bases, is difficult to protect. The sheer amount of power needed to outfit the distant outposts, combined with the uncertainty as to the location and timing of potential attacks, makes it impossible to have an impermeable frontier. When a power assesses threats, the key questions of "where, when, and by whom" are directly related to the length of the imperial frontier. A regional power has well-delimited borders and a clear idea of who the rival is. For instance, from the final decade of the nineteenth century on, Germany was burdened with the possibility of a two-front war, with France on one side and Russia on the other; a serious problem of military planning caused by poor diplomacy but not a source of strategic confusion. For a global power, it is that strategic clarity that is missing, resulting in the need to prepare for multiple contingencies and ultimately to stretch resources in several theaters of potential action.[17] While imperial Germany could concentrate on its two-front problem, Great Britain at the turn of the twentieth century had to consider threats from Russia (in Central Asia, pushing toward India), Japan (in the Asian littoral sphere), France (in Africa as well as the Mediterranean), and Germany (in Europe and the North Sea in particular). Through deft diplomacy, it managed to neutralize the first three, allowing it to focus on the German naval threat, thereby limiting its "frontier problem."

In practice, probing the periphery of a rival's great power often translates into testing the strength of its alliances. Most great powers, or empires, expand their influence in informal ways, through political arrangements with local elites and formal alliances.[18] The security of these great powers, in particular of ones with global reach, therefore resides not only in the safety of their borders but in their ability to hold rivals at a distance and thwart their challenges to faraway interests. They do so only in part through their own forces and rely heavily on the presence of allies that provide additional military strength and local deterrence (see chapter 5). Allies are at the periphery of influence and strength of great powers, and it is there that the powers' commitment and influence are at their weakest. It is clear that a state will respond to an encroachment on its territorial possessions or to an attack against its forward deployed forces. It is less certain, however, that a state will respond in the same strong fashion to similar actions directed against its allies and their interests. The security guarantee extended to them, the foundation of the alliance, is a promissory note that carries a high degree of uncertainty. Placing bases with troops on the territory of an ally is a time-tested way of diminishing this uncertainty. As Thomas Schelling put it, the role of U.S. troops in South Korea was simply to die, buttressing the American security guarantee to its ally.[19] The loss of American soldiers to an initial attack by the enemy would, so the argument goes, create powerful pressures for Washington to respond. French general Ferdinand Foch, when asked before World War I how many British troops would be needed for the security of France, replied, "One single private soldier . . . and we would take good care that he was killed."[20]

Probes by the revisionist power are not attacks against these bases and forces that underwrite the credibility of the extended deterrent. Rather, they target areas that may be of great importance to the ally but not necessarily to the security patron. That is the periphery of the periphery, so to speak, the tip of the great power's commitment.

The United States has a particularly pronounced "periphery" problem. There are few direct threats to the continental United States, short of a large-scale assault with weapons of mass destruction or the tragic yet relatively small and isolated terrorist attack. While the absence of a contiguous threat is a geopolitical blessing, it also means that most of the menaces to U.S. interests and security are outside of the North American continent. Hence, in the competitive international environment, "the strategic position of the United States rests ultimately on its ability to project power over great distances. "[21] In practice this entails managing alliances that maintain stability and keep U.S. rivals on the defensive in key regions of the world, in particular along an arc from Europe to East Asia through the Middle East. And historically this has been, and continues to be, achieved by extending U.S. deterrence beyond the North American continent to the countries, some allied by treaty and some neutral. Such an extended deterrence is a "'three-nation problem' involving an aggressor nation, the United States, and some smaller nation which is the object of the aggressor's designs and which Washington seeks to protect. "[22] Probing by an "aggressor nation" aims to test U.S. commitment to these "smaller nations," which constitute the periphery of American interests and power.

In the most successful case, probing could achieve a dual purpose: first, it tests the level and credibility of the commitment of the distant security patron, and second, it can weaken the rival alliance. It does so by targeting the foundation of the alliance, the belief that the alliance is beneficial to both parties and that it is effective. As Michael Mandelbaum has observed, alliances need to manage two concurrent fears: one of entrapment, namely, of being dragged into undesirable wars of limited significance and local interest, and one of abandonment, the apprehension of often the weaker ally of being abandoned by its security provider when the need comes. [23] Probing aims to increase the rival's fear of entrapment while at the same time stoking worries of abandonment among its weaker and more dependent partners. By harassing the local interests of the rival's peripheral allies, the revisionist power wants to drive up the risk of a local war, perceived by the rival as a distraction and a potential drain of resources. At the same time, it wants to indicate to the smaller allies that they may not rely on their security provider to defend their local, narrow interest, and that they may be abandoned. The goal is to drive a wedge in the opposing alliance by leveraging the fundamental dilemma of alliances—the fears of entrapment and abandonment.

This is where probing becomes more than a simple test of the rival's strength. By targeting the outer edges of the existing hegemon, and thus harassing its alliance system, the revisionist is engaging in a much more significant endeavor. The contest for regional, or global, control is in the end a contest for allies. A.J.P. Taylor observed that when Germany "was bidding for the domination of Europe" in the decade before the outbreak of World War I, "her chosen method was to isolate the independent Powers one from another."[24] As we point out in chapter 5, allies are, among other things, an extension of the distant patron's power. Were they to peel away from the side of their security guarantor—or vice versa, were the security guarantor to decide that the risk of continued support of a distant ally pressured by a regional revisionist power is too big—it would in either case signify a retrenchment of power for that offshore patron. The loss of allies is both a confirmation of the waning sway of that rival great power as well as a further reduction in its reach. To be alone in international relations is to be vulnerable, inviting further aggressive behavior from the rival. Walter Lippmann observed in 1943, "No one knew, not Hitler, not Stalin, not Chamberlain or Daladier, the relative strength of the Axis and of the opposing combination. Only when Hitler succeeded at Munich in separating the Franco-British allies from Russia, had he so altered the balance of power in his favor that a war for the conquest of Europe was from his point of view a good risk."[25] War is an extension of successful probing.

The benefits of targeting allies of a rival, rather than the rival itself, are well recognized in history. The astute observer of history and politics Niccolò Machiavelli noted in his *Discourses* that attacking a rival's ally is always a preferred option: "For I know especially that if I assault his friend, either he will resent it and I will have my intention of making war with him, or by not resenting it he will uncover his weakness or faithlessness in not defending a client of his. Both the one and the other of these two things are able to take away his reputation and to make my plans easier."[26] In the strategic behavior we describe, the probing power is not interested in "making war" with the rival, and therefore a probe is not a full-out attack on a rival's ally or supported state. The risks of activating the security guarantees or assurances that ought to be at the foundation of that alliance are too big. But it is an offensive act of sorts, which threatens the interests of the rival's ally. The security patron will either respond, thereby disproving the perception of its weakness, or will not, "taking away his reputation" and undermining its alliance.

China has been particularly astute in picking geographic objectives that are important to U.S. allies but only indirectly important to the United States, such as the shoals and reefs around the Spratly and Paracel Islands. By ratcheting up the pressure in these areas, China causes the targeted states to intensify their demands for American assurance while diminishing U.S. willingness to back allies over seemingly petty issues that could lead to a larger conflict. Americans do not want to risk their lives for insignificant and distant rocks.

Russia achieves a similar effect by reigniting NATO's eastern frontier through its attack on Ukraine and a series of threats against exposed NATO members around the Baltic Sea. Those are areas that until recently have not been prominent on the U.S. strategic radar screen but are naturally vital to those smaller states inhabiting the region, which in turn are driven to make increasingly vocal requests for security reassurances from Washington. As in the case of the South China Sea, however, the local and limited nature of the rival's probes generates in Washington as much a perception of threat as fear of a larger conflict, raising doubts about the benefits of extending security guarantees to these allies and partners. In the end, these peripheral probes pursued by U.S. rivals can create a wedge between Washington and its regional friends and allies.

These three features—low intensity, low risk but high reward, peripheral—point also to the timing of the probing behavior. Probing is a strategic behavior that arises out of an uncertain assessment of power relations. It is the product of doubt, not confidence, in the resilience of the existing international order. As such it arises early on in the transition of power, when perceptions of rise and decline are not firm. The vagueness of the security environment creates among revisionist powers the perception of opportunities that a probing behavior aims to test. Hence probing should occur with less frequency in the immediate aftermath of a war, when, as we point out, an assessment of relative power carries the weight of the ultimate test, war. A defeated power may have all the incentives to upset the existing order, but unless it has no ability to evaluate its clearly weakened position, it has no capacity to do so. After a defeat probing may be tempting but is unfeasible. Such states are more likely to pursue a policy of *recueil-lement* (introspection, a moment of pause and strengthening), charac-terized by internal reforms, modernization, and very limited foreign engagements mostly aimed at dividing the opposing alliance.[27]

When, however, the perceived weakening of the founding power puts in doubt the existing international settlement, the desire to re-vise it is matched by the possibility of doing so. The perception of American weakening, or at least retrenchment, therefore opens up a window of opportunity for those powers that aspire to expand their own influence and resent the Western order and its institutions.

THE AUDIENCES OF PROBING

Another useful way of looking at the strategic behavior of probing is by considering the audiences involved. As we argued, a revisionist power pursues probing behavior to check whether new boundaries of influence are feasible given the perceived weakening of the rival. The main purpose is therefore to elicit a response from the targeted audiences. That response, or lack thereof, supplies information nec-essary to draw the new outline of the geopolitical map. Probing is first and foremost a violent and risky didactic exercise.

The most direct audience is the immediate target of the probing behavior, usually an ally, or an aspirant to be an ally, of the rival great power. Probing here seeks to gauge the willingness and capacity of the targeted state to withstand pressure, and ultimately it aims to push that state to sever itself from its security patron. As we exam-ine in chapter 4, vulnerable frontier allies of a great power actively consider alternative strategic options, especially when they perceive themselves to be under threat from a neighboring revisionist power and to have a fraying security guarantee from a distant patron. A probe is meant to ratchet up the threat perception while also attempt-ing to establish a sense of strategic isolation and separation from the security provider.

Hence as important as, if not more important than, the first audi-ence is the second one: the distant but more powerful ally and secu-rity provider. Probing tests indirectly the regional staying power of the rival hegemon. While carefully avoiding direct confrontation, the revisionist power wants to assess the commitment of the opposing great power to its ally in the near neighborhood. What the revisionist is testing, therefore, is not the rival's *resolve* to oppose other great powers, but the rival's *reliability* to its own allies.[28] Resolve is the willingness to risk war to achieve one's own objectives: the more diffuse and distant the threatened interests, the less the resolve. Given that the target of probes is peripheral and not the rival's homeland or troops and bases, the resolve is assumed to be small. Direct war between the revisionist probing state and the rival great power is unlikely to erupt as a result. Moreover, the probing state is not interested in finding out whether the rival has the will to fight a direct war: the stakes would be simply too high and the outcome too uncertain. A direct challenge would test the resolve of the rival. Poking around the periphery, therefore, is a poor test of the rival's willingness to fight a war. History seems to confirm this. For instance, as scholars have pointed out, Soviet leaders did not think that U.S. responses to peripheral threats (e.g., in the Third World) could serve as indicators of future American behavior when its core interests (NATO allies, Japan, or the U.S. homeland) were threatened.[29] Whether the United States responded militarily or not to a Soviet foray in Angola or Ethiopia could not be easily translated into expectations of future American behavior in Europe. But it does affect the perception of whether the United States wants to fight in other peripheral areas. "If Soviet leaders were to gain the impression that the United States is firmly set upon a course of neo-isolationism and the absolute avoidance of intervention in local wars, they might become dangerously adventurous in the Middle East and elsewhere."[30]

Probing, however, tests the reliability of the rival great power— that is, its willingness to protect and stand by its ally or aspiring allies. The immediate target is not a test of the rival's general credibility but only of its commitment to the security ties to the state. Probing wants to elicit a response (or lack thereof) from the rival great power regarding the seriousness of its commitment to the directly targeted state. To be perceived as a reliable ally means to instill the belief that promised security guarantees will hold even in cases of heightened tensions and, in final analysis, of conflict.

Consequently a perception of low reliability results in the belief that the alliance is fragile and that it may be in the small state's interest to seek accommodation with the nearby revisionist power. As delineated above, probes are carefully tailored to split the distant security patron from its regional allies, showing it to be unreliable.

Even if it achieves nothing else, probing can introduce doubts about the security guarantees, forcing the security patron to renew its promises. The less reliable the security patron is perceived by its allies, the more insistent are their demands for continued security guarantees. Probing thus imposes an immediate cost on the rival great power by reactivating a frontier region that until then was dormant and by pressing the rival to expend more resources and political capital to reassert its security guarantees.

Finally, the third audience is composed of the geopolitical onlookers, states that are watching the behavior and derive their own conclusions about the resilience of the existing great power. The strategic interaction spurred by a probe does not directly affect them, but they perceive it as a regionally circumscribed development with potentially more global repercussions. That is, a probe is limited to a specific region but has radiating effects as others also see it for what it really is: a test of the resilience and reliability of the great power that may be analogous in other regions.

Recent academic literature puts in doubt the idea that reputation for commitment is interdependent. Thomas Schelling, among others, articulated that idea in his classic work from 1966 where he argued that U.S. reputation was global, and a loss in one region would have negative impact in other areas. Reputation was not compartmentalized in different regions, in large measure because the rival, the Soviet Union, was one and the same across the world map. Hence "we tell the Soviets that we have to react here because, if we did not, they would not believe us when we say that we will react there."[31] Academics have relentlessly questioned this argument, resulting in copious writings asserting that reputation is not interdependent and, according to some, does not even matter.[32] Reputation is merely a cult and does not exist in international relations.[33] Policy makers, however, disagree and continue to speak of reputation for resolve and reliability as something that not only matters and requires constant work but also is interdependent. They prefer to rely on time-tested authors, from Thucydides to Machiavelli, who consider reputation as indispensable to political power.[34] In brief, there is a deep gap between academics and policy makers on the issue of reputation.

By observing recent events in the three frontier regions—Central Europe, the Middle East, and East Asia—we think that the truth is closer to Schelling's view. It is clear that the effects of probing behavior do not remain confined to the immediate actors involved (the probing power, the direct target—usually a rival's ally—and the rival great power). Other actors in the region are keenly aware of the revisionist state's probing and of the responses of the United States. For instance, other states, from the Baltics to Poland and Ukraine, observed Russia's war against Georgia in 2008 and its invasion of Crimea in 2014 with great trepidation.[35] These wars were symptoms of a more assertive Russia; a source of worry in themselves. But they were also meant to elicit an answer from the United States. Any sign of American hesitation to respond quickly and firmly to Russian small wars in the two states was perceived as affecting directly these other states, not directly involved in the probing event. America's reputation for reliability, in other words, was at stake, even though Georgia and Ukraine were not NATO members but only aspiring to closer security and political relations with the United States and the EU. Similarly, Pacific nations from Japan to Australia follow with great attention China's probing behavior in the South China Sea that puts pressure on Vietnam, the Philippines, and Taiwan. They too seek to figure out whether the United States has the will to remain as a security provider in this region and to the "global commons" in general. How the United States responds to a probe in a particular region therefore affects its regional image.

The question is whether there is also a wider, global audience to regional probes. Do Middle Eastern leaders watch American responses to Russia's probing in Eastern Europe? Do Kremlin elites draw lessons from U.S. actions along the "first chain of islands" in East Asia? Or, do Chinese neo-Mahanian leaders think the United States is on the wane if it accommodates Putin's imperial fantasies? According to the latest academic literature, the answer should be negative: how the United States is perceived to be doing in one region does not

translate into a similar perception elsewhere. The practical implica-
tion of such a view is that the United States should not have fought
in Vietnam to prove that it would stand its ground in Europe; similarly, it ought not to oppose Putin around the Black Sea basin simply
to demonstrate that it will oppose China in the South China Sea.

But we are not so confident that there are no connections between
regional demonstrations of will and power. It is at least plausible, and
perhaps safer, to argue that there are wider, global effects of probing.
First, the world is indeed global, and regions are not hermetically
separated from each other. As Nicholas Spykman observed, "Global
war, as well as global peace, means that all fronts and all areas are interrelated. No matter how remote they are from each other, success
or failure in one will have an immediate and determining effect on
the others. It is necessary, therefore, to see the world as a whole and
to weigh the measures taken to achieve victory in the light of conditions in all theaters."[36] Leaders watch and learn from other regions,
more than previously in history when conflicts were limited by technology and geographic knowledge to a contiguous region. Because
of their domestic opacity, it is difficult to prove that America's rivals
learn from U.S. behavior in other regions, but the question whether
they do so needs to be asked. Chinese military officials, for example,
have commented publicly on lessons for China from the U.S. handling of the war in Ukraine.[37] As one analyst noted, "It might be
impossible to determine definitively whether the Ukraine Crisis has
impacted China's risk calculus in hotspots such as the South and
East China Sea, but the evidence . . . certainly suggests that such eastern reverberations are quite plausible."[38] At a minimum we have to
recognize that some cross-regional analyses do occur, and it is safer
to assume that the U.S. reputation does not stay limited to a region.

Second, the much stronger effect of probing appears to be on U.S.
allies and friends, the key geopolitical spectators. They watch how
the United States treats other allies and form an opinion regarding American reliability. The former director of Saudi intelligence
summed up the view of many officials from U.S. allied states in
the Persian Gulf when he said in reaction to the Russian seizure of
Crimea, "While the wolf is eating the sheep, there is no shepherd to
come to the rescue."[39] Israel was interested in the war in Georgia;

Japanese analysts followed the Obama administration's decision to cancel the Ballistic Missile Defense (BMD) program in Central Europe; and Polish experts watch U.S. moves in East Asia.[40] The probing by revisionist states is first and foremost an attempt to test the strength of their rival's commitment to its allies and friends.

In sum, probing behavior by revisionist states targets these specific audiences in order to elicit responses from them. The goal is to figure out whether and how to draw the new map of power. And it puts the burden on the targeted audiences: their responses determine whether the probe is successful.

EVALUATION OF PROBING: SUCCESS OR FAILURE

From the perspective of the revisionist power that engages in probing, whether a probe has achieved its objectives determines its success or failure. The minimum objective of the probing state is to measure the rival's staying power in its neighboring region, an objective that is achieved whether the targeted powers respond or not, but it is difficult to interpret. The targeted rival may be tempted to ignore the probe not out of a sense of its own weakness but in the belief that ignoring the test will send a signal of strategic insouciance from its pedestal of power. Also, because of the local and limited nature of a probe, directly involving only the regional actors, it is tempting for the distant security provider to leave the response to its allies and friends. A direct and strong intervention by the offshore patron would escalate the interaction, raising the chances of a larger war, an outcome that neither party desires. But the shrewdness of a probing strategy is that it puts the targeted rival power in the position of having either to escalate the tensions in order to respond or to choose a less confrontational approach but one that risks weakening its alliances. The response to the probe, not the probe itself, is perceived as a potential cause of war. This creates strong disincentives for the tested great power to react by opposing the revisionist state's probe in a direct and forceful way, or to respond at all. For instance, in the case of China's probing actions in the South China Sea, the Obama administration's approach seems to have been to accommodate Beijing, acknowledging a decline in U.S. naval capabilities and welcoming a greater Chinese role in providing security to the global commons.[41] Similarly, after Russia's takeover of Crimea, Washington's first response was to turn the episode into a strictly regional affair. As President Obama put it in February 2014, "Any violation of Ukraine's sovereignty and territorial integrity would be deeply destabilizing, which is not in the interest of Ukraine, Russia, or Europe," tellingly not including the United States in the list of the affected parties.[42]

The problem is that the temptation of the existing great power to either ignore or regionalize the tension stemming from the revisionist state's probes—an attempt to de-escalate the strategic interaction—also constitutes a response. It may, however, be one that serves for the revisionist power as a confirmation of its initial suspicion that the rival's commitment to the region was on the wane. An unanswered—ignored or regionalized—probe is an indication that the existing map of power is open to revisions. Another way to put this is that a probe is a question of sorts: does the existing hegemon have the will and capacity to oppose the revisionist power? An attempt to dismiss the question or to let allies respond to it is a tacit admission by the tested great power that its interest in maintaining a strong foothold and influence in the region is in decline. Silence in response to a probe is telling. Probing, therefore, always elicits some sort of answer, and in this narrow sense it is a success.

The purpose of a probe is also to attain a secondary, albeit crucial, goal of beginning to redraw the map of influence without generating counterbalancing pressures from the tested great power and its allies. The most successful probe would be one that pushes the targeted small states and other regional spectators closer to the revisionist power (or at least convinces them to distance themselves from their existing security patron, the rival great power) while at the same time convincing the rival great power that it is too costly to maintain its political influence and provide security in the region. Hence the probe needs to be evaluated on what it achieves in the three audiences: the directly targeted neighboring small state, the distant security patron, and the geopolitical onlookers (in particular other states in the region). The success or failure of a revisionist state's probe depends on the actions by these three groups, and, arguably, it can attain partial success by achieving a revision of the status quo in one audience but not the other.

For instance, a probe can succeed in extending the revisionist power's influence over the immediate target, the ally or would-be ally of the rival, but at the same time it may generate more vigorous efforts by regional onlookers to counterbalance it through a variety of strategies, ranging from military modernization to tighter defense cooperation with the distant security patron. This seems to be the case for Russia's takeover of Crimea. Moscow quickly conquered Crimea and destabilized Ukraine's easternmost oblast, successfully demonstrating its ability and willingness to use force to achieve limited territorial adjustments. While Kiev maintains its political independence, it has also been shown to be weak and unable to oppose Russian pressures. The quasi–civil war in the eastern regions and Russia's conquest of Crimea make Ukraine an unlikely candidate for a closer relationship with the EU and NATO, even if Ukrainian political elites and public opinion may continue to be in favor of it. Russia's probe, in the form of its intervention in Crimea and eastern Ukraine, has thus been successful in neutering the westward drift of Kiev. The EU, and in particular states such as France and Germany, have now an even smaller desire to bring Ukraine closer, as it is deemed too dangerous and risky; Ukraine is not worth losing business deals with Russia, not to mention starting a war with Russia.

The Ukraine War has also damaged American credibility in the region. Washington after all had given assurances (not "guarantees," which are reserved for NATO members) to the Ukrainian government in the Budapest Memorandum of 1994. This is undoubtedly a Russian success. But there are also other consequences of Russia's probing, unintended and unwelcome by Moscow. Some states in the Central European region, in particular Poland and the Baltic states, have awakened from the geopolitical vacation of the past two decades. The 1990s and the 2000s were characterized by a widespread sense that threats to the territorial security of the region were minimal, and most of the strategic focus was on economic cooperation with the EU and on keeping in the good graces of the United States through participation in wars in Iraq and Afghanistan. This is over, at least in part. While strengthening the EU continues to be a priority in Central European capitals, there is simply no more interest in "out-of-area" operations, which drain resources and time from territorial defense. From this perspective, Russian probes have altered the geostrategic outlook of some Central European states. The eastern frontier is what really matters to them now, as their threat assessment has changed. Russia, in other words, has reached an upper threshold in its probes, creating a backlash among some of the states in the region, which are pursuing diplomatic counterbalancing and defense modernization. They are also calling for more visible and permanent NATO (and in particular, U.S.) security presence on their territories to shore up the extended deterrent against Russia.

It appears therefore that Russia is less successful than the other revisionist power, China. Moscow is less subtle in its probes, choosing dramatic military interventions (Georgia and Crimea) that generate growing fear and opposition among some European states as well as the United States. In part Moscow's more aggressive behavior is a result of a Russian assessment of the weakness and divisions of the West. But in part the seeming Russian rush to restore influence over its "near neighborhood" is due to internal demographic, economic, and political problems. The growing weakness of Russia, a great power more by courtesy and by nuclear weapons than by economic and political strength, gives little time to Putin to shore up his country's position facing China's rapid economic growth and Europe's political appeal. It is a short-term approach of large probes, and it may be successful only by extending influence over its most immediate nearby target.[43]

China, on the other hand, may have a different time frame, allowing it to probe in a much more indirect and less violent way, though this could change in the months ahead. It is therefore more careful and guarded, pursuing a long-term strategy of small probes over, quite literally, small rocks in the South China Sea. The U.S. "pivot" or "rebalancing" to Asia makes American presence and resolve more pronounced, increasing the doubt of a U.S. retrenchment and thus, from China's perspective, the need to be cautious in testing the limits of American influence and commitment. Moreover, the counterbalancing efforts of regional onlookers, from Japan to the Philippines and Vietnam, are increasing in intensity, in both the rhetoric used and the arms buildup. Similarly, unlike Russia in Crimea, Beijing has not succeeded in extending its direct control over a large piece of real estate. But in the end it may be more successful, because it is establishing a gradual change in the map of power, visible only after a decade-long period. Through its probes, China is pursuing a classic example of "salami tactics." As Thomas Schelling describes them, "If there is no sharp qualitative division between a minor transgression and a major affront, but a continuous gradation of activity, one can begin his intrusion on a scale too small to provoke a reaction, and increase it by imperceptible degrees, never quite presenting a sudden, dramatic challenge that would invoke the committed response."[44] Many small probes into areas of contested influence do not individually invite a strong response, but they erode steadily the perception and in the end the reality of the opponent's influence.

Moreover, a continuing sequence of gradual probes signals the seriousness of the revisionist's intent to alter the status quo. In the mind of the hegemon, the steady drumbeat of low-intensity and peripheral incidents creates the impression that the revisionist both has special claims for and may someday be willing to fight over a particular piece of real estate. These claims are often backed up by legal, historical, or ethnic justifications and a creeping physical presence—in Ukraine, Russian forces and equipment; in the South China Sea, artificially created reefs. Over time, this places the onus of a response on the shoulders of the hegemon and its allies in the region for why the status quo should be maintained. For a weary hegemon like the United States today, probes communicate that the act of supporting the regional status quo is no longer cost free but will require a level of exertion that was not needed in the past, inevitably leading to questions of whether such effort and resulting escalation are worthwhile.

Nonetheless, it is certainly possible to see failed instances of probing, which achieve the opposite of the revisionist power's intentions. The historic scorecard of probing states is mixed. A clear failure of probing would be if the targeted regional states and offshore security patron responded strongly, tightening their alliance and even initiating a direct war. This is an unintended consequence of a probe and can take several forms, from a tightening of alliances countering the revisionist power to increased military contingency planning and rearming. In the worst-case scenario, it results in a combination of actions that counterbalance the revisionist state more effectively and forcefully than before the probing behavior started. The revisionist state did not want nor expect this response before engaging in probing. It amounts to a disconfirmation of the initial hypothesis that the rival great power is in decline and retreat, and in the end it worsens the strategic position of the probing state.

The biggest loser may thus be the probing power, which puts in motion a series of strategic interactions that undermine its own strength. This was the case of Germany in the early twentieth century. Kaiser Wilhelm's visit to Tangier in 1905 initiated the first Moroccan crisis, manufactured by Berlin to, among other objectives, probe the strength of the brand new and untested Franco-British Entente Cordiale.[45] By challenging French interests in Morocco in a nonviolent way, Berlin wanted to pressure Paris, "the weakest link in the surrounding chain" of states opposing Germany.[46] But it desired to do that in an area and in a way that were expected not to draw Great Britain into a direct confrontation, so that Germany could demonstrate to Paris that the entente was in effect useless. Morocco was important to France but not to Great Britain, and the German Foreign Office expected that London would not back Paris. Great Britain after all was also seen as retrenching after a bloody war with the Boers and unable and unwilling to project power on land to guarantee the security of its French quasi-ally. As Friedrich von Holstein put it, the French would seek a rapprochement with Germany, in effect bandwagoning, "when they have seen that English friendship . . . is not enough to gain Germany's agreement to the French seizure of Morocco, but rather that Germany wishes to be loved on its own account."[47] Germany, however, greatly miscalculated the British need for a continental ally and resulting commitment to France. The Moroccan crisis was resolved in a multilateral conference in Algeciras where Berlin ended in a position that was considerably worse than before the crisis: its only support was from the weak Austro-Hungarian Empire, while London was firmly and actively on the side of Paris. Instead of weakening the nascent strategic friendship between Britain and France, "German bullying" strengthened it.[48] From then on, the "European

Balance of Power, which had been ignored for forty years, again dominated British foreign policy; and henceforth every German move was interpreted as a bid for continental hegemony."[49] London reoriented its attention away from the empire and toward the European continent, gradually planning to ready an expeditionary force to come to France's defense.[50] Berlin's probe in Morocco turned into a clear failure.[51]

Probing is low risk, insofar as it is tailored to minimize a strong reaction of the rival, but it is not danger free for the revisionist state. Despite the fact that it arises out of a desire to clarify an allegedly new map of power, the effects of probing are difficult to interpret. All parties involved—the revisionist power and the targeted states—can miscalculate their reactions. In a case of moral hazard, the smaller states, directly targeted by the revisionist power, may respond violently to the low-intensity probe, feeling secure thanks to the alliance with a more powerful patron. Or, sensing that their distant patron is no longer capable of maintaining its influence, they may decide the exact opposite and accept the hegemony of the rival. This was the case of Athenian allies in Thrace, switching sides under General Brasidas's pressure and persuasion. They were mistaken because their "judgment was based more upon blind wishing than upon any sound prediction."[52] Athens rallied and sent large forces north to restore its sway.

The probing power can also be the one to miscalculate, either not seeing the success or ignoring the failure. The nature of probing is such that the effects are often not visible immediately and require time to alter the perceptions and realities of power. The episode of Spartan commander Brasidas is again telling. Sparta did not follow up on his successes, in part because Spartan kings were jealous of his military exploits, but in part because they thought the damage inflicted on Athens was sufficient to strike a deal and end the war.[53] They were of course wrong, as the war continued for decades. Alternatively, despite being checked, the probing power may simply up the ante, seeking some gain. This may have been the case of Germany, which did not stop challenging France and Britain after 1905, despite its diplomatic isolation, the military conundrum of a two-front war, and a robust Franco-British entente. In brief, there is no easy single interpretation of a probe and its effects.

A related risk is that a probe may lead to an unintended and untimely escalation of the strategic rivalry. As we described, the purpose of probing is to see how permissive the geopolitical order is, and to that goal a probe is limited in geographic reach and means used. It targets an issue presumed peripheral to the rival great power, seeking, for instance, a small territorial adjustment that is costly to the weaker neighboring state but not deemed worthy of a direct conflict by the distant and more powerful security patron. But the limited nature of the probe is somewhat at odds with its ultimate purpose to check the limits of an allegedly declining rival great power. A probe is a low-intensity, local pinprick with wider repercussions; limited geographically yet potentially global in outcome. The probing state has a strong interest in keeping the crisis limited and circumscribed to the narrowly defined area, but it is also poking the rival great power to see what the reaction may be. It is banking on the fact that the probe is on the periphery of the rival's influence and interests, and thus that the rival will not escalate the interaction. The probing challenger, in other words, is betting that its great power rival will fear entrapment, being involved in an undesirable conflict, more than loss of prestige, reputation, or influence. The revisionist power seeks to use the fact of alliances (which it lacks itself) as a source of competitive disadvantage for the hegemon. This is based on two reinforcing perceptions—first, that the commitment involved in their maintenance is an encumbrance depriving the hegemon of strategic flexibility; and second, that the hegemon's temptation to devalue its own alliances suggests that it feels the weight of this encumbrance.

Probes therefore arise from a view that entrapment is the congenital flaw of alliances. They are the ultimate act of attempting to expose the dangers of entrapment to hegemon and ally alike. This is ultimately a gamble—an expectation, not a certainty. And the gamble can backfire, as there is always the possibility that a probe will result in a dramatic escalation since it is targeted at multiple audiences. There is thus a clear recognition that a probe has a much wider purpose than its immediate action may convey, and consequently the desire to keep it limited runs against the desire to have a much larger demonstrative effect. As a result, the interaction a probe initiates has an inherent risk of escalating into a much larger confrontation.[54]

The revisionist state neither desires nor expects the escalation, but its possibility and perhaps likelihood are a direct outcome of probing. A probe by definition crosses a limit, a tacit or an explicit line of influence, in the expectation that it no longer reflects the actual will and power of the rival state. The revisionist power tests limits that until then were accepted and unchallenged and takes the first step in an "escalatory ladder" of competitive behavior. For instance, Kaiser Wilhelm's support of Boer independence in 1896 was a test of British strength in what Berlin wrongly thought was a peripheral area of the British Empire. Similarly, the Moroccan crisis in 1905 was a test of British commitment to France in a region that should have been of no importance to London. Both, however, were a "move in the European Balance of Power," and that, beyond the details of the individual probes, was becoming of paramount concern to Great Britain.[55] Both were met by a strong British response, intensifying the Anglo-British rivalry. Escalation here was a willful choice of the targeted power.

Finally, probing can be in many cases a violent act, raising even further the likelihood of escalation and war. Probing is a political act first and foremost, only at times pursued by military means, but it does involve a careful application of violence or threat of violence. This requires strict political control, which is easier to maintain if the probe is not militarized and violent. But the more violent it becomes, the more difficult it is to keep it under political control. The logic of war may overwhelm the political rationale. Bismarck was keenly aware that the limited wars he fought, such as the Franco-Prussian one in 1870, would result in political outcomes that were different from his objectives were other great powers to become involved. But his greatest obstacle was the German military, resentful of civilian interference in what they deemed to be affairs in their exclusive purview. Political control over a limited war is paramount, because otherwise operational war objectives can overwhelm the larger political goals.[56] The fact that Russia and China probe through a variety of nontraditional means, such as fishing vessels in the South China Sea and specially formed battalions (*Vostok*) of Chechens, makes political control more difficult. There is an incentive to use such means in a more aggressive way than would be warranted by official state forces, because in case of defeat one can always deny control over them and claim that they are simply individual citizens. Moreover, the "civilian" paramilitary forces that the probing power uses (e.g., the "Russian separatists" in eastern Ukraine) may not be easily recalled if the conflict ceases to be useful. The civilianization of conflict has its own risks. This makes probing behavior inherently destabilizing to an international order, as it sets forces in motion that, once unleashed, can be hard to control.

Probing can, moreover, spiral into war, unexpected and perhaps unwanted by the revisionist power. For instance, in the third century BC, Rome started to probe Carthaginian power in Sicily. It extended protection to Messana (or, more precisely, to a band of mercenaries, the Mamertines, who controlled it), thereby asserting Roman influence in northern Sicily. The peaceful withdrawal of the Punic garrison from the area seemed to suggest that a war was avoidable and the probe successful in attaining a low-cost revision to the balance of power. But the Romans miscalculated and were emboldened by this small success. As Polybius put it, they "now cherished the hope that they could drive the Carthaginians out of Sicily altogether, and that once this goal was attained their own power would be greatly increased."[57] Carthage sent a large force to Sicily and solidified its alliance with Syracuse against Rome and its new ally Messana. Rome then escalated and sent a large army to besiege Syracuse, starting the first Punic war, which lasted more than twenty years.[58] What started as a low-cost, low-risk probe turned into a long and costly slugfest.

To sum up, the risk of probing is that it may result in a slide toward a direct clash. Miscalculation and escalation by all parties involved can elevate what is a small, localized harassment into a wider, more violent war. Moreover, a pattern of probing may gradually lead all sides to accept war as necessary and perhaps inevitable, as each probe and reaction escalates the competitive interaction.

THE BENEFITS OF PROBING FOR THE STATUS QUO POWER

Probing does not guarantee to the revisionist state a successful extension of its influence. And albeit it presents a serious challenge to the targeted great power and its allies, the rise of probing behavior is also a strategic opportunity. There are four related benefits of probing. The first two point to the possibility of worse alternatives, namely, a direct, violent, all-out confrontation and a more subversive diplomatic campaign, and thus are benefits in a relative sense. The other two benefits present probing as a pattern-breaking behavior that, first, makes explicit the intentions of the revisionist power and, second, creates incentives to counterbalance it.

A state bent on revising the geopolitical status quo can choose alternative and more dangerous paths to try to attain its goals. The alternative to probing, that is, is not necessarily inaction and continued acceptance of the regional or international order established and maintained by the hegemon. On a spectrum of possible strategies pursued by a revisionist power, whether Russia or China, probing is somewhere in the middle in terms of violence as well as effectiveness. The first alternative that is undoubtedly worse than probing is an outright war; a direct clash between the revisionist state and the great power. The fact that the revisionist power engages in probing behavior is a symptom of its uncertainty about the disposition of relative power; it is a question, not an answer. And it stems from the firm desire to avoid, or at least to postpone, a direct confrontation.

In fact, the low-intensity interactions between revisionist and status-quo powers can lead to relatively peaceful coexistence. The strongest case of this is perhaps the Russo-British rivalry in the second half of the nineteenth century, which, at least from the British perspective, was a key geostrategic concern given the Russian threat to the British position in India. And yet this "Great Game" did not result in a great-power war. Surely Japan's defeat of Russia in 1905, combined with the rise of Germany, a threat to both Moscow and London, contributed to the Anglo-Russian rapprochement and the Convention of 1907. But another reason was that Russian attempts to push outward toward British spheres of influence had failed. As Ludwig Dehio observed, the "great Continental power [Russia] simply kept on probing along the entire Asian-Balkan front, switching pressure from one point to another. Undeniably crowned with success in the depths of the Continent, Russia was checked at, or driven back from, the coasts wherever she impinged on the spheres of interest of the naval power."[59] When successfully countered by the targeted states, probing can lead to an accommodation of interests in the form of more stable and accepted frontiers.

The Cold War was another example of constant probing, made even more careful because of the shadow of a nuclear war, that resulted in a prolonged contest always short of total war. Throughout the decades-long confrontation, Moscow continued to follow Stalin's belief that, in the words of Charles Bohlen, you "have to probe with a bayonet. If you meet mush, you push farther. You meet steel, you pull back."[60] Whenever Soviet leaders perceived an opening, provided by an absence of formal and credible U.S. commitment to the defense of a region or a country, or by an assessment that the "correlation of forces" was to their advantage, they pursued a probing approach. By putting pressure in peripheral areas, they tested their hypothesis of American neglect or withdrawal and sought low-cost revisions to the existing balance of power.[61] The Berlin Crisis of 1948 was a case in point. The purpose was to pressure Western powers not to create an independent West Germany, as well as to test the uncertain American commitment to the continent. A successful Soviet push would have severed the transatlantic connection and divided European states, opening the door to Moscow's "taking one country at a time as [it] had so successfully done in Eastern Europe."[62]

The other alternative to probing, and thus its second indirect benefit, is a much quieter, subversive approach that undermines the strength of the rival great power, in particular by depriving it of allies. The revisionist's low-level cunning diplomacy that silently recruits allies to its side through elite bribery, internal destabilization, or economic pressuring is dangerous because it happens surreptitiously, and its effects are visible only when it becomes too late to alter them. A classic example comes from the end of the Persian Wars that pitted Persia against a coalition of Greek cities led by Sparta. In 478 BC, when he was tasked to continue the war against Persia, the Athenian general Aristides noticed how the Spartan commanders, Pausanias in particular, were arrogant and rude toward their Greek allies. By presenting himself as accommodating and gentle, he succeeded in depriving the Spartans of their leading position before they realized it, and he did this, in Plutarch's words, "neither by weapons, ships, or horses, but by equity and wise policy."[63] Had Aristides used troops and ships, Sparta could have noticed and opposed the Athenian quest for leadership. Subversion at the right times can be more effective in breaking alliances than a more aggressive behavior.

This does not imply that these alternative strategies, and in particular the latter, are mutually exclusive of probing. Probing, as we described earlier, can escalate into a war and also can be conducted together with the low-level approach of "equity and wise policy." Both Russia and China are pursuing a mix of policies that aim at quietly subverting American alliances without the use of force or even the threat of use of force. Moscow in particular has been adept at building political support in Europe through financial largesse, energy leverage, and commercial deals.[64] By buying or hiring political elites (e.g., former German chancellor Schroeder joining a Russian gas pipeline subsidiary), subsidizing pro-disarmament groups (e.g., the anti-BMD Czech group), and inking commercial deals (e.g., French Mistral, with promises of more defense acquisitions), Russia has managed to split the Western alliance and to win tacit French and German acceptance of its advances into eastern Ukraine (and its conquest of Crimea). The point here is that such policies sow divisions within the rival alliance, weakening the position of the opponent and allowing a more aggressive revisionist probing. It is a policy of slow and gradual undermining of the foundations of strength, namely, of allies, of the rival. As a British correspondent put it in 1900, Germany was looking at Great Britain and its global influence "as upon an artichoke to be pulled to pieces leaf by leaf."[65] Alliances are fragile and can be destroyed by cunning diplomacy that disrupts them by bribing, coaxing, and persuading.

From the point of view of the status quo power, such an "artichoke" strategy is more treacherous because it deprives its allies of incentives to counter the revisionist state. Or, the flip side of this point, probing alone is less successful at weakening an alliance because it is more visible and affects more directly the interests of the allies located in the most immediate vicinity of the revisionist power. This, the creation of incentives to counterbalance, is the third benefit of probing.

A probe is a clear challenge to the existing geopolitical order and to the alliance structure that underpins it. While it is meant to create a fissure between the immediately targeted state and its offshore security patron, a probe is a form of pressure that can generate comparable counter-pressure. It is a form of warning that the revisionist state does not accept the existing frontiers of influence and will push to change them. Winston Churchill put it best when writing about Germany in the years before the outbreak of World War I. The aggressiveness of Berlin and its naval buildup "closed the ranks of the Entente. With every rivet that von Tirpitz drove into his ships of war, he united British opinion.... The hammers that clanged at Kiel and Wilhelmshaven were forging the coalition of nations by which Germany was to be resisted and finally overthrown. Every threatening gesture that she made, every attempt to shock or shake the loosely knit structure of the Entente made it close and fit together more tightly."[66]

Finally, the fourth benefit is related to the previous one. When a revisionist state embarks on probing, it creates a discontinuity in its behavior, and by doing so it exposes its own intentions.[67] The pattern-breaking behavior of probing is a sign that the rival perceives an opportunity supplied by a permissive international situation. The intention of challenging the order may have already existed, but the revisionist state did not act on it earlier because a belief that the rival great power was in decline did not accompany the desire to alter the status quo. Probing, a change in the revisionist state's behavior, thus has the unintended consequence of revealing the intention of the revisionist state and of making those states appear as overly aggressive aspirants of geopolitical change.

Probes, in other words, identify the rival. They suggest answers to the key questions of who the threat is, where the threat may materialize, and what its intentions are. They lift the "fog of peace." Without the ability to identify clearly the rival and its geostrategy, one is left with a confusing array of possibilities and contingencies, with unclear threats and uncertain alliances. It is impossible to build defensive measures *tous azimuts*, and planners need to narrow down the possible scenarios. In some cases this may mean focusing on the wrong threat, as the British did in the 1920s: the navy "continued to prepare doggedly for a war with Japan, as the Royal Air Force continued to prepare doggedly for a war with France. The Army showed little interest in either."[68] In other cases, as perhaps our present one, the inability or unwillingness to point to a threatening rival pushes one to engage in "wars" with a variety of abstractions, from "terrorism" to "climate change." When the rival is identified, the purpose of a state's strategy becomes clearer and there is renewed interest in strengthening counterbalancing alliances. The result is that the targeted states often seem to steel their positions, tightening their existing security arrangements, beefing up their military capabilities, and seeking new and stronger alliance combinations. In brief, probing may diminish alliance uncertainty—assuming, that is, that threatened small states see the United States as a committed, credible, and capable protector.[69] As we will argue in the next chapter, this is increasingly not the case.

CHAPTER 4

RESPONSES OF U.S. ALLIES

We have run with the angels; now we shall hunt with the wolves.
—Czech general Jan Syrový, 1938

Small, rich, vulnerable countries do not want to be the ones who stick their fingers in the big bully's eye, if nobody's going to come to their support.
—Yousef al-Otaiba, UAE ambassador
to the United States, 2010

Perceived American retrenchment and intensifying revisionist probes are leading many long-standing U.S. allies to rethink the basic assumptions that have guided their foreign and defense policies for the past several decades. Since the Second World War, American allies have operated on the premise that the United States was and would remain a reliable guarantor of their security and of stability in the world's major regions for the foreseeable future. They based this calculation on two assumptions: that the United States would be physically capable of repelling attempts at large-power aggression; and that it would be politically willing to do so if the security of even the smallest of its allies was threatened. The credibility of the first assumption was grounded in America's maintenance of a large military establishment, its strategic nuclear weapons arsenal, and the forward deployment of U.S. troops and fleets in the Eurasian rimlands. The credibility of the second assumption was based on formal security guarantees like NATO's Article 5 and similar bilateral treaty commitments in Asia, as well as informal guarantees in the form of U.S. military assistance and a culture of close communication and coordination between Washington and allied capitals.

Together, U.S. military strength and political commitments have made up the backbone of American extended deterrent. This is as much a psychological construct as a physical reality, consisting in the belief that the United States is willing and able to take retaliatory action—if necessary, using nuclear weapons—to guarantee the territorial integrity of its allies. This produced a sense of strategic certainty that is an anomaly in frontier regions and has enabled allies to focus on economic development and growth and virtually ignore traditional geopolitics, under the assurance that an active U.S. security presence would underwrite their national security. In exchange for this protection, allies have aligned their diplomacy with U.S. interests, oriented their military doctrines toward American habits of war, maintained generally open economic policies, and provided support for U.S. initiatives outside their own regions. Significantly, frontline states have done so while forgoing the typical behaviors that threatened states have traditionally used to ensure their safety, such as building large armies or engaging in friendly diplomacy with big rivals, on the calculation that the benefits of the U.S.-led order were greater than any conceivable alternative. The result, from America's standpoint, has been a durably stable and favorable configuration in the world's major regions that has promoted its core interest of preventing hostile coalitions in Eurasia.

THE WEAKENING OF EXTENDED DETERRENCE

America's system of extended deterrence is still working (allies have not been invaded), but it is weakening—and with it, key elements of security in the world's regions as we have known them for the past seventy years. First, as outlined in chapter 2, U.S. allies are increasingly the targets of aggressive probing from U.S. rivals, a sign that the barriers to challenging states under the American security umbrella are weaker than they were in the past. Second, allies doubt the political willingness of the United States to intervene on their behalf in the event of a military crisis. These misgivings are rooted in allies' recognition of the growing capabilities of American rivals, as well as reemergent currents of isolationism in American politics and signals from U.S. policy makers suggesting a downgrading of alliances in American strategy in favor of closer engagement with large powers. Third, allies increasingly doubt America's ability to deter and defeat its challengers. This concern stems from changes to the global military balance brought about by reductions in U.S. defense spending and the rise in spending and capabilities in other powers, notably China and Russia. But it also reflects allies' worries about the ability of the United States to counter the new probing tactics outlined in chapter 3. Limited war techniques like those on display in Crimea represent a type of threat well below the threshold of conflict that extended deterrence was designed to answer, stoking concerns among frontline states that the United States would not be able to prevent incursions by Russian "little green men" or Chinese fishing trawlers with traditional means such as trip wires, even if it wanted to.

Together, these changes have weakened American extended deterrence, and with it the assurance to the exposed states whose independence has been essential to the stability of the U.S.-led global order for the past seventy years. From the standpoint of U.S. allies, this change presents an unexpected new challenge. At just the moment when large powers are growing more determined in their efforts to contest the international status quo, the one power on earth that is capable of guaranteeing their safety is showing signs of political introversion, strategic ambivalence, and diminishing power. Historically, such moments involving the diminution of an existing system leader, whether forced or self-imposed, have been especially dangerous for small states, which "have been most endangered when the balance has been unstable or askew."[1] As Robert Rothstein notes, when nineteenth-century Britain "concentrated on internal affairs, and ignored its continental interests, the normal result has been the destruction of one or more small powers." The danger is greatest for those states at the outer limits of American military reach, which have the highest exposure to rival probes and are most dependent on the continued efficacy of U.S. guarantees. For states like Israel,

Taiwan, and Poland, the diminishing utility of extended deterrence represents a grave national-security problem that, unless somehow mitigated, could eventually pose a threat to their prosperity, political independence, or even continued existence as states.

In response, many U.S. allies have begun to reexamine their strategic options in search of new methods for ensuring national survival—if necessary, without the United States. From East Asia to the Middle East and Eastern Europe, American allies are hurriedly altering their diplomatic postures, military capabilities, and national strategic outlook in response to rapidly changing security environments and their assessment of American behavior. While still relying on the United States as their primary source of security, many have begun to revisit the full range of methods that small, threatened states have used throughout history to cope with extreme changes in their security environment. Some are building up their militaries to supplement the weakening U.S. deterrent, forming alliances with neighbors who share their predicament, or even considering the acquisition of nuclear weapons to improve their security position. Others are attempting to reduce exposure to conflict by pursuing more neutral stances in regional diplomacy, seeking outright accommodation with rising powers, or even positioning themselves to profit from any territorial revisions that may occur. In many cases U.S. allies are pursuing a mixture of these approaches simultaneously—creating diversified strategic "menu cards" characterized by a number of separate options that allow them to reduce their reliance on the United States without fully committing to a single alternative in its place. While analytically distinct, the various strategies are all driven by the organizing problem: the need to find new methods to ensure state survival and success in the absence of predictable U.S. support.

MILITARY SELF-HELP

By far the most common and significant reaction of frontline U.S. allies has been to improve their ability to defend themselves in the event of a crisis. Historically, this has usually been the option of first resort for vulnerable states faced with a rapid deterioration in their strategic surroundings. For centuries states of all sizes have built up their armed forces when threatened by stronger neighbors and lacking in credible alliance options. In the early modern period European kingdoms like Burgundy and the Swiss cantons built small but potent militaries in an attempt to resist absorption by neighboring empires. Prior to World War I Belgium created a sophisticated army and defensive network to repel German or French attacks. And in the 1930s the Polish Second Republic developed a large army and an offensive war-fighting doctrine to counter Russia and Germany—in part because of the failure of Western democracies to provide effective offshore security support. In all these cases, small states were acting on the simple strategic calculation of self-defense—that "maintaining a high level of military preparedness and possessing a reputation for military virtues might turn them into an unattractive target, promising an aggressor costs incommensurate with any potential gains."[2]

A notable feature of the post–Cold War global security setting has been the relative absence of such behavior among the world's smaller states. For allies under the U.S. umbrella in particular, there simply has not been a need to build up large militaries, given the extensiveness and presumed permanence of American military power and the relative quiescence of any potentially threatening powers in the international system. So deep has been the impression of military safety under the U.S.-led system that many American allies have, as noted in chapter 3, ceased to invest significant sums of money in their own defense, to the consternation of U.S. defense planners. But this pattern is changing. As large powers like China, Iran, and Russia gain in military strength and traditional forms of U.S. deterrence and assurance weaken, many frontline states have begun to move away from planning on the basis that they can entrust their physical safety solely to the United States. For the first time in decades, many small powers have begun to augment their national defenses—in some cases dramatically. The result is a series of rapidly intensifying regional military competitions that mark a dramatic and potentially dangerous shift from the conditions of stability that we came to take for granted in the post–Cold War era.

The New Asian Arms Race

The trend toward military self-help is most pronounced in Asia, where regional economic growth, shrinking U.S. defense budgets, and increased tensions over regional waterways have created conditions for a region-wide arms race. Despite some claims to the contrary, Asian countries have invested consistently more in defense in the period since the end of the Cold War, and in particular over the past few years.[3] Driving the trend is the rapid growth in Chinese defense spending, which has increased by 170 percent since 2003 and is now doubling every five years.[4] At the same time, as noted in chapter 3, the U.S. defense budget has faced unprecedented reductions, and, in light of fiscal realities, it is likely to continue declining in the future.[5] In response, U.S. allies across Asia are increasingly taking the responsibility for national defense into their own hands, launching ambitious acquisition and modernization efforts to expand their militaries and keep pace with China's surging capabilities.

Leading the pack are countries in the eastern approaches of the Asian mainland that lie within easy reach of Chinese air and naval power. In 2013 alone Japan raised spending by $83 billion—a dramatic spike after a prolonged period of relatively low growth in defense spending that indicates the degree of concern generated by Chinese behavior.[6] In Southeast Asia, where tensions have mounted over congested waterways, U.S. allies raised spending by more than 13 percent in 2011 and again by nearly 9 percent in 2013 (see figure 4.1). The Philippines—traditionally among the most dependent of Asian states on U.S. protection—doubled its budget in 2012 and increased it again by 17 percent in 2013. Indonesia tripled its defense budget between 2006 and 2012 and increased it again in 2013 by an incredible 26.5 percent.[7] While figures for Vietnam are unreliable, the country increased spending by 70 percent between 2010 and 2011.[8] Tiny Singapore was the world's fifth-largest importer of weapons between 2008 and 2012, making it the first state in the region to rank among the world's top ten arms importers since the Vietnam War.[9]

As significant as the amount of money being spent is the sophistication of weaponry being purchased. In a dramatic break from its

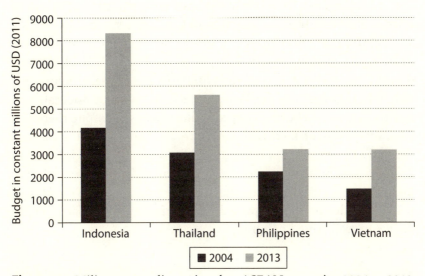

Figure 4.1. Military expenditures in select ASEAN countries, 2004 vs. 2013.
Source: Stockholm International Peace Research Institute, http://www.sipri.org/research
/armaments/milex/milex_database.

post–World War II, constitutionally mandated self-defense posture,
Japan has undertaken a transformation of its Ground and Maritime
Self Defense Forces that in 2014 alone included purchases of destroy-
ers, submarines, patrol aircraft, two Aegis cruisers, early warning aircraft, amphibious landing vehicles, tanks, refueling aircraft, unmanned
aerial vehicles (UAVs), tilt-rotor aircraft, and twenty-eight F-35A joint-
strike fighters.[10] Taiwan is acquiring air and missile defense capabilities, attack helicopters, tanks, maritime patrol aircraft, mine-hunting
ships, and anti-ship and anti-aircraft missiles.[11] Vietnam has acquired
six Russian Kilo-class submarines, long-range aircraft, and seven frig-
ates; Indonesia has bought advanced U.S. and Russian fighter aircraft,
new ships, and diesel-electric attack submarines; and Singapore has
acquired air and missile defense components, F-16 fighter aircraft, and
attack submarines.

These shopping sprees are strategically notable for the United States
for three reasons. First, they signal an end to the period of "free riding"
through low defense spending that marked this region in the past; increasingly, Asian allies are concerned enough about security to divert
national wealth away from economic growth toward defense. Second,

they are actions that few of these states would have viewed as necessary a decade ago—even at the highpoint of U.S.-Chinese tensions over the Taiwan Straits confrontation in 1995 or the Hainan Island incident in 2001, U.S. allies were sufficiently convinced of U.S. credibility that they did not increase defense spending; that baseline assumption has clearly changed. Third, the U.S. pivot to Asia has not noticeably affected these allies' efforts to improve their defenses; despite rhetorical announcements of increased American attention to that continent, the regional arms race is intensifying. For virtually every U.S. ally in Asia, the goal is the same: to quickly and tangibly improve their ability to do for themselves what they can no longer assume the United States will do for them—provide protection against a large, confident, and well-armed neighbor.

Middle East: Race for Containment

The situation in the Middle East is similar. As in the case of China, Iran's growing military ambitions and aggressive moves over the past few years have fueled anxiety among U.S. allies about the future stability of the region. To a greater extent than elsewhere, states here have perceived a weakening of interest from the United States in continuing its traditional role as the regional ordering power in the wake of the Iraq War.[12] Regional allies Israel and the Gulf states have been dismayed by the reluctance of the United States to intervene decisively to interrupt Tehran's efforts to acquire military nuclear capabilities. U.S. leaders have "struggled to reassure Gulf States over an interim nuclear deal with Iran that [they] worry will embolden Tehran."[13] Saudi Arabia in particular stands to lose from the spread of Iranian influence into neighboring Iraq, Lebanon, and Syria and is concerned about Tehran's growing pressure on offshore Saudi oil fields and access routes. Heavily dependent on the sea for survival, Saudi Arabia and the other Gulf states are threatened by the expansion of Iranian strategic presence capable of disrupting traffic in the Suez Canal, Strait of Hormuz, Bab Al Mandab, Gulf of Aden, and Arabian Sea.[14]

U.S. allies in the Middle East are worried about the growth of Iranian defense spending (which was projected to increase by 127 per-

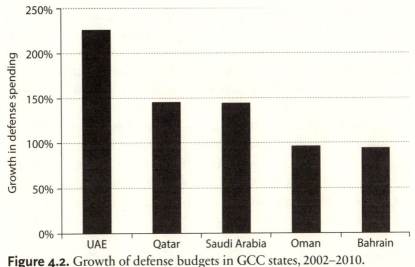

Figure 4.2. Growth of defense budgets in GCC states, 2002–2010.
Source: Stockholm International Peace Research Institute, http://www.sipri.org/research/ armaments/milex/milex_database.

cent in 2012) and would be potential targets of any future Iranian nuclear weapons.[15] To counterbalance the growth of Iranian capabilities, they have engaged in military buildups like those of U.S allies in other regions. Over the past decade, the region has developed the characteristics of a conventional arms race second in scale only to Asia, with six of the world's top ten fastest growing national defense markets. Measured as a percentage of GDP, the Gulf states have become the biggest defense spenders on earth, allocating 10 percent apiece of their annual economies to defense (compared to 4.5 percent for the United States and a global average of 2.5 percent).[16] Saudi Arabia has increased spending by 300 percent since 2004, while it and Oman have both raised spending by 30 percent since 2011 alone (see figure 4.2).[17] Israel spends proportionally more than any state in the region (about 18 percent of the annual national budget), with a 400 percent increase in the offensive capabilities of the Israeli Air Force between 2012 and 2014 and spending hikes of $289 million planned for 2014.[18]

Unlike in Asia, where naval assets are a priority, the common thread in buildups among the Gulf states has tended to be long-range strike systems and anti–ballistic missile defense to lend extra credibility to the U.S. extended deterrence. Anticipating a future war with a nuclear-armed Iran, U.S. allies in the region want to be able to attack conventional and nuclear targets on the ground and shoot down Iranian missile strikes, with or without U.S. help. To this end the Gulf states have purchased large quantities of fighter aircraft, precision-guided munitions, and defensive missile systems, primarily from the United States. Between 2010 and 2014—a period coinciding with numerous setbacks in efforts to halt the Iranian nuclear program—the Gulf states accumulated the world's largest regional air and missile defense (AMD) network, with UAE, Kuwait, Qatar, and Saudi Arabia bolstering their Patriot and terminal high altitude area defense (THAAD) missile systems and accompanying early warning radar assets.[19]

The preference of the Gulf states for balancing against Iran is consistent with their history of resisting bids for regional hegemony. The tribal kingdoms of the western Persian Gulf successfully fought incorporation into the Persian Empire and fought with Britain against Iraq and Saudi Arabia in the post-colonial period and with the United States and Iraq against revolutionary-era Iran.[20] Nevertheless, as in Asia, the scale and speed of their current turn toward military self-help suggest a degree of strategic uncertainty that would not have been present at earlier stages of the post–Cold War era, when U.S. military commitments were more certain and aspirants for regional leadership more easily containable. The mainly rhetorical efforts of U.S. officials to provide strategic reassurance have not stemmed this uneasiness; as in Asia, allies in the Middle East may be reaffirming their alliance with the United States rhetorically, but their frantic efforts to arm suggest that they doubt America's ability to protect them.[21]

Central and Eastern Europe: Remilitarized Frontier

The trend toward military self-help in the Asia Pacific and the Middle East has been under way for a while and is closely followed in the U.S. defense community. More surprising to many observers has been the sudden appearance of similar behavior among U.S. allies along the eastern borders of NATO. Following the Cold War, the territory of the former Soviet Empire and its East-Central satellite states ceased to be a fulcrum of global geopolitical competition and acquired the characteristics of a deactivated geopolitical zone for the United States. With Russia militarily weak and in a state of advanced economic decay, it has not, until recently, seemed to pose as serious a threat to America's Central and Eastern European (CEE) allies as China or Iran pose to U.S. allies in their respective neighborhoods. Moreover, the extension of Western security guarantees to the states of Central and Eastern Europe following the 2004 and 2007 eastern enlargements of NATO appeared to permanently ameliorate the region's security dilemma. The result has been widespread strategic complacency among all but the most exposed frontline states, steep reductions in European military budgets, and a reorientation of U.S. political and military attention to other regions.

But this is changing. The re-emergence of Russia as an active and determined revisionist force in regional politics has prompted greater seriousness about traditional security among many frontline U.S. allies in the region. The confluence of the Russian invasion of Georgia in fall 2008 and the U.S. cancellation in spring 2009 of plans to build third-site missile defense sites in Poland and the Czech Republic signified to many states the onset of a new and less predictable regional security climate. Already Poland and Estonia, two of the region's most vulnerable states, had been spending well above the European average on defense. Following the Georgia War, Poland and the Baltic states became even more serious about finding ways to strengthen their security. Most notably, Poland launched a ten-year, $40 billion military modernization program with the explicit aim of increasing its ability to deter or repel a Russian attack, if necessary by itself.[22]

As recently as the beginning of 2014, Poland and Estonia were unique in Central and Eastern Europe in their strong emphasis on national defense. But the Russian invasion of Ukraine, to an even greater extent than the Georgia War, stirred regional states from their twenty-five-year complacency on matters of security. In its aftermath, most frontline NATO states have introduced or announced significant increases in defense spending (see figure 4.3). Latvia, with a

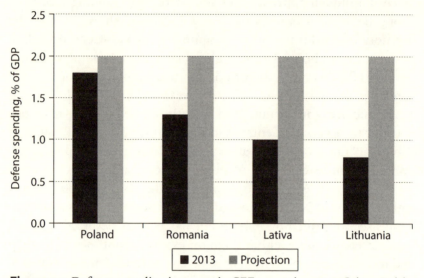

Figure 4.3. Defense spending increases in CEE countries, post–Crimea crisis. *Sources*: Stockholm International Peace Research Institute, *Defense News*, and *Balkan Insight*, http://www.sipri.org/research/armaments/milex/milex_database, http://www.defensenews.com /article/20140607/DEFREG01/306070013/Russian-NATO-Arms-Race-Takes-Shape, http://www .defensenews.com/apps/pbcs.dll/article?AID=2014304260024,http://www.balkaninsight.com/en /article/romania-to-raise-2014-defence-budget.

large ethnic Russian population and exposure to Ukraine-style in-cursions, announced plans to increase military spending by 12 per-cent.[23] Lithuania introduced increases of 30 percent for 2014 and planned a further 40 percent increase in 2015.[24] Poland, the primary target in most Russian threats and military exercises, announced a further increase to its already substantial defense budget. Romania, which shares a border with Ukraine and could face Russian provoca-tions in neighboring Moldova, has announced an increase of 15 per-cent.[25] The Czech Republic, though less exposed than its neighbors, announced increases that would bring its stagnating defense budget from 1.0 to 1.4 percent of GDP.[26] Hungary and Bulgaria are pub-licly considering increases, and only Slovakia has ruled them out altogether.

The sudden tendency toward heightened military self-help in Cen-tral and Eastern Europe is emblematic of the rapid change that is under way in global perceptions of U.S. strategic reliability. It marks a significant break from the dominant and long-standing European trend of flat-lining defense budgets in order to prioritize social programs or economic growth.[27] To an even greater extent than similar behavior in Asia or the Middle East, the new focus on local defense in CEE states would have been inconceivable—and ultimately unnecessary—at any previous point in the post–Cold War era. In the absence of reliable deterrence from the United States, states in the region are taking steps that they assumed, after the enlargement of NATO, would never be needed again, building larger armies, navies, and air forces to supplement the traditional U.S. security umbrella and, if necessary, survive for as long as possible without it. While this tendency is visible among most frontline CEE states, it is most pronounced among the handful that, like the Gulf states and littoral Asian allies, have direct geographic exposure to the threat, have a history of conflict with the revisionist power, and stand to lose the most should traditional U.S. security fail.

The End of Expeditionary Allies in Europe

America's allies are not only rethinking how much to spend on their militaries, they are also rethinking how to use them on the battlefield. Throughout the post–Cold War era, the overwhelming focus in European allied militaries has been to develop postures and weapons that maximize their interoperability with the U.S. military for conducting out-of-area operations. The doctrinal emphasis of this type of warfare is light, maneuverable units that can be rapidly deployed in support of counterinsurgency operations in theaters outside the territory of the ally itself—primarily in Central Asia and the Middle East. This has led to a preoccupation in allied procurements on light armored vehicles, helicopters, and other expeditionary equipment. The tendency has been reinforced by allied participation in the International Security Assistance Force (ISAF) mission in Afghanistan and pressure from the United States to plan and spend with similar future operations in mind.

Recent changes in the international security climate, however, have led allies to jettison expeditionary war fighting in favor of renewed emphasis on traditional territorial defense. With large adversaries engaged in military buildups close to home, it simply no longer makes sense for U.S. allies to devote scarce national security resources to improving performance in American-led foreign wars that, from their perspective, ultimately involve secondary strategic interests. Increasingly, they envision fighting wars not against insurgents backed by nonstate networks but against the conventional forces of more powerful states attempting to invade or control their territory. While some weapons systems can be used for both purposes, the central doctrinal focus and technologies of expeditionary wars are not well suited to territorial defense. In response, many U.S. allies are building heavier and more defensively minded armies.

Poland typifies this trend. A major contributor of forces to the U.S.-led operations in Iraq and Afghanistan, the Polish military has undertaken a comprehensive effort to retool itself for territorial defense. Polish and other CEE defense planners took note of the tactical difficulties that Georgian Army units, which had been trained and equipped for light counterinsurgency warfare, faced when attempting to repel heavy Russian land units. In the wake of the ISAF mission, regional militaries have begun to plan for a different kind of war. As President Komorowski said in 2013, "There'll be no more easy sending of our troops half a world away." Similarly, where the Estonian National Security Concept of 2004 emphasized "international crisis management and peace operations," the Concept of 2011 stresses "conventional threats," stating that "small countries must account for the possibility that an unfavorable concurrence of events may result in the international community failing to pay attention to their security issues"[28] Most notably, Polish officials talked of a new "Komorowski Doctrine," which would seek to improve the Polish Army's survivability in the event of a conventional Russian attack on Polish soil. Warsaw is acquiring AMD systems similar to those used by U.S. allies in the Gulf and Asia and a force of one thousand tanks that will give it the heaviest land army in Europe.[29]

Emphasis on territorial defense among frontline U.S. allies has gone hand in hand with a new prioritization of "stand-off" defensive capabilities that would maximize allied survival in the event that extended deterrence fails. The widespread adoption of so-called anti-access area denial (A2AD) strategies is one of the main patterns to emerge in recent U.S. alliance behavior. The goal of A2AD is to use large numbers of precise, inexpensive, and overlapping munitions to create "no-go zones" that limit the freedom of maneuver and offensive options of a more powerful force.[30] While pioneered by China with the aim of disrupting U.S. maritime power projection in the western Pacific, the concept is ideal for smaller states using limited means to ward off larger militaries.[31] For a threatened state, such a capability would represent a cost-effective alternative for achieving a localized deterrent that drives up the costs of attack beyond what even a determined adversary would be willing to pay.

Pursuit of A2AD capabilities has become a major focus for many U.S. allies. All but a handful of frontline U.S. allies, for example, currently possess or are seeking to acquire AMD assets such as Patriot or THAAD. Asian allies are investing in anti-ship missiles to hamper the Chinese Navy's access to that region's narrow waterways. The Gulf states are building extensive AMD systems to defeat Iranian rockets. And Poland is purchasing stockpiles of anti-tank, anti-ship, and anti-air missiles to stop Russian tanks from advancing across the North Central European Plain. In all three cases, U.S. allies are actively preparing for scenarios in which their national survival would depend, in the final analysis, more on their own defensive capabilities than on the timely intervention of the United States. The fact that they are making these preparations—at the cost of billions of dollars in expenditure diverted from other national priorities—is an indication of the extent to which the effectiveness of traditional U.S. deterrence has come into question.

The Rise of Offensive Doctrines

Not all allied attempts at military self-help are defensive in nature. Some vulnerable states are considering more aggressive strategies aimed at imposing penalties on potential attackers with or without the help of the United States. While strategically defensive, these states have developed tactically offensive doctrines (often publicly stated) on the calculation that offensive strike capabilities under national control are more likely to dissuade a large power than is a passive defensive stance that waits on America support that may never come. States with extreme military vulnerability, irreconcilable ideological or ethnic differences with the threatening state, and a lack of viable external allies have often taken such an approach. One such case was interwar Poland, which developed plans in the early 1930s for a preemptive war against Germany to forestall that country's rearmament and growth into a more serious military threat.[32]

The goal of such strategies is not to seize territory for its own sake but to dislocate the revisionist state's offensive efforts before they can form while simultaneously increasing the small state's attractiveness to larger powers as potential allies. Perhaps the prime example of a small-state offensive strategy today is the state of Israel. Surrounded by state and nonstate enemies and lacking a formal security pledge from the United States that would be usable across the range of politically charged crises facing the state, Israel has developed a highly offensive military doctrine that stresses the use of disproportionate force applied through sudden strikes deep into enemy territory to dissuade or punish attacks on Israel. The logic behind the strategy is threefold:

> First, Israel's small size [makes] it too sensitive to human casualties to allow the home front or the standing army to absorb too many attacks in long wars of attrition. Second, Israel's lack of territorial depth also [makes] it necessary to take the fight to enemy territory by preemption if need be. And, third, the need to deter initiation of new waves of attacks [necessitates] that every round of hostilities end with a crushing blow to the Arab adversaries.[33]

Developed in the early days of Israeli statehood, the doctrine was reinforced by Israeli lessons during the Yom Kippur War in 1973 when Israeli forces suffered heavy casualties after failing to deter or preempt Arab armies. Reintroduced during the war with Lebanon in 2006 (and dubbed the Dahiya Doctrine after the destruction of a Beirut suburb by that name), the doctrine seeks to change the cost-benefit ratio of aggression by "inflicting damage and meting out punishment to an extent that will demand long and expensive reconstruction processes"—in effect, using prompt and devastating reprisals to create an independent conventional deterrent.[34]

Another small state possessing an offensive military posture, though considerably less aggressive than Israel, is Finland. Like Israel, Finland occupies a position of extreme geographic exposure and a history of invasion from a nearby larger power. It shares Israel's predicament of being an informal ally of the United States that lacks explicit security guarantees against attack. A neutral state outside the NATO alliance, Finland is essentially a northern version of Poland without Article 5. To cope with its vulnerability, it maintains a small professional army backed by universal male conscription. If invaded, it would likely employ a defense-in-depth strategy, using its large spaces to slow and sap larger Russian forces as it did in the Second World War. Unlike in the past, however, Finland also increasingly possesses offensive strike capabilities, including F-18 Hornets, special operations forces, and a growing catalog of advanced missiles. A Finnish Defense Forces study in 2004 identified heavy missile launchers and air-to-surface missiles as the most crucial weapons systems for the country's defense.[35] The country is seeking to acquire long-range strike tools such as the so-called JASSM and ATACM tactical missiles. Used in combination with special forces, these stand-off capabilities would enable Finland to conduct assaults deep into Russia territory to disrupt command and control. Though unlikely to be used preemptively, these weapons go well beyond the needs of border defense and suggest the growth of an offensive mind-set to cope with worsening security conditions after the war in Ukraine.

The path taken by Israel and Finland of using offensive capabilities to deter larger states in the absence of a credible U.S. security guarantee could spread to other U.S. allies in the years ahead, as the effects of a weakening American deterrent are felt across regions. Already there are signs that some U.S. allies might someday consider such a strategy—notably, Japan, Saudi Arabia, and Poland. These states have similar characteristics to Israel and Finland, being unusually exposed and possessing alliance arrangements with the United States that are perceived as becoming less dependable over time. All three are purchasing weapons that would enable them to project offensive power and are taking baby steps toward the creation of new doctrines that would allow them to take a more independent course from the United States if necessary.

The Japanese military, for example, is developing a new "Defensive Attack Force" composed of two expeditionary divisions and two brigades that would be capable of projecting offensive amphibious power beyond the home islands for the first time since the 1940s.[36] Japan is also considering preemptive strike weapons capable of knocking out North Korean or Chinese missiles on the mainland.[37] Similarly, Saudi Arabia is considering a more offensive stance in response to Iranian military preparations. It is acquiring one of the world's largest fleets of fighter-attack aircraft, considering an expansion of the "Fahd Line" asserting Saudi protection over Persian Gulf offshore oil sites, and developing a new military doctrine centered on preemption and power projection "to establish itself as an alternative to Western military interventionism in the Arab world."[38] It has a growing stockpile of ballistic missiles, and in 2013 alone, Saudi Arabia and UAE bought some six thousand GBU-39 bunker buster bombs from the United States—weapons that could be used to strike hardened underground Iranian nuclear sites.[39] Even NATO memberstate Poland has shown interest in following Finland's path to acquiring strike capabilities. The country is developing a combination of semi-stealthy cruise missiles, fighter aircraft, special operations forces, and combat drones—known collectively as Polish Fangs— that could someday evolve to enable Poland to inflict damage on Russian home territory in the event of an attack.[40]

In a handful of cases, it is possible that allies' responses may not remain in the realm of conventional war. In Japan and Saudi Arabia, for example, there are ongoing discussions about developing military nuclear capabilities. Japan has opened a large plutonium reprocessing plant and, in an internal government report, signaled its intention to explore "the possibility of domestically producing nuclear weapons."[41] Saudi officials have publicly stated their intention to produce nuclear weapons if conventional capabilities are deemed insufficient to deter a nuclear Iran.[42] As a paper on Saudi defense put it in 2014, "The Kingdom of Saudi Arabia will have to invest in a nuclear deterrent in order to establish a counter to Iran's atomic program. Of course, if Iran gets nuclear weapons . . . [we] will be forced to follow suit."[43]

To a greater extent than any other allied behavior, this growing tendency toward offensive or conventional or even nuclear self-help illustrates how deeply the credibility American extended deterrent has been eroded. Across these regions, states that until now have not needed to possess offensive weapons or doctrinal mind-sets are beginning to do so. While not yet at the level of seriousness or capability of Israel's Dahiya Doctrine, the Japanese Defensive Attack Force, Saudi preemptive steps, and Polish Fangs are tentative steps toward creating indigenous strike capabilities that could grow with time and, in the Japanese and Saudi cases, assume extreme proportions if regional security conditions continue to worsen.

REGIONAL CAUCUSING

Military self-help is not the only method that U.S. allies are using to improve their security. Many are also forming regional alliances to strengthen their defenses against regional aggressors. Historically, this has been one of the most common response strategies of small states faced with geopolitical change. During the interwar period, for example, the countries of Central and Eastern Europe formed groupings such as the "Little Entente"—Czechoslovakia, Romania, and Yugoslavia—and the "Baltic Entente"—Latvia, Estonia, Poland, and Finland—to bolster their positions against Russia and Germany. The objective of such alliances is to accumulate greater defensive capabilities than any one regional state would possess in order to deter attacks while also making the region's otherwise isolated states more attractive as prospective alliance partners to outside Western powers. The same tendencies can be seen in the world's major regions today.

Asia: Toward an "Eastern NATO"

In Asia, the period since the onset of more aggressive Chinese behavior has coincided with a series of efforts to intensify military, industrial, and political cooperation among the region's small states. This is a noteworthy trend for a group of countries that have tended to be less cooperative than states in other regions as a result of their maritime geography and, in a few cases, disputes with one another. For decades the prevailing wisdom has been that U.S. Asian allies possess "insufficient solidarity" to form security groupings against China.[44] But in recent years states across North and Southeast Asia have been investing in a growing array of bilateral and multilateral arrangements aimed at strengthening political and military coordination.

One example of this trend is the thickening of defense ties within the Association of Southeast Asian Nations (ASEAN), a grouping of states that includes Singapore, Thailand, Vietnam, Philippines, and Malaysia. Traditionally lacking a strong security dimension, the group in recent years began to transition from a catch-all regional dialogue platform to a mechanism for containing Chinese hard power. With four member states involved in ongoing disputes with China over the South China Sea, ASEAN is becoming a rallying point for coordinating opposition to Chinese assertions of sovereignty over regional waterways. The group's security cooperation has expanded from the long-standing and largely symbolic Malacca Strait Patrol to a "defense spider web" of joint air and naval exercises, shared access to military facilities, heightened defense-industrial cooperation, and defense-ministerial consultations. Recent examples include Thai-Singaporean-Filipino air training missions, Malaysian-Filipino bilateral defense agreements, Singaporean-Indonesian naval exercises, Malaysian-Singaporean efforts to create an Integrated Air Defense System, and Malaysian-Thai maritime and air patrols.[45]

Similar linkages are forming between Japan and its neighbors. The reinterpretation of Japan's Article 9—the constitutional provision prohibiting military aid to other countries—and cancellation of the long-standing ban on the export of Japanese military equipment have gone hand in hand with intensified Japanese diplomatic outreach to and material supply of neighboring states threatened by China's rise. In recent years Tokyo has provided Vietnam and the Philippines with patrol ships, surveillance equipment, and training for regional coast guards.[46] It has worked to establish a common front with Taipei over the South China Sea and moved to establish a "Japanese version of the Taiwan Relations Act" that would enable it to formalize relations and provide a basis for broadened political and economic cooperation.[47]

While U.S. policy has occasionally encouraged linkages among allies in Asia, states in the region themselves have organically driven the emergence of heightened security cooperation. As with military self-help, these groupings are being explored as a means of coping with eventual reduced American strategic presence, irrespective of the messaging of the "pivot." Spurred by Chinese probes, the pace of security caucusing has led to discussions of creating formal mechanisms of joint military command and collective security guarantees similar to those in Europe. The need for such mechanisms would not have existed at an earlier and more stable phase of the post–Cold War era. They would face numerous obstacles—not least the deep political and historical divisions that exist between U.S. regional allies.[48] Nevertheless, the experience of postwar Europe shows the power that the emergence of a common strategic threat can have in overcoming even the deepest historical animosities to achieve greater security.

Middle East: Toward a Gulf Union

Iranian military ambitions have had a similar effect in prompting cooperation among U.S. allies in the Gulf. Like ASEAN, the Gulf Cooperation Council (GCC)—a grouping of Saudi Arabia, Bahrain, Oman, UAE, Kuwait, and Qatar—has existed for years without achieving much in the way of security coordination. However, as in Asia, the emergence of a revisionist power has demonstrated the potential benefits of regional alliances. Fueling these efforts have been America's growing political distance from the Middle East following the Iraq War and the perceived destabilization of the region by the Arab Spring uprisings. As with American allies in East Asia, the Gulf states share a common interest in counterbalancing Iran—especially its nuclear armaments and growing naval presence in the Persian Gulf. In addition, they are unified by the common ideological goal of curtailing radical elements that could undermine the stability of their own political establishments at home as they have done in neighboring Egypt, Tunisia, and Yemen. To an extent, this shared interest has also led to informal alliance linkages between the GCC states and Israel.[49]

In recent years GCC cooperation has expanded beyond the levels attained in ASEAN to include a joint military organization (the Peninsula Shield Force), Joint Defense Council, and common military academy. Gulf states have increased coordination in defense technology procurements, especially in the realm of AMD, and increasingly approach the United States on issues of security from a common position. Saudi Arabia is working to create an initiative for a formal political and economic entity—the so-called Gulf Union—that would have a joint military command and shared combat units, as well as common structures in missile defense, border security, weapons procurement, and intelligence. Based in Saudi Arabia, the Gulf Union Military Force would comprise a "deterrent force" of 100,000 soldiers whose mission in the immediate term is to prevent acts of military aggression against Gulf states or their allies and to "subdue Iranian influence in the Arab world over the medium- to long-term."[50] The creation of this force is the strongest attempt to date by U.S. frontline allies at forming a military "backstop" to traditional American military guarantees—a visible indication of how little faith the states of this region increasingly have that the United States will be able either to disarm Iran or to effectively guard them against its new nuclear capability in a future regional conflict.[51]

In pursuit of regional cooperation, the Gulf states possess several advantages over similar groupings in Asia and Central Europe. Unlike the states of ASEAN, which are geographically diffuse and ethno-linguistically diverse, the Gulf states have proximate territory and for the most part a shared identity; all but Oman are majority Sunni states threatened by the spread of Iranian Shia influence. Like regional groupings elsewhere, they have a history of intermittent cooperation, with various regional tribal confederations being used to defend against Persian and later Ottoman influence, and unlike U.S. allies in Asia, they suffer from few outright territorial disputes that could form a barrier to cooperation. They also share an ideological basis as conservative monarchies threatened by the spread of revolt in the Arab Spring. These common linkages have translated into a greater tendency toward regional "caucusing" as the preferred coping mechanism for the Gulf states than in other regions.

Central and Eastern Europe: Back to the "Intermarium"

As in the Persian Gulf and East Asia, U.S. allies in Central and Eastern Europe have responded to recent geopolitical turmoil by seeking closer defense ties with one another. While a number of regional groupings have existed in the region since the end of the Cold War, like ASEAN and the GCC they have performed mainly symbolic functions as forums for ad hoc consultation on non-vital interests. With entry into NATO and the EU, CEE states lacked a compelling strategic reason to engage in regional cooperation—indeed, it became a potential political impediment to breaking from their post-communist identity and establishing their credentials as new EU member states. But as in other regions, the return of traditional geopolitical competition has acted as a driver to attempts at security collaboration at the regional level. In a period roughly coinciding with the resurgence of Russian revisionism under Vladimir Putin and the downscaling of the U.S. presence in Europe, CEE states have begun to invest greater political capital in regional alliance formats as supplements to their Article 5 defense guarantee.

One example of this behavior is the Visegrád Group (V4), a regional bloc that includes Poland, Czech Republic, Slovakia, and Hungary. Shortly after the Russia-Georgia War of 2008, the V4 began to ratchet up coordination on issues in defense and energy policy normally reserved for the NATO and EU. In 2011 the V4 formed a regional Battle Group under Polish leadership that is scheduled to field joint combat units by 2016. Other steps have included efforts at shared defense procurement, construction of interconnecting gas pipelines to alleviate exposure to Russian supply interruptions, and coordination of policies in NATO and the EU. As in other regions, revisionist behavior has acted as a spur to deeper V4 cooperation; in the aftermath of the Russian invasion of Ukraine, group leader Poland intensified efforts at joint military planning, pushing for closer V4 coordination with Romania and working to forge a unified message among regional capitals in support of strengthening the alliance's eastern flank ahead of the NATO Summit in 2014.[52]

Another example of CEE regional cooperation is the Nordic-Baltic Group, an informal military alliance that includes Latvia, Lithuania, Estonia, Sweden, Finland, Norway, and Denmark. Formed one year after the Georgia War, the group aims to toughen the defenses of Europe's northeastern flank against Russian military incursions. Though not as formal as the V4, it engages in a higher degree of practical military cooperation, including regular consultation in defense planning and intelligence, coordination in force posture, pooling and sharing of military equipment, and frequent military exercises.[53] As in other regions, efforts at security cooperation in the Nordic-Baltic Group have increased in correlation to instability in the regional security landscape. Following the Russian invasion of Ukraine, members have engaged in a wider range of steps to bolster regional security than the less-exposed V4 Group, including intraregional repositioning of air defense assets, acceleration of shared military acquisitions, increased defense spending throughout the group, and intensification of efforts to ensure NATO entry for Sweden and Finland.[54]

Both the V4 and Baltic groupings have acquired the characteristics of sub-alliances within the European security order. To a greater degree than states in ASEAN or the GCC, CEE states have a history of forming such groupings; the Polish-Lithuanian Commonwealth, Austria-Hungary, and Little Entente are all examples of CEE states pulling together in different formats to augment their capabilities for survival or in some cases conquest. During the interwar period the concept emerged under Polish marshal Jozef Pilsudski of combining the various CEE sub-groupings to form a bulwark of states between the Baltic and Black Seas (the so-called Intermarium) against Bolshevik Russia and National Socialist Germany. The fact that similar "Baltic-to-Black" alliance concepts are surfacing today in response to Russian aggression in Georgia and Ukraine, although highly unworkable politically, is an indication of the degree of uncertainty that Russian revisionism has generated as well as the lack of confidence that CEE states place in NATO or the EU to ensure their safety.

As in other regions, the goal of CEE caucusing is twofold: to advertise the region's attractiveness as allies to potential outside patrons by showing its seriousness and defensibility, and if that fails, to jointly deter and defend the region against the nearby aggressor—if necessary, without the United States. In the case of CEE, the drive toward sub-alliances has been uneven: strongest in parts of the region with the highest exposure to Russian pressure but weaker in areas where the risk is lower or the history of resistance is less pronounced. In some ways the Nordic-Baltic Group—with its cultural similarity and extreme frontline positioning—resembles the GCC in its (comparative) ease of reaching joint positions and achieving military coordination. By contrast, the Visegrád Group has often resembled ASEAN, with efforts at synchronizing policy hampered by strategic disagreements over how to best respond to the Russian threat that are rooted in cultural, historical, and geographic differences. In all three regions, recent and historical experience has shown that there are steep obstacles to effective strategic coordination among small states, even when they are confronted with an obvious danger to their mutual security. Successful regional counterbalancing by small states requires the support of a strong external patron.

STRATEGIES OF ACCOMMODATION

Not all U.S. allies are placing all of their eggs in the basket of resistance to the rise of revisionist powers. While most frontline states are engaged in one form or another of balancing through military self-help or regional alliance building, a few are also hedging their bets by pursuing strategies aimed at mollifying or accommodating the nearby threatening state. Importantly, they are doing so without formally renouncing their security link with the United States or relinquishing close ties with neighboring small powers. This is distinguished from classic bandwagoning behavior, which commits the small state diplomatically or even militarily to supporting the goals of the revisionist state in hope of obtaining territorial spoils or other benefits.[55] Instead, the aim is to maintain a diversified menu card that resists the revisionist where necessary while avoiding a degree of confrontation that could limit the small state's strategic options down the road. In a few cases U.S. allies are going one step further, engaging in backdoor diplomacy to maximize their economic and energy linkages with the revisionist and avoid fallout from geopolitical tensions. The goal is to ensure that they are positioned to survive in the event that the United States exits the region, other "backup" mechanisms fail, and the revisionist power becomes the new regional hegemon.

This is consistent with the behavior of small states historically, which have sometimes chosen to pacify or even assist rising powers on the calculation that if they "followed a non-provocative policy, [they] might be ignored" by the aggressor and avoid hardship.[56] Small powers during the interwar period, for example, pursued a wide variety of accommodationist strategies to reduce their exposure to German, Russian, and Japanese revisionism. Several CEE states were able to avoid the fates of neighboring Poland and Czechoslovakia by eschewing alignment with the Little Entente and offering assistance to Germany. Following Britain's failure to back French opposition to the remilitarization of the Rhineland, Belgium opted for neutrality on the calculation that nobody was willing to oppose Germany.[57] Hungary chose a more actively accommodationist stance, siding with Germany in exchange for territorial gains at the expense of neighboring small powers. Thailand pursued a similar course in East Asia, jettisoning its customary pro-British diplomatic stance at the last minute to provide Japan access to the Malaysian peninsula in its attack on the Allied naval base at Singapore.

In the current setting, there is no evidence of overt small-state bandwagoning on this scale. Nevertheless, while not assisting the rising power in territorial terms as occurred in the 1930s, some states are avoiding open resistance on the scale that would seem to be desirable given their geographic position and the stances adopted by their neighbors. Their behavior spans a spectrum from passive defense policies and abstention from confrontational allied stances to de facto neutrality or "equidistancing," diplomatic accommodation, and (in a very small number of cases) open support for revisionist states' aims. In some states, these impulses exist not as formal policies but as options favored by some portion of the domestic political establishment that could grow stronger if security competition breaks out between the neighboring revisionist and the United States. While rare in comparison to the overall amount of balancing behavior among U.S. allies, these early forms of accommodation could become more common in the years ahead if geopolitical circumstances change.

East Asia: China's Self-Defeating Probes

The tendency toward accommodation is weakest among the states of East Asia—in part because of Chinese bellicosity, in part because of the region's nascent nationalism, and in part because of the inherent defensibility of its mainly maritime geography. China's move toward a more assertive stance in territorial disputes has had the effect of driving the region's small states together militarily and closer toward the United States and diminishing the attractiveness of bandwagoning as a strategic option. Virtually every U.S. ally in Asia is engaged in some form or another of classic balancing behavior, using military buildups and regional alliances to limit China's options for expansion. Notably, this is even true for states that have close economic or historic relationships with China—an indication that security concerns are trumping other considerations of national policy. So lopsided is the tendency toward balancing that Chinese behavior has pushed even states traditionally aligned diplomatically with China toward the United States. Notable examples include Malaysia, which has moved away from its past anti-American stances, and Vietnam, which is seeking a formal military alliance despite its history of military conflict with the United States.

Beneath the surface, however, there are accommodationist currents in many Asian states that were present in the recent past and could reappear if regional power dynamics shift. Until the early part of this decade, most analysts believed that U.S. regional allies were overwhelmingly choosing *not* to resist China but to accommodate its rise.[58] One study in 2010 found that "East Asian states today have neither forged military alliances with each other nor with the United States for the singular purpose of balancing against China."[59]

To varying degrees, most states in the region are economically dependent on China for some combination of markets, labor, and raw materials. Prior to the onset of greater Chinese assertiveness, most preferred to walk a careful line between confrontation on areas of core interest and cooperation in economic policy, seeking to "maximize maneuvering room by positioning themselves to benefit from ties with both China and the United States."[60]

In the current setting, the region generally breaks into "staunch balancers" like Japan and the Philippines that have primary interests threatened by China's rise and therefore consistently resist its maneuvers; states like Taiwan that are threatened but prefer if possible to keep a low profile; and states that have less to lose from Chinese hegemony and are more prone to pursue noncommittal diplomatic stances that change as circumstances necessitate. One example of the latter is Thailand, which for years has pursued a "bend in the wind" diplomatic strategy aimed at "accommodating—and seeking advantage from—both China and the United States." In recent years the Thais have updated this strategy to "'blow the wind,' as well as bend with it" by strengthening commercial and strategic linkages with both China and the United States simultaneously.[61]

Even in the period since onset of more aggressive Chinese tactics, Thailand has continued to keep its options open, increasing defense spending and cooperating with the United States while maintaining close military links with China and taking ambivalent positions on regional territorial disputes—including most recently in the South China Sea disagreement between China and Philippines. The Thai government has sought Chinese support for its position in the dispute with Cambodia over Khao Praviharn/Phrea-Vihear as an implied parallel to Chinese claims in the South China Sea.[62] Referring to Thailand's mixed messages on Taiwan, one study asked, "How reliable will the American ally be when it counts?"[63]

Malaysia has also hedged its bets in recent Asian geopolitical squabbles. While building up a strong military with close political links to Washington, it has also carefully nurtured what many Chinese officials refer to as a "special relationship" with Beijing. Malaysian leaders reacted passively to the Zhengmu Reef incident in 2013 involving Chinese warships in Malaysian territorial waters and have chosen a less confrontational response than Vietnam's to competing Chinese claims over Borneo natural-gas fields off the Malaysian coast.[64] The country's general approach, as one Australian analyst put it, has been to "embrace China's rise and give it the benefit of the doubt" and "downplay regional anxieties about China's military build-up" while keeping the option open for greater resistance in the future if Chinese behavior grows more aggressive.[65]

While Taiwan's main strategy has been to counterbalance China militarily in order to maintain its independence, many analysts see signs that Taipei may begin to lean toward a strategy of "self-Finlandization," distancing itself from U.S. military support and regional networks in favor of a more neutral stance that increases political engagement with Beijing.[66] For Taiwan and other vulnerable states in the region, the main approach has been to resist China's assertions of dominance by investing sufficiently in self-defense to convince the United States of the value of continued strategic investment. However, should the circumstances facing these states change—say, through a softening of Chinese military behavior, new evidence of American retrenchment, or an unexpected demonstration of Chinese generosity (e.g., in response to a tsunami or second financial crisis)—it is reasonable to expect that the incentives for bandwagoning will increase.

Despite its recent military assertiveness, China often seeks to encourage these accommodationist tendencies in U.S. allies. One way it has done so is through soft power. In the aftermath of the global financial crisis of 2008, Beijing engaged in intensive financial diplomacy to demonstrate its ability to supplant the traditional U.S. role as regional benign hegemon, establishing a $10 billion China-ASEAN investment cooperation fund and $15 billion in credits to economically distressed U.S. allies in the region.[67] Another way is through implied territorial reciprocity aimed at the region's more pliable states. For example, Beijing has cultivated sympathies in the Thai military and stoked expectations of possible support for Thai territorial claims in Cambodia in exchange for acquiescence in Chinese maritime claims against other ASEAN states. Beijing has "treated Malaysia with kid gloves on their overlapping maritime claims," withholding public objections to Malaysian explorations in the South China

Sea of the sort that it has frequently used to denounce the actions of the Philippines and Vietnam. A third way is through threats. Chinese officials have repeatedly warned U.S. regional allies that the United States would not come to their defense in a war with China; in June 2014, for example, Chinese major general Zhu Chenghu told China's neighbors that the United States had developed an "erectile dysfunction" that would prevent it from being a reliable ally in a crisis.[68]

Persian Gulf: Breaking Ranks in GCC

There is also growing evidence of accommodationism among U.S. allies in the Persian Gulf. As in Asia, states here have primarily favored balancing strategies to curb Iran's nuclear ambitions. Nevertheless, some members of the GCC have maintained flexible diplomatic positions or even openly friendly relations with Tehran in an attempt to act as intermediaries or benefit from Iran's continued rise. This behavior has tended to go hand in hand with formal declarations of support for U.S.-backed defense arrangements and commitments to GCC solidarity against Iranian assertiveness—for example, in the push to create a militarized Gulf Union with cooperation in AMD. However, the tendency of states in the region to look for ways to hedge their bets has grown stronger at moments of perceived weakness in American diplomacy with Iran, with noticeable movements in this direction in the period since the Obama administration opened direct talks with Tehran on an interim nuclear agreement.

One example of such behavior can be seen in the foreign policy of Oman. For years this small kingdom at the southwestern entrance to the Persian Gulf has conducted a flexible foreign policy between Iran and the West that is not unlike Thailand's strategy of bending with the wind. On one hand, the country is host to numerous U.S. military bases, providing a hub for Air Expeditionary Force deployments, anti-submarine patrols, and a joint U.S.-Omani air installation. At the same time, Oman maintains close ties with Tehran, providing an economic lifeline to Iran through port towns that bypass international sanctions. Muscat has acted as a diplomatic intermediary in Iran's nuclear standoff with the West, hosting back-channel meetings that paved the way for the signing of the interim nuclear agreement in Geneva in November 2012.[69] Like Thailand, Oman has been more inclined than other GCC states to acquiesce to the naval moves of the nearby revisionist state, with which it shares sovereignty over the Strait of Hormuz. In both cases the basic strategy is to resist the rising power where necessary while providing intermediary services that lessen the small state's exposure to conflict. This approach of playing off its more powerful neighbors' political divisions has allowed Oman to maintain favor in both Iran and the West while benefiting indirectly from sanctions—at least for now.[70]

A second example is Qatar. Like Oman, Qatar hosts significant U.S. forces, including the forward headquarters of CENTCOM, from which the United States conducted operations during the Second Gulf War. It also participates in GCC missile defense plans and has increased defense spending to counter Iran's rise. But, also like Oman, it has a considerably lower threat perception of Iran than the rest of the region does and does not share the concerns of Saudi Arabia, Bahrain, and UAE about the spread of Iranian political and ideological influence.[71] In addition to maintaining close ties with Tehran, Qatar has provided financial, moral, and military support for extremist organizations across the region—including terror groups in Gaza, Syria, Egypt, and Libya—and is home to the al Jazeera media network. The extent of these relationships has led both U.S. and GCC officials to publicly question Qatar's reliability in future conflict scenarios; as Vice Admiral Kevin Cosgriff, former commander of the U.S. Fifth Fleet, commented, it is not clear whether Qatar would "take the shot" against Iranian missiles fired at another Gulf State.[72]

In less dramatic ways, other Gulf states are also hedging their bets on Iran. As U.S. efforts to reach a compromise agreement on the Iranian nuclear program have progressed, even staunch balancers in the region have begun to explore avenues of accommodation. While viewing the interim nuclear agreement as overly permissive for the continuation of Iran's nuclear program, many GCC states have nevertheless used it as an opening for their own forms of détente with Tehran. UAE gave the earliest public backing for the agreement, engaging in high-level talks that led to a new settlement on UAE-Iranian territorial disputes.[73] Despite its vocal leadership of the regional anti-Iranian coalition, Saudi Arabia did "a bit of band-wagoning" after Geneva, "trying to lower the flames with Iran and test the waters of a future rapprochement. While not actually joining Iran, it is trying to hedge its bets by just getting along."[74] For its part, Kuwait is widely seen as being "indifferent about Iranian intentions and capabilities, despite what Kuwaiti leaders say about Tehran."[75]

Like China, Iran has occasionally sought to stoke accommodation-ist impulses among U.S. allies in its neighborhood. Under the gov-ernment of Hassan Rouhani, Tehran has engaged in regional "charm offensives" and offered incentives to nearby kingdoms willing to strengthen their ties with Iran at the expense of the GCC and the United States. Like Beijing, it has focused these efforts on regional fence-sitters, bypassing Saudi Arabia and singling out Oman, Qatar, and UAE for special treatment. Also like Beijing, Tehran has used ter-ritorial and other enticements in its diplomacy to demonstrate the payoff of future bandwagoning. In an "attempt to lure Oman away from the United States/GCC campaign against Iran, Tehran has sought to offer Muscat rewards to maintain its relative independence," including a natural gas transfer project and a role for Oman in an Iranian undersea pipeline project to provide gas to India.[76] Similarly, Iran "rewarded" UAE for its prompt outreach following the Geneva agreement, removing its fighter planes from Abu Musa, one of the disputed Hormuz islands, and eventually offering a diplomatic reso-lution that returned the Greater and Lesser Tunbs to UAE.[77]

Such behavior is consistent with the pattern in other regions, where some small states are looking for ways to do just enough to maintain their alliance with the United States without closing the door to a future accommodation with the nearby rising power. In the case of the Gulf, the tendency toward accommodation is likely to increase in proportion to the degree of weakness that states perceive in the strategic behavior of the United States. Should Washington fail to halt or significantly slow the Iranian nuclear program, as now appears likely, many regional allies may conclude that America is "unwilling to stand up to Iran on their behalf" and choose to "cozy up to Tehran, accommodate its wishes, even appease it."[78] As the UAE ambassador to the United States said in 2010, "There are many coun-tries in the region who, if they lack the assurance the United States is willing to confront Iran, will start running for cover towards Iran. [S]mall, rich, vulnerable countries do not want to be the ones who stick their fingers in the big bully's eye, if nobody's going to come to their support."[79]

Central and Eastern Europe: Strategic Diversification

Accommodationist currents are also emerging in Central and Eastern Europe. Unlike allies in the Persian Gulf or East Asia, the small states of CEE have a recent history of military occupation by or political coexistence with the nearby revisionist state. As noted above, most CEE states are already engaging in some form of balancing against Russia, either by boosting their defense spending or by investing in regional alliance frameworks. All have remained committed to their NATO roles and continue to publicly affirm their alliances with the United States as a primary security option. However, many states in the region are also quietly investing in alternative diplomatic strategies to supplement their traditional foreign policy pillars and, if necessary, hedge against an eventual U.S. retrenchment from the region.

Even before the Russian invasion of Crimea, some CEE states had begun to take more flexible approaches to their relationship with Russia, pursuing pragmatic stances that occasionally broke from the EU consensus.[80] Bulgaria has maintained especially close ties to Russia in the period since its NATO entry, participating in Russian energy projects such as the South Stream gas pipeline that circumvent EU antimonopoly regulations. Hungary has in recent years followed what one Hungarian official described as a "marriage of convenience" with Russia, signing a $14 billion, thirty-year nuclear deal with Moscow and providing political support for the South Stream pipeline despite protests from other CEE states.[81] While such tendencies predate the Obama administration, they have intensified in the period since the onset of the U.S.-Russia reset and the U.S. pivot to Asia. Indeed, as part of the former policy, Washington has actually pushed CEE states to improve their relations with Russia, prompting even prominent regional Atlanticists Poland and Romania to invest in half-hearted efforts at détente with Moscow.[82]

Like Asia, the CEE region increasingly breaks down into two broad camps: "balancers" like Poland, the Baltic states, and Romania that have preferred a consistent policy of military resistance and the rest of the region, which to varying degrees has tended to "maintain a close relationship with Russia and . . . put their business interests above political goals."[83] As in Asia, the regional dissimilarities tend to be rooted in divergent threat assessments, which are linked to geography. Poland and the Baltic states have direct exposure to possible Russian threats owing to their position on the North Central European Plain and proximity to the Russian oblast of Kaliningrad. Romania is exposed to Russian pressure in neighboring Moldova. By contrast, the southern Visegrád states enjoy relative insulation behind the Carpathian Mountains. Bulgaria has historically seen Russian support as an alternative to nearby Turkey.

The war in Ukraine has brought these differences dramatically to the fore. After a joint diplomatic rebuke of Russian actions in Ukraine early in the crisis, the Visegrád Group splintered in its members' strategic priorities and preferred responses.[84] While Hungary, Slovakia, and the Czech Republic have remained publicly supportive of NATO and EU positions, beneath the surface these states differ significantly from Poland, both in the degree of threat they believe that Russia poses and in the extent of resistance they would like to see the West offer to Putin's moves. Hungarian officials, for example, have criticized the Ukrainian national government in terms reminiscent of Moscow's stance, emphasized the rights of Magyar ethnic minorities in Trans-Carpathia over security risks to Poland, and resisted U.S. efforts at tougher economic sanctions against Russia.[85] Slovak president Robert Fico cast public doubts on whether Slovakia would come to Poland's defense in the event of a crisis.[86] Czech President Milos Zeman attacked Western sanctions against Russia and characterized the Ukraine conflict as a civil war rather than Russian invasion—positions that Czech diplomats later clarified are not those of the government. Bulgaria has pursued what its prime minister describes as a "balanced position," symbolically backing Western pressure on Russia but resisting additional sanctions and providing unofficial support for the invasion of Crimea.[87]

To a much greater extent than China or Iran, Russia has worked to encourage these accommodationist tendencies. Moscow employs a combination of loans from state-owned banks and bribery to purchase leverage in small-state foreign policies that divide NATO and the EU. Not unlike China in its stoking of Thailand's territorial claims in Cambodia, Russia has encouraged implicit parallels between Hungarian ethnic irredentism in Trans-Carpathia and Russian separatism in Crimea and eastern Ukraine.[88] Moscow bluntly offered CEE states sections of Ukrainian territory if they would join in a partition of the country.[89] Less publicly, Moscow has provided funding for anti-Western (especially far-right) parties across the region and bankrolled popular movements such as Czech resistance to U.S. missile defense and Polish, Romanian, and Bulgarian opposition to gas exploration by American companies. It has used lucrative business arrangements to entice states in southeastern Europe into various energy projects that would bypass EU energy regulations. Like its large-power counterparts in Asia and the Persian Gulf, Russia aims to reward fence-sitters and isolate those states—primarily Poland and the Baltic states—that are most resistant to its policies. As the aftermath of the Ukraine crisis shows, these efforts are succeeding; U.S. allies in CEE today are more divided over basic strategic priorities than at any point since the end of the Cold War.

NET ASSESSMENT

All the behaviors described above, whether balancing in the form of military self-help and regional alliance formation or bandwagoning in the form of accommodation and self-Finlandization, are different methods by which small states are attempting to cope with the same problem of aggressive revisionists and declining U.S. strategic presence (see figure 4.4). In all three regions, U.S. allies are responding to this set of problems by engaging in forms of behavior that would not have been seen as necessary at previous stages of the post–Cold War era. In some cases the tactics that they are using have not been seen in their regions since the 1930s. The increasingly frantic efforts

Competition	Accommodation	Avoidance or "hedging"	Military self-help	Regional caucusing
1930s: UK & France vs. Germany	Hungary Bulgaria	Czechoslovakia Romania Belgium	Poland	Little Entente Balkan Entente Baltic Entente
2010s: US vs. Russia/China/Iran	Thailand Qatar Bulgaria Hungary	Oman Taiwan Slovakia Czech Republic Malaysia	Poland Estonia Lithuania Romania Israel Japan Saudi Arabia Philippines South Korea	Visegrad Group Nordic-Baltic Group ASEAN GCC

Degree of resistance

Low ◄ – ► High
Opportunity   Fear

Response to weakening deterrence

Figure 4.4. Menu card: allied coping strategies.

of many of these states to arm, build regional coalitions, or find ways to collaborate with the nearby threatening power (or, in some cases, do all three simultaneously) illustrate just how much both military and political components of extended deterrence have weakened in the world's major regions.

While most frontline allies' first choice remains U.S. security, and most are attempting to strengthen ties with Washington, their questions about the credibility or capacity of American power are fundamental. They have become serious enough to convince states of the need to divert resources away from economic growth and internal development and begin creating backup security mechanisms to cope with the possible failure of deterrence. All states worry about worst-case scenarios, but exposed U.S. allies are increasingly planning for such contingencies in the near term and not some distant future. From the standpoint of these states, the burden of proof rests with the United States to demonstrate that deterrence has as much credibility under conditions of contested U.S. primacy, with numerous rising challengers, as it had in previous eras characterized by one large challenger—or none at all. Allied behavior suggests that states are not convinced this is the case.

Their responses are taking many forms, some of which are more problematic from the standpoint of U.S. interests than others. Accommodationist behavior almost always results in negative outcomes for regional stability. While various forms of engagement have occurred between U.S. allies and rivals for decades, the new wave of accommodation is different in two ways. First, it increasingly involves behaviors that undermine the primary interests of other nearby U.S. allies (including territorial self-defense). Whether it takes the form of muted reactions to revisionist probes (much of the CEE region, Thailand, Malaysia), attempts at self-Finlandization (Oman, or perhaps eventually Taiwan), or collaboration (Bulgaria, Thailand, Qatar), allied cheating makes it harder for other states to form coherent regional alliances. Witness the effects of Omani and Qatari obstruction in stalling movement toward a Gulf Union; lack of CEE solidarity in supporting Poland's efforts to attract NATO permanent basing after Crimea; and Thai and Malaysian resistance to a stronger ASEAN line against China in the South China Sea. Such cleavages make it less likely that local coalitions will be capable of stopping revisionism in its early stages, thereby increasing the burden on the United States to provide resistance to the aggressive state. They also make allied regions and nearby U.S. military assets harder to defend in the event of a conflict. Would Qatar "take the shot" against an Iranian missile bound for Saudi Arabia or an American installation? Would Thailand support Taiwan in the event of a Chinese move across the strait? Would Bulgaria support Poland if Article 5 were invoked? The answer is unclear.

Second, the new accommodationism could with time turn into outright bandwagoning. It would involve support by some small states for the revisionist powers' goal of *altering* the status quo. A movement in this direction would be a dramatic departure from the previous post–Cold War paradigm. In the past, whatever differences they had with the United States, U.S. allies, particularly vulnerable ones at the frontier, saw themselves as chief beneficiaries of the territorial status quo and were unambiguously invested in its perpetuation. In a few instances that appears to be changing. Though still early, a pattern is emerging in which revisionist powers are able to find pockets of dissatisfaction among U.S. allies with the status quo.

It is not hard to imagine a scenario in which Thailand seeks backing for its claims against Cambodia in the Khao Praviharn/Phrea-Vihear dispute in exchange for a softened Thai stance against China's South China Sea claims, or in which Hungarian concerns about ethnic Magyars in Trans-Carpathia translate into de facto support for Russian policies in support of ethnic Russian grievances in the former Soviet Union. Both are instances, unimaginable only a few years ago, in which a U.S. ally has more in common with a revisionist power's territorial interests than it perceives itself to have with the United States or other allies. Should revisionist powers aggressively exploit these parallels, as they did in the 1930s, it is not unconceivable that some allied accommodationism could morph into full-fledged bandwagoning. The result would be highly destabilizing for regional security orders, stymieing U.S. efforts at containment, fueling disputes among allies, and creating a greater "critical mass" in support of revisionism in the global balance of power.

Though less corrosive in the immediate term, allied balancing behaviors are also not necessarily positive for the United States or regional stability. On one hand, the tendency toward military self-help has eased the long-standing "free rider" problem of allies using U.S. security to justify lower defense spending at home. In all three regions, frontline states are almost unanimously returning to traditional defense in ways that could lighten the defense load for the United States. Moreover, much of this effort is being directed at acquiring the kinds of A2AD defensive systems that ease the U.S. task of protecting allies and make their militaries more valuable. But balancing behavior may take other, more dangerous forms. Rather than prompting defensive postures, U.S. strategic withdrawal may lead states to favor offensive stances similar to those of Israel and Finland. As the military debates in Saudi Arabia, Poland, and Japan demonstrate, this is a natural choice for extremely vulnerable states because it offers the possibility of disrupting the revisionist power early, before it can develop into a threat. It also provides a cost-effective way of reinforcing or even supplanting the fading U.S. deterrent and can be used to induce the United States to take the ally more seriously, as a more effective (and potentially independent) partner. For the United States, such approaches are potentially dangerous because they reduce U.S. strategic control over the behavior of allies while spreading offensive capabilities and escalatory mind-sets that increase the odds of an eventual regional clash that could draw in U.S. forces.

Some states may go even further, investing in their own nuclear weapons technology. While a handful of scholars have argued that nuclear proliferation among U.S. allies could exert a stabilizing presence in the world's regions (and perhaps even obviate the need for alliances at all), this is unlikely.[90] From a U.S. standpoint, such a development would translate into a faster pace of global nuclear proliferation and, ultimately, a larger number of nuclear-armed states (and nuclear weapons). The idea that this would result in stability assumes that the new regional nuclear arms races would be characterized by the same degree of self-restraint that has existed between the superpowers. But this does not account for the range of often highly emotional territorial, historical, and ethnic disputes that characterize relations between regional powers and were largely absent in superpower relations during the Cold War. Moreover, multiple small states possessing limited nuclear arsenals could generate instability; because of their vulnerability to surprise attacks, small arsenals produce incentives for first-strike posture.

As with offensive doctrines generally, a trend in this direction would reduce U.S. influence over the military actions of its allies—an essential but often overlooked ingredient in global stability. It could also fuel nuclear arms races between revisionist powers and U.S. allies and, in some cases, even between U.S. allies themselves. The resulting dynamic of numerous states in every major region possessing catastrophic capabilities would raise the stakes of even minor regional geopolitical competitions, increasing the chances that conflicts that occur could result in catastrophic loss for other powers—and possibly the United States.

Rethinking Offshore Balancing

Both military self-help and accommodationism are examples of temptations that arise in regional security orders when states traditionally secured by the United States perceive that they may have to fend for themselves in a not-so-distant future. Both tendencies have always existed beneath the surface in one form or another. Both are dangerous. Without the moderating influence of U.S. extended deterrence, these tendencies can rapidly metastasize into forms that make regions less rather than more stable and complicate U.S. interests or even endanger the safety of the United States itself.

These behaviors and their consequences are very different from what advocates of offshore balancing argued would happen if the United States reduced or withdrew its security umbrella from allied regions. As noted in chapter 2, offshore balancers have held for years that less American military presence would lead allies to overwhelmingly balance against potential revisionists in ways that resulted in *greater* stability than that provided by the United States. Real-world events are now testing these claims for the first time. The recent behavior of U.S. allies shows that the reality is more complicated and inherently dangerous than expected. Rather than balancing against threats, many states are choosing to acquiesce in or even abet their rise, either in hopes of avoiding conflict, in expectation of eventual gains for themselves, or both. And while most U.S. allies are indeed spending more on their own militaries, many are gravitating toward offensive weapons and doctrines that could lead to more rather than less potential for future conflict. What advocates of offshore balancing overlooked is the unintended consequences of U.S. strategic withdrawal: that allied responses can take many forms, not all of which lead to stability or would allow the United States to safely withdraw into North America without negative strategic consequences to itself. In all three regions, emerging trends in state behavior show that, in order to lead to stability, allied "coping" responses need to be channeled, and the only way to do this is through a U.S. security presence. It is precisely this presence that, as we will argue in the next chapter, has been a key stabilizing feature for the past several decades in the world's major regions.

CHAPTER 5

THE BENEFITS OF ALLIANCES

The means will be, first, the acquisition of allies, Hellenic or barbarian it matters not, so long as they are an accession to our strength naval or pecuniary.

—Speech of Archidamus, *The Peloponnesian Wars*

[It is] cheaper in the long run to remain a working member of the European power zone than to withdraw for short intermissions to our insular domain only to be forced to apply later the whole of our national strength to redress a balance that might have needed but a slight weight at the beginning.

—Nicholas Spykman, *America's Strategy in World Politics*

As discussed in chapter 2, arguments in favor of an isolationist stance typically stress the ability of the United States to defend itself without relying on allies, while pointing to the dangers of being pulled into conflicts in faraway regions. Alliances with small, vulnerable states are seen as offering a particularly low return on America's strategic investment because of the size, remoteness, and presumed indefensibility of the states. Countervailing statements of the exact benefit that the United States derives from these relationships are less common.[1] So deeply ingrained have alliances become in U.S. thinking about the world that even their defenders often overlook the *strategic* reasons for having and maintaining them; more often, statements of their worth to the United States take the form of vague affirmations of shared interests, are assumed to be self-evident (e.g., "more friends are better than few"), or are simply treated as inherited artifacts of past practice worth perpetuating.

In reality, America's worldwide network of alliances offers a number of vital strategic benefits to the United States, both materially, as for instance sources of advantage over military competitors, and politically, as supporting bulwarks in the U.S.-led global order. Many of the benefits that America derives from its allies are similar to those that large, status quo states have obtained from alliances throughout history: the combined firepower and deterrent effect of defensive networks; the availability of foreign bases for projecting power; the control of choke points that regulate the flow of resources. But some are also unique to the United States, including support for a set of values and international trade practices that favor the U.S. economy and make possible America's large national debt. Far from sentimentality or antique prestige, a cold-blooded pursuit of these benefits has led U.S. leaders to form America's alliances for the past seventy years. Rivals like China or Russia lack the attractant power, military reach, or credibility to organize similar networks, and they have few allies. This puts them at a profound disadvantage relative to the United States and forces them to target the American-led alliance system using, among other methods, probing, as we discussed in chapter 3. For the United States, rather than a hindrance, these networks are a strategic necessity, providing geopolitical, military, and economic advantages that have played an important role in America's seventy-year winning streak and are likely to be crucial for extending its primacy in the competitive conditions of the twenty-first century.

THE GEOPOLITICAL BENEFITS OF U.S. ALLIANCES

The most important benefit that the United States derives from alliances is through their use as tools of geopolitical management that enhance its ability to compete against other states. For reasons rooted in its geographic placement and system of government, the United States needs such relationships more than other powers do. As a maritime power of continental scope, America is both blessed and cursed by geography: it is far enough away from the world's major regions to be physically safe but not so far away that it cannot easily project influence in the rest of the world when it needs to do so. Herein lies the organizing strategic problem for America: it possesses sufficient power to dominate its own hemisphere but not enough to affect developments in that portion of the Eurasian landmass that contains the demographic and industrial potential to directly affect American security—what early twentieth-century British geopolitical writer Sir Harold Mackinder famously called "the World Island."

From this geographic problem emerges the main imperative of U.S. grand strategy: to prevent the emergence of a power or combination of powers within the Eurasian landmass that could invade or economically dominate the United States. America has three basic options for how it does so: direct containment (maintaining large military forces directly next to the territory of its rivals to prevent it from becoming a threat); retreat and reentry (ceding important regions to its competitors in peacetime and waiting to intervene until they have begun to achieve regional dominance); and alliances (maintaining a sufficient presence in the world's most important regions to affect outcomes without sapping economic strength over the long term).

The first strategy offers the advantage of strategic control but imposes enormous military and financial burdens that are hard to sustain, as the Roman Empire found when it transitioned from an alliance-based grand strategy to a system of militarized frontiers in the first century.[2] The second strategy aims to create a self-perpetuating balance of power by pitting regional states against one another and intervening only when necessary. It is cheap at first but presents high costs over the long term as large hostile powers gain ascendancy and break down the indigenous balance, making strategic reentry more difficult, as Great Britain found when it was forced to abandon this strategy in favor of permanent alliances to contain German land power in the twentieth century.[3] While American intervention in the First and Second World Wars ultimately succeeded, these conflicts also demonstrated that the natural strategy of choice for the United States—hanging back in the Western Hemisphere until the European and Asian balances had been disrupted and then wading back in to restore them, usually at the last minute—is costly, inefficient, and ultimately dangerous.

Beginning in 1940s, halfway through America's second such strategic escapade in a generation, U.S. strategic thinkers began to search for a smarter strategy. Arguing from the premise that prevention is cheaper than reaction, geostrategist Nicholas Spykman challenged the contemporary notion that hemispheric defense was sufficient to guarantee long-term U.S. survival and prosperity. Instead, Spykman argued that, for a maritime power like the United States, the key to success in geopolitics was to maintain a steady presence in and around the ingress routes to Mackinder's World Island—the coastal zones possessing the largest and most industrially rich power centers in western and eastern Eurasia, or rimlands as Spykman called them.[4] Only when the United States had found a way to sustainably project its influence in these regions abutting the Eurasian continental core, Spykman reasoned, could it hope to head off future attempts at hegemony at their source and bring to an end the cycle of retrenchment and reentry that had destabilized global geopolitics in the twentieth century. The way to do this, short of attempting to form an empire or relying on the limited reach of the U.S. Navy, is through the cultivation of onshore allies.

Geopolitically, the chief characteristic of alliances for a large power is the access they provide into remote equations beyond its direct control. This can be either an advantage or an encumbrance, depending on the strategic needs of the patron. For a power in the remote geographic position of the United States, alliances translate into a tool for global management that allows it to project a degree of influence into places beyond the confines of North America that it would otherwise not possess. To a greater extent than any other asset at America's disposal, alliances act as a curb on the ambitions of its rivals and a hedge against the chaos of interstate rivalry, resource competition, and great-power confrontation that have characterized previous eras of geopolitical history. Historically, and for the United States today, they have performed this geopolitical function in three main ways: by deterring war, by checking the growth of large-power rivals, and by attracting small powers to the side of the global status quo. In performing these functions, the U.S. alliance network has helped to address America's central grand-strategic need to prevent the emergence of hostile coalitions in Eurasia while providing a general benefit not only to that continent's weaker states but to the international system as a whole.

Alliances as War-Prevention Mechanisms

It is customary to think of alliances as being most valuable strategically after a war breaks out, when a country needs the direct military support of friendly states to defeat an opponent. But perhaps the most important geopolitical benefit they provide to the United States is in heading off conflict before it begins. Defensive alliances deter aggression by combining the military resources of multiple states, ensuring that a would-be revisionist will have to contend with numerous opponents rather than being able to concentrate its attention against one vulnerable target at a time. In the classic formulation, alliances "increase the amount of firepower confronting the aggressor, which in turn increases the likelihood that deterrence will work."[5] To a greater extent than a single army or a strong defensive position, alliances shift the military balance in favor of the status quo, driving up the costs of aggression and reducing the potential payoff that a revisionist state can expect to achieve from an expansionist military policy. In geopolitics as in everyday life, bullies are "likely to be deterred much more effectively by superior power than merely equal power."[6] Through aggregation of superior power combination *in advance* of a possible conflict, alliances perform an inherently conservative geopolitical role, discouraging disruption and aiding in the perpetuation of a stable international system.

This has been the main purpose of alliances for much of history—to dissuade the restless and powerful from attacking the peaceful or weak. From the time of antiquity, states have formed defensive pacts to prevent land-hungry neighbors from attempting to take their territory. This war-preventing feature of alliances has been obscured by the modern fixation on alliances as triggers to conflict, as in the role that Europe's complex systems of counter-alliances had in fueling the outbreak of the First World War.[7] But more often alliances have acted as "defensive instruments aimed at containing an actual threat to the balance of power."[8] Historically, security orders built on defensive alliances have been characterized by infrequent great-power war and the preservation of small states, while those in which defensive alliances have not existed or have broken down have tended toward entropy and eventual military hegemony by strong states. As Spykman wrote, Western geopolitical history has been characterized by a long series of attempts by defensive alliances to thwart hegemonic power-grabs *du jour*:

> The weak states of the Tigris-Euphrates valley allied themselves against their stronger rivals and preserved their independence for centuries. . . . The Greek city-states maintained a precarious balance by means of the Delian and Peloponnesian Leagues under the leadership of Athens and Sparta, but they failed to combine against the menace of Macedonia. Rome found no league to stem her vast expansion and defeated her enemies one by one. Had they known how to combine, Carthage, Egypt, and Macedonia might have preserved their independence far longer and confined Rome within the boundaries of Europe. When the House of Hapsburg under Charles V attained such vast domains that it threatened to become a menace to other states, these states combined to check its ascendancy. Similar was the fate of the hegemonic aspirations of Spain under Philip II, France under Louis XIV and Napoleon, and Germany under Kaiser Wilhelm II.[9]

The presence of defensive alliances is no guarantee against the outbreak of war. But they have acted more often in history as preventives to conflict than as geopolitical straightjackets entrapping their members in escalatory feuds. Historically, there is a strong correlation between the existence of alliances in a given region and the effectiveness of deterrence against a threatening power. A review of the Alliance Treaty Obligations and Provisions (ATOP) dataset for the years between 1816 and 1944 found that "potential challengers are less likely to initiate a militarized dispute against a potential target if the target has one or more allies committed to intervene on behalf of the target if attacked by this challenger."[10] Another study examining fifty-four cases between 1900 and 1980 determined that defensive alliances characterized by close political ties and even small amounts of trade succeeded in deterring aggression seven times out of eight. In cases where states within an alliance maintained strong military assistance and defense trade links, the odds were even higher; "deterrence is more likely to be effective," the authors wrote, "the greater the defender's visible and symbolic stake in the protégé."[11]

The effectiveness of defensive alliances in deterring conflict is visible in the fact that the two longest periods of international peace in modern history—the nineteenth century and the Cold War—coincided with the existence of extensive, well-regulated defensive alliance systems. The elaborate Central European alliance systems engineered first by Metternich and later by Bismarck allowed Europe to avoid a generalized great-power conflict for a hundred years between the Napoleonic Wars and the First World War.[12] Similarly, in the twentieth century the U.S.-led NATO alliance helped to deter Soviet aggression and maintain peace in Europe for more than seventy years. The success and longevity of both systems were anchored in defensive arrangements that favored the status quo and presented unacceptably high military costs to any state attempting to undertake large-scale territorial aggression.

The continued functioning of post–Cold War U.S. alliances has helped to prevent war in the modern era. Though less often touted than the economic benefits of the *Pax Americana*, the conflict-suppressing qualities of U.S. defensive networks are a major part of the explanation for why there has been neither a direct challenge to American supremacy nor a major regional war in the quarter century since the end of the Cold War. In Europe, the extension of the NATO alliance into the former communist countries of Central and Eastern Europe removed the sources of conflict that had made this region the birthplace of three global wars in the twentieth century. It was the failure to create such arrangements in the 1930s that created the conditions for the Second World War. NATO's presence in CEE has helped to dissuade Russian military adventures and to suppress tensions between regional states over disputed territory. Had the United States allowed this region to become a Finlandized "gray zone" as many pundits argued in the 1990s, today's CEE landscape might contain many of the same characteristics as the states of the former Soviet Union, including unstable internal politics, simmering irredentist feuds, and perennial Russian invasions—with negative consequences for the European security order. With NATO's Article 5 security guarantee in place, Russian threats to take military action against the Baltic states or Poland have (so far) remained rhetorical.

Post–Cold War U.S. alliances have also had a calming effect in Asia. As in CEE, American security linkages with the region's small coastal states have acted as a hedge against hegemonic aspirations by the area's largest land power, China, while assuaging tensions between U.S. allies (i.e., Thailand and Singapore or Japan and South Korea). U.S.-backed defensive alliances along the Asian coastline helped to channel China's latent power potential into the grand strategy of a "peaceful rise" that for many decades allowed this region to avoid military buildups, confrontation, and geopolitical instability. As with Russia in CEE following NATO enlargement, the presence of extensive alliances has for years simply made the costs to China of attempting to improve its regional position through traditional military revisionism too high to be worth the trouble. Of the six wars that China has fought in the period since the founding of the communist state in 1949, all have been with states on China's frontiers (Vietnam, Tibet, India) lacking alliances with the United States and therefore involving lower risks for Beijing. Much as the presence of NATO has deterred Russia from attempting Georgia War–style military incursions in Central Europe, defensive alliances in Asia have helped to restrict China's aggressive intentions to posturing.[13]

Defensive alliances also exert a stabilizing influence in the Middle East. During the Cold War America's military backing of regional states was instrumental after the colonial powers' exit in maintaining a regional balance of power and deterring a generalized conflict involving Soviet intervention—most notably during the Yom Kippur War of 1973. Since the Cold War the perpetuation of U.S. alliance structures has helped to deter the region's largest powers from attempting bids at regional supremacy or exerting control over the region's primary oil-producing sectors. The U.S. alliance with Israel has been a fundamental component in the stability of the region, providing the basis for a sustainable peace with Egypt and discouraging the region's large states from coalescing in support of an exterminationist war like those attempted in 1948, 1967, and 1973 (prior to the establishment of closer links with Washington).[14] Similarly, America's informal alliances with the Gulf states, by supplying offshore military strength that these mostly small countries would not otherwise possess, have enabled them to act as a hedge against the ambitions of two powers—Iraq and Iran—to seek military dominance over regional oil fields. During the invasion of Kuwait in 1991, it was the U.S. security relationship with Saudi Arabia that deterred Iraq from attempting a wider offensive, which it would otherwise likely have attempted—and possibly won.[15] More recently, U.S. security backing of the Gulf states has acted as a bulwark against Iran seeking to assert military control of the western and southern shores of the Persian Gulf—and with it, dominance of the world's most important energy route.

In all three regions, the presence of U.S. alliances has been a central ingredient in making the post–Cold War era free of major regional or global war. In all three cases, defensive alliances are performing the role of war prevention that they have played for centuries, changing the calculus of revisionism in ways that reduce the potential payoff of aggression and make the regional order more peaceful than it would likely otherwise be. The much-touted costs of maintaining alliances must be weighed against the savings that they bring in both lives and treasure through avoiding costly conflicts.

Alliances as Containment Tools

A second and related way that alliances help the United States geopolitically is by limiting the physical reach of large rivals to their own neighborhoods. By maintaining numerous client states, however small, close to the borders, resource arteries, and historical expansion zones of large powers like Russia, China, and Iran, the United States can contain these potential rivals for long periods of time at relatively low financial or military cost to itself. Using alliances in this way places "embedded checks" on the ambitions of potential troublemakers while giving the United States onshore sources of influence that share its interest in system stability. Put differently, it's not just that possessing defensive alliances deters war, it's that possessing defensive alliances with states *located near a rival* hinders that state's ability to accumulate and project power beyond its immediate environment in ways that would threaten the United States. Alliances do this in two ways—one geographic and one political.

First, alliances deny large powers access to important geography. By supporting the survival of weak states in strategically vital locations that an expanding neighbor would otherwise subsume, alliances prevent Eurasia's largest states from accumulating the natural resources, population, and geographic access to directly challenge the United States. Through the medium of alliances, America is able to encourage geopolitical pluralism in historically pivotal geographic zones that keep strategic control divided between multiple polities while providing the additional benefit of ensuring political self-determination for the (mostly democratic) states inhabiting these areas. The kaleidoscopic political geography of the three global hinge points that are the subject of this book is an example of this strategy at work. In any one of these regions, expanded geographic control by a large power over areas that U.S. allies currently occupy would bring political co-optation or extinction for the countries in question and a broadened material basis for sustaining global power projection and competition with the United States.

Throughout history status quo powers seeking to contain revisionist rivals have employed the strategy of using alliances with small states to ensure divided control over important regions. For three centuries Britain took advantage of alliances with the Low Countries to deny first the Habsburgs, then France, and later Germany control over the strategically vital Scheldt Estuary, which would have enabled these powers to threaten British security and employ Holland's deepwater ports for global power projection.[16] Austria engaged a similar strategy with small Balkan states to prevent Russian control over the approaches to the Bosporus Strait and domination of the Black Sea basin.[17] In the seventeenth century Cardinal Richelieu employed alliances with the small German principalities to maintain a Middle European buffer zone denying the Habsburgs access to the European heartland.[18] In the eighteenth century Louis XV used alliances with Sweden, Poland, and Turkey to create a "barrier" denying Russia's westward expansion toward the warm-water ports of the Baltic and Black Seas.[19] And in the twentieth century the French Fourth Republic implemented a similar policy in its husbanding of the Little Entente in Central and Eastern Europe in an effort to deny expansion zones to both Germany and Russia.[20]

In all these cases, alliances were used to prop up small states in critical locations that, if possessed by a larger neighbor, would have provided the building blocks for regional dominance and created conditions for extra-regional power projection. U.S. alliances perform a similar function today, denying America's rivals access to coastal zones, waterways, and strategic hinterlands that would likely fall under their sway without outside support. The international landscape is dotted with examples of modern-day equivalents of "Low Countries"—strategically placed enclaves that, if controlled by a hostile power, could dramatically alter the character of the regional military balance and global competition to America's disadvantage. In all three regions that are the focus of this book, U.S. allies occupy geography that revisionist powers covet in part because of the effect that its absorption, whether through invasion, state capture, or co-optation, would hold for their regional and international power positions.

In Europe, for example, U.S. alliances in CEE ensure geopolitical pluralism in the thousand-mile stretch of territory that has been the traditional empire maker for large continental powers of both East and West. NATO's presence in this region blocks Russian reentry into and control over a collection of territories that were indispensable elements in Russian power under the tsarist empire and communist regime. These include the Baltic states, Russia's traditional warm-water ingress into the Baltic Sea and window onto northern Europe; Poland, the historic gate to mainland Europe, control of which is necessary for exerting Russian land power in the European balance of power; the Bohemian highlands, a westward-facing Slavic salient that Bismarck called the most defensible real estate in Europe; Hungary and Slovakia, the keys to control of the upper Danube River basin and supporting energy and transit routes that are linchpins of the European economic space; and Romania and Bulgaria, which occupy the westward approaches to the Black Sea Straits, access to which is necessary for Russia to project naval power into the eastern Mediterranean—the unending object of Russian nineteenth-century diplomacy.

Historically, the possession or neutralization of these territories has been a necessary precondition to Russian great-power status. At its apogee, with these territories under its direct control, Russia was more than just a European power—it was a Eurasian superpower with sufficient resources to shape its external environment and equipped with the territorial portals to project that power outward into the wider world. In geopolitical terms, it represented a kind of supersized version of Bismarck's Germany: an entity too powerful to be restrained by the total combined resources of the indigenous European balance of power and, on that basis, the only state in history to have so far been capable of directly threatening the survival of the United States. Without control of these territories, Russia becomes just another large Eurasian state. In the words of a group of senior experts from the Section for Geopolitics and Security at the Russian Academy of Natural Sciences, it is "no longer functionally a great power" but a state that is transformed from "geopolitical extrovert" to "geopolitical introvert": a "shrunken Russia . . . deprived of key elements of its strategic early warning system and shut off as a 'northern-continental country' like some obscure corner of Europe." With U.S. alliances embedded in its Western approaches, Russia's geopolitical growth is checked, limiting it to the status of a large and occasionally difficult but ultimately quarantined Eurasian state.[21]

The pattern in the Asia-Pacific region is similar. Viewed from a Chinese geopolitical perspective, practically all maritime zones that the country would need to control in order to ascend to first-rank status as a global power are inhabited by allies of the United States. In the contemporary Chinese strategic debate, the string of U.S.-aligned coastal states and islands along the length of the Asian coast—the so-called first island chain—are seen as containment mechanisms that hem China into the Asia mainland.[22] The de facto territorial access-denial role that these allies play performs a valuable service to the United States as an offshore power attempting to manage the distant Asian geostrategic environment. Much like the small states of CEE, U.S. littoral allies in Asia act as built-in blocking mechanisms that impede the growth of a rival power to proportions that could challenge the United States globally. These include Taiwan, the watchtower of the Asian coastline straddling shipping lanes to both north and south; Singapore, the choke point connecting Persian Gulf energy transit routes to Asia; South Korea, the peninsula from which a controlling power can project naval power into the East China Sea and threaten Japan; the Philippines, linchpin of the South China Sea connecting the maritime lines of communication from Singapore to Taiwan; and Australia, the extra-regional depot that has served as the historic foundation of British and later U.S. strategy in Asia.[23] With some combination of these territories directly or indirectly under its control, China would be able to create an Asian Mediterranean from which to project naval power beyond the first island chain into the Pacific Ocean ("breaking through the thistles," in the current Chinese military parlance), becoming a global power virtually overnight.[24] With these territories in the hands of governments allied to the United States, China remains virtual landlocked, hedged into the Asian mainland, and deprived of access to expansion routes.[25]

U.S. allies play a similar role in the political geography of the Middle East. Like Russia and China, Iran is a historical imperial power constrained in the current security setting from reentering traditional expansion routes by the presence of strategically placed small states with close security ties to the United States. To its west lies a fragmented Arab world interspersed with American allies Israel and Jordan, and (potentially) U.S.-supported Iraq. Historically, this space has played a role for Iran similar to the role that CEE plays for Russia: if weak and unsupported, it offers an arena for Iranian expansion; if unified or backed by an outside power, it becomes a de facto containment mechanism.[26] To Iran's south and southwest, it is hedged in by U.S. allies Saudi Arabia, Kuwait, Bahrain, Qatar, Oman, and UAE. Historically, possession of the western shore of the Persian Gulf either directly or through the medium of client states was a vital object of Persian imperial policy—not unlike Russia's historic quest to reach the mouth of the Baltic Sea. With this real estate under its sway, Iran would be able to control global energy arteries and project naval power into the Indian Ocean. With U.S. allies occupying this real estate, Iran remains a large but essentially quarantined regional power.

In all three cases—Russia, China, and Iran—the maintenance of U.S.-backed alliances in geopolitically sensitive territory helps to prevent a large power from acquiring a regionally dominant position from which it would be capable of threatening primary interests of the United States. Importantly, this role is a largely passive one—through their very existence as independent entities, the small states that the United States supports deny access to territory that their larger neighbors would need to be able to dominate the region and threaten the United States more directly. In all three cases, the real estate in question is primarily maritime. Whether it is the Baltic and Black Seas, Persian Gulf, or East and South China Seas, the principal *geographic* value of American allies in these places is that they either prevent or complicate a large power's access to the ocean. In the cases of Russia and China in particular, the nearby presence of U.S. allies helps to forestall large land powers from attaining the attributes of large maritime powers—a key condition for preventing the emergence of rival sea powers able to harness large industrial bases that Mackinder warned about. With U.S. allies in place along the world's coastlines and land-necks, three of Eurasia's largest land powers are effectively blocked in their (sometimes centuries-long) quest for unfettered ingress to the world's major waterways. The result is a triple containment at low direct cost to the United States—an important benefit to a power like America that is otherwise distant from these regional equations and one that is rarely accounted for in cost-benefit assessments of U.S. alliances. By blocking the expansion of rivals in Eurasia, U.S. allies reinforce the other bank of the oceanic moats that naturally but imperfectly protect the North American continent.

Alliances as Balancing Tools

A second containment function of alliances is that they help the United States counterbalance the ambitions of large powers. Unlike the access-denial role described above, which is primarily geographic and passive in nature, the balancing function is political and active. It's not just that by virtue of their independent existence these U.S. allies prevent geopolitically important territory from falling under the sway of larger powers. It's that the policies pursued by their governments actively work to curtail attempts at regional hegemony. Motivated by the desire to retain political independence and territorial sovereignty, threatened states will use a variety of military and diplomatic strategies (see chapter 4) to resist the growth of large powers in their neighborhood. The stronger the revisionist power's efforts at expansion become, the more likely they are to trigger reactions from nearby states. This is one of the positive effects of the probing behavior by U.S. rivals, as we observed in chapter 3. By providing military and diplomatic support to these threatened players, the United States can use their natural hostility toward large powers to its advantage, creating built-in "regulators" that check the growth of hegemonic ambitions.

For centuries great powers have used alliances with weaker states located close to rivals in this way. "Far back into antiquity," Spykman wrote, "goes the practice of strong states protecting small countries [to] stop the expansion of some great state which after further growth might become a menace."[27] The closer the small state is to the rival, the more useful it is likely to prove as a balancing agent, under "the eternal logic that dictates that alliances are best made with the unfriendly neighbors of unfriendly neighbors."[28] Hence the Romans famously used Armenia to hamper Sassanid Persian expansion into Syria and the Byzantines formed alliances with the lesser Turkic tribes located near their main adversaries in the Asian steppe and with the Khazars against the Muslim Arabs.[29]

Most famously, Britain coalesced small-state coalitions to balance against challengers on the European continent. Britain's strategy was to empower local groupings of minor powers that were alarmed by their larger neighbors' ambitions but did not possess the power or courage to resist them without the help of a strong patron. This strategy succeeded in part because it worked with the momentum of local power balances, using preexisting fears and geopolitical rhythms to the offshore state's advantage. Like Rome and Byzantium, London aligned with states that, for their own reasons, shared Britain's enemy and wanted to prevent its growth in power status. As a briefing book for young British diplomats pointed out in 1917, "the general tendency of British policy . . . was to support the smaller nations of Europe against the interference of the great autocratic empires. . . . Greece, Spain, Belgium and Italy owed the maintenance of their independence largely to British help."[30] By publicly and consistently supporting the weaker side in Europe's conflicts, it is likely that Britain made it more feasible for weak states to choose resistance over compliance. This defrayed the costs that Britain would have to pay for effective management of the European system. The opposite is certainly true: episodes when Britain failed to resist aggression made it more likely that Europe's small states would choose neutrality or accommodation.[31]

America's global strategy since the Second World War has been based on a similar logic. Like Britain, the United States, through its status as a system-leading maritime power, has a compelling strategic interest in maintaining a balance of power in the world's major regions at the lowest possible cost to itself. If anything, the wider geographic dispersion of America's global competitors makes its ability to activate local counterbalancing coalitions more important for the maintenance of its global power position than was the case for Britain, which faced only one region (mainland Europe) with the potential to threaten its existence. By contrast, the United States faces three regions of potential existential concern: Europe/Russia, Asia-Pacific, and, in the era of nuclear proliferation, the Middle East. In all three regions, America's practice of taking the side of the smaller states allows it to work with the natural rhythm of local balances of power.

Weak states in the world's major regions already fear the emergence of a neighboring hegemon, whose expansion would likely lead to the loss of their territory or sovereignty, more than they fear a distant offshore power like the United States. This puts the United States in a position to use regional states as balancing mechanisms against potential rivals more quickly and cheaply than these rivals would be able to use such mechanisms against the United States. The fact that Japan or Poland is willing to spend its own diplomatic and military resources against China or Russia reduces the money, time, and effort that the United States would have to spend on this task on its own. America's regional allies already possess incentives to monitor and limit the growth of their larger neighbors; the support of the United States merely reinforces these preexisting dynamics, making the weaker states more effective and ensuring that, when the United States does weigh into these equations, it will have a greater preponderance of strength on its side in the competition. Through alliances the United States can outsource a portion of the costs of global leadership and defray the cost of containing its rivals. Critically, it is through the medium of alliances that America has the option of *containing* its rivals—using local forces to hedge the growth of a large state early on rather than waiting to combat them once they have assumed proportions that would threaten the United States.

As they did for Britain, small-state alliances also improve the range of options for U.S. strategy. By activating local power from frontline allies as a first line of defense against emerging rivals, the United States has an early warning system that buys time and improves its ability to manage multiple peripheries simultaneously. This ultimately makes U.S. containment of its rivals more cost-effective. As for previous hegemons, America's use of alliances is built on an implicit bargain with weaker states: they will accept the risk of openly opposing a stronger nearby state (thereby forgoing the options of a more flexible diplomacy) in exchange for the United States providing a guarantee of effective opposition against threats that may emerge to the weaker state's survival. This alleviates the ally's fears of extinction and lessens America's burden of having to be present everywhere at the same time to ensure system stability.

With such alliances in place, America can maintain a relatively thin military presence at the periphery and wait to bring its main weight to bear against big problems when and where they arise. The global power of the United States is made possible by its allies who can hold the line in their own region while American power is occupied in another theater. Not unlike the Roman Empire's use of client states to secure the military frontier, America's frontline alliances allow it to "surge" in the critical spot at the right moment using a combination of its own military power and that of its allies to restore the regional balance without concern of sacrificing its influence in other regions. This allows American power to achieve an impact in more places, with fewer opportunity costs and to greater overall strategic effect, than would be possible by relying solely on the U.S. military. It translates into lower overall costs of system management since it allows America to keep the bulk of its forces at home, concentrate resources where they are needed most, and avoid the high start-up costs of reentering regions each time a new threat emerges. The Obama administration's famous Asia pivot, while ill-timed and poorly executed, nevertheless symbolized the flexibility that alliances can give to a maritime power. That America was able to plausibly consider shifting military focus from one important region to another without forfeiting the former was based on the logic that it could rely on allies (and a reduced U.S. force presence) to handle the quieter of the two peripheries. Without alliances, such a strategy would have been unthinkable. A large American rebalancing to Asia will be impossible, or highly risky, if, for instance, CEE states are unable or unwilling to hinder Russian revisionism in Europe.

Using alliances in this way to manage multiple peripheries is especially important for the United States, given the size and distance separating the regions that it must successfully monitor to ensure its security. Such a strategy allows America to achieve economy of force in the disposition and application of its power, maximizing limited military resources against numerous rivals. Using alliances, the United States can shift from reaction to prevention, disrupting its rivals' growth in the critical early phases. This is cheaper in the long run and avoids the full costs that would be required to achieve system leadership on its own strength alone. Without extensive alliances, America would be tied to a reactive strategy that required recurrent interventions in the regional "firetraps" of Europe and Asia once they became too strong to contain locally. By maintaining forward alliances and positioning some portion of its strength near its rivals, it is able to address imbalances early on, before they have "gone global," while exerting influence to prevent crises from erupting in the first place. It is the equivalent of installing fire sprinklers rather than waiting to get a hose until a fire has already started. This is cheaper than attempting to maintain a large, active American defensive presence across major regions, which, as Rome discovered, eventually outstrips the ability of any hegemon to bear. It is also ultimately more effective than the offshore balancing strategy, which, as Britain discovered, is cheap in the short run but imposes high costs of reentry from repeatedly assembling new coalitions from scratch once a region has deteriorated, wasting opportunities to disrupt a rival's growth early on and gradually eroding confidence in the maritime power's credibility.

Alliances as Status Quo Preservers

Part of the reason that defensive alliances succeed and are beneficial to the United States today is that they tend to act as natural rallying mechanisms to other states with a vested interest in preserving the geopolitical status quo. As noted above, small states in particular are negatively affected when systemic disruption occurs. As weak polities that are unable to directly shape outcomes in the environment around them, they stand to lose the most when the status quo fails. Whereas the rise of a revisionist might damage a large status quo power's interests, for small states it could mean the loss of their very existence as sovereign entities. This is particularly problematic for small powers on the frontier that have neither the geographic distance nor sufficient power to protect them from aggression in even its earliest phases. Historically, such states have tended to be the first to face extinction when revisionist powers succeed and the greatest beneficiaries of durable arrangements made to prolong a stable international system.

Small states have a dual relationship with the balance of power. First, the existence of independent small entities is an indicator of the overall health of a geopolitical ecosystem. If the system's weakest entities are numerous and prospering, it is an indication that relations between the large powers are stable and war is being averted. Second, small states actively participate in this outcome. While they themselves may not be directly concerned with the abstract question of global systemic stability, their interest in survival coincides with and reinforces the desire of the United States to achieve a stable global geopolitical and economic order. Hence for most of the eighteenth and nineteenth centuries, Britain and its small-power allies were "the only 'true' defenders of the Balance of Power"; for other powers, "security seemed to reside in a favorable *imbalance* of power."[32] Then as now, small powers are most likely to fight to maintain the status quo—a tendency that a large patron like the United States can harness to create natural, built-in suppressors to revisionism that, by the very virtue of their existence, narrow the range of options available to aggressive states.[33]

However, while small states are naturally inclined to side with guardians of the status quo, they do not always do so. Although the logic of balancing assumes that regional states threatened by the growth in power status of a potential hegemon will offer resistance, the opposite can also be true: if unconvinced that resistance will succeed, some states will seek to avoid conflict or even accommodate a powerful state's ascent. Alliances help to address this problem by signaling the intention of a large and powerful state to defend the regional status quo. For small states, the certain knowledge that the United States will actively resist efforts at hegemony tips the calculus of costs and benefits in favor of resistance. Put differently, balancing does not always happen by itself. It is not the automatic law of international relations that political scientist Kenneth Waltz posited.[34] The view that medium or small states have no choice but to balance against the growing neighbor—either alone or together with other powers—and thus will likely side with the status quo power is based on a blind faith in balancing. As Paul Schroeder argues, "No matter what neo-realist international relations theorists may say, balancing against growing or threatening powers is not a natural or necessary response for either small or great powers in international politics, an unchanging bedrock rule for survival in international politics over the centuries."[35] Indeed, balancing is often the result of an extraregional chaperone inspiring confidence in states that would otherwise be persuaded to consider other options. The key is the expectation of America's likely behavior in future conflicts.

Because of their implied permanence, formal alliance commitments are more effective at incentivizing resistance than are ad hoc coalitions. Britain often waited to form alliances until after a war had broken out, by which time some potential allies had chosen accommodation or been invaded. By contrast, America's standing security arrangements enable it to mobilize anti-hegemonic aspirations and encode them into the fabric of regional security orders well in advance of a conflict. This gives the United States the moral advantage over its competitors of being on the side of the global underdog. It helps to ensure that the largest number of states possible are on the side of the status quo, that they are as active as possible in supporting it, and that they are bringing their diplomatic weight to bear early rather than late in the game—considerable advantages for a power like the United States with a vested interest in system stability.

THE MILITARY BENEFITS OF ALLIANCES

The arguments above have focused on the benefits that alliances provide in avoiding war—by deterring aggression, containing rather than confronting rivals, and maximizing the range of strategic options and number of supporters available to a status quo power. But alliances also benefit the United States in a more direct way, by making it more likely that it will win if and when a war does break out. This has been the most basic rationale for forming alliances throughout history; as writers from Sun Tzu to Machiavelli have noted, allies are good to have because they fill gaps in one's own capabilities. In the case of the United States, this gap is twofold: (1) physical— having the human and material resources to win on land, air, and sea against potentially multiple military rivals in the various strategic environments of the world's regions—and (2) geographic—having the ability to overcome space and effectively project power into the distant reaches of Eurasia. To varying degrees, America's allies help to address both gaps.

Alliances as Capability Aggregators

At root, alliances are tools for accumulating greater military capabilities than a state would possess on its own. "The first standard by which to evaluate alliances," as Arnold Wolfers wrote, "is whether the allies can offer something worthwhile in terms of military assistance" and thereby increase the odds of competing successfully with other states.[36] Measured in this way, U.S. alliances represent a significant multiplier to American power. Today's United States commands the largest and best-armed military alliance in history. Viewed collectively, the military capabilities of the United States and its allies are formidable: fifty nations spending almost $1.2 trillion on defense—about 67 percent of global military spending—and deploying more than 7 million troops worldwide.[37] By comparison, the combined total for America's principal competitors China, Russia, and Iran is about 13 percent of global defense spending and 18 percent of global military manpower.[38]

At a regional level, the combined forces of American and allied militaries outstrip the forces of large competitors in virtually any conceivable military contest by a wide margin. In Asia, the United States and its allies combined account for 4.3 million troops and $767 billion in annual defense spending compared to 2.3 million active armed forces and $126 billion for China—a disparity of 47 percent in troops and 84 percent in spending. In Europe, the United States and its allies account for 3.8 million troops and $905 billion in annual defense spending compared to about 766,000 men and $76.6 billion for Russia—a disparity of 80 percent in troops and 92 percent in spending. And in the Middle East, the United States and its allies account for 2.4 million troops and $721 billion dollars in annual defense spending compared to 545,000 active armed forces and $6.3 billion for Iran—a disparity of 77 percent in troops and 99 percent in spending.[39]

Without alliances, the United States would lose a significant chunk of world military capabilities. While America would remain the most capable military power in the world, its margin of superiority against rivals in regional competitions would diminish—especially in Asia. These margins will matter more in the coming decades than they did in the previous post–Cold War era, as the United States and its major allies spend less on defense relative to the rest of the world and as targeted increases in Russian and Chinese military spending narrow the gap in the size and sophistication of rival militaries (see figure 5.1). The Russian defense budget, for example, increased by 4.8 percent in 2013 to $87.8 billion (about 4 percent of GDP)—the first time in more than a decade that Russia has spent a larger share of its overall economy on arms than the United States. Additionally, Moscow has introduced a decade-long infusion of $700 billion for

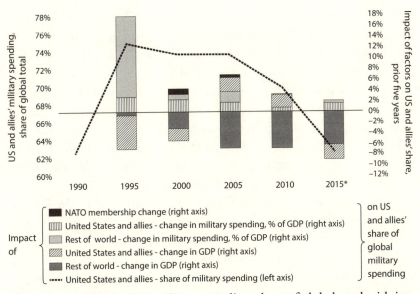

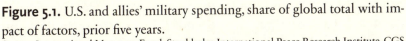

Figure 5.1. U.S. and allies' military spending, share of global total with impact of factors, prior five years.

Sources: International Monetary Fund, Stockholm International Peace Research Institute, CGS estimates.

Note: Allies include NATO, Japan, South Korea, Israel, and Saudi Arabia. Projection based on IMF growth estimates, assuming static military spending as percent of GDP after 2013.

military modernization.[40] The Chinese defense budget is also growing, with overall spending doubling every five years and current projections of surpassing U.S. defense spending by 2035.[41]

As America's military advantage over large land power rivals narrows, the military value that it derives from alliances will increase. Part of the reason is technology. With the proliferation of sophisticated capabilities—nuclear weapons, advanced missiles, satellites, guided munitions—the United States will be able to count less on the dominance of its own military for deterring or overcoming competitors and will need the help of others more. The spread of lethal technologies makes American technological supremacy more difficult to sustain, increasing the value of allies. Great Britain had less strategic use for allies in the eighteenth and early nineteenth centuries, when the Royal Navy enjoyed wide numerical and technological superiority over its continental rivals, than in the early twentieth century, when French, Russian, and especially German advances in fleet construction had eroded this advantage. For the United States, the proliferation of advanced conventional war-fighting technologies to competitors like China necessitates, to a certain extent, the proliferation of these same technologies to U.S. allies. Since proliferation is occurring anyhow, it is in the interests of the United States that it take place in ways that benefit friendly states to create the widest possible array of countervailing capabilities on America's side of the ledger in the event of a conflict. This requires alliances.

Another reason that the military value of alliances to the United States is likely to increase is the growing shift in many frontline allied states toward defensive capabilities that augment the long-range military assets of the United States. Historically, the most effective alliances have been those that not only add raw fighting abilities but provide a force capability that their patron lacks. Hence, Thucydides noted that Corinth's navy depended for its success on the "land forces furnished by their barbarian allies."[42] In its confrontation with Athens, Sparta could not have won the Peloponnesian War had it not been aided by Persian naval power. The Roman Army depended on allied auxiliary contingents specializing in tactical capabilities—archers, slingers, and above all cavalry—that complemented Rome's heavy legions. Similarly, Britain's large Royal Navy and small expeditionary army were most effective when waging European wars in combination with allied land armies—whether Austria in the wars against Louis XIV, Portugal in the Peninsular campaign against Napoleon, or the French Army against Germany in 1914.

The degree of military complementarity between U.S. forces and the militaries of American allies is generally considered to be low.[43] This is largely based on U.S. military experience during the wars in Iraq and Afghanistan, where allied contingents sometimes performed poorly in combat, added to the supply costs and difficulties of U.S. forces, and in a few cases even interfered with important operations. Allied contributions in both conflicts often consisted of units specializing in unneeded or redundant tactical duties, with a low degree of complementarity to U.S. forces that added little if anything to the success of the campaign. These experiences contributed to a widely negative impression of allies' military capabilities among both senior and junior U.S. military personnel during these conflicts and fueled the impression that American forces would have been more effective *without* the hindering presence of allies.

However, this track record is an unreliable gauge for measuring the military value of allies to the United States for two reasons. First, focusing on negative tactical experiences has the effect of undercounting the positive strategic effect that allied militaries had in these conflicts. Taken collectively, U.S. allies had suffered 1,114 casualties in Afghanistan by the beginning of 2014—about a third of total U.S. fatalities during the same period.[44] Allies contributed billions of dollars to the financing of these wars and, perhaps more important, provided a foundation of international diplomatic legitimacy for U.S. military actions. Even if not as tactically capable as the U.S. military, allied forces in Iraq and Afghanistan allowed the United States to achieve and maintain military control over a wider territory and concentrate its forces on high-value sectors and offensives without sacrificing gains elsewhere. Without allies, the United States would either have had a thinner overall position on the ground or have had to send more American troops, with greater expense for U.S. taxpayers. Either way, U.S. forces would likely have been less successful in both conflicts and would have lacked some of the critical mass that allowed them to sustain viable, long-term missions.

Second, criticisms of allied military contributions are based entirely on experiences from expeditionary operations and therefore underrepresent the fighting abilities that these states would bring to bear in conflicts closer to home. As the British found at Gallipoli in 1915–1916 and the United States found in various coalition campaigns (e.g., Kosovo or the Iraq War of 1991), allied expeditionary operations are among the most complex and difficult forms of warfare. Inevitably, some parties have better capabilities and a stronger motivation to participate than others. While many U.S. allies in Iraq and Afghanistan contributed their best units, others did not; for all, the missions were a fractional representation of the capabilities that they would field in defense of their own territory. More important, the motivation of these militaries to *win* in faraway conflicts involving an abstract threat that concerned primarily the United States was inevitably lower than the motivation they would possess for defending home territory against an attack. Allies do not perform well in global roles, focused as they are on their own region.

It is in the category of territorial defense that the military utility of allies to the United States must ultimately be assessed—and where their capabilities are now undergoing the most growth. Strengthening American military competitiveness against a large power *in its own region* has been the organizing purpose for the United States to form defensive alliances—not primarily to recruit support for out-of-area expeditions. This fact has tended to be obscured for the past two decades by the combination of a permissive global geopolitical environment, a seemingly unassailable American lead in military capabilities, and a hyperfocus on operations in Iraq and Afghanistan. These conditions have created strong incentives for U.S. allies to reduce spending on defense and to produce forces that are of limited direct military value to the United States in its foreign campaigns. By comparison, the emerging twenty-first-century military landscape is likely to be characterized by a growth in capabilities among large powers, a diminishing of the U.S. lead in critical military technologies, and a refocusing of competition to U.S. allies' own neighborhoods.

Not surprisingly, these factors are leading many U.S. allies—particularly those located at the frontier—to reassess their defense postures in favor of larger budgets and enhanced capabilities to conduct territorial defense rather than out-of-area operations. In Central Europe, for example, Poland has launched a $40 billion, decade-long defense modernization program aimed at strengthening the country's capacity for conventional deterrence and defense. This represents a shift in doctrine and technological emphasis away from the light, quickly deployable forces like those that Poland used in Afghanistan toward less mobile but better-armed land warfare forces. Similarly, in Asia, many frontline U.S. allies are developing anti-access area denial (A2AD) capabilities consisting of advanced anti-aircraft and anti-ship missiles that would increase their ability to defend home territory against conventional attack.

To a greater extent than is commonly appreciated, this turn toward defensive capabilities will increase allies' military value to the United

States. Positioned on home turf with advanced stand-off capabilities, frontline states are likely to be more effective in inhibiting the ambitions of revisionist powers in their own neighborhoods than they were as half-hearted fellow-travelers in support of America's foreign wars. Properly supported, they can act as a global first line of defense against large-state aggression in the twenty-first century. Larger defense budgets signal a reduced political assumption on the part of allied governments that the United States will shoulder the burden of their defense. Bigger and better-munitioned allied forces suggest an increased emphasis on local defense, which translates into reduced reliance on American-supplied extended deterrence while at the same time strengthening U.S. effectiveness against the "limited war" techniques on display in Crimea and the South China Sea.[45] Stronger allied militaries deter conflict more effectively by raising the visible cost of attack while giving frontline states higher resiliency during an attack. This buys time for the United States to respond in a crisis and increases its strategic options for conducting an effective global perimeter defense with what will inevitably be a smaller American military.

A global frontier sprinkled with well-armed allies will also benefit the United States by allowing it to focus scarce defense resources on areas of comparative advantage, such as long-range airpower and sea assets. This is the central concept, for example, of the "Air Sea Battle" in contemporary U.S. defense thinking. In such a scheme, allies would offer the ultimate in complementarity for the American military since they would focus on home defense—their natural inclination and comparative advantage as small states near large rivals. The United States would concentrate on higher-end military assets that allow it to backstop resilient frontline allies. Such a utilization of alliances would constitute a potentially significant structural advantage to a power in America's position that must find ways to leverage its extensive inherited security obligations into sources of strength against proliferating sources of geopolitical competition.

The ability of the United States to consider using allies in this way, as forward-deployed ravelins integrated into the posture and doctrine of a reconfigured U.S. military, is a reflection of the high degree of interoperability that allied forces have built up with the U.S.

military in recent decades. Interoperability is one of the most important benefits of alliances; by incentivizing military cooperation, they help to make allied militaries more conversant with one another's weapons, doctrines, and tactics. This is particularly true of standing alliances, which provide predictability through long time horizons of training and operations. The necessity of such interactions has only increased with modern war-fighting technology, which requires a higher degree of training and unit-level battlefield integration for armies to be effective. Because this process needs to have begun long before a conflict erupts, alliances are a necessity for modern states to achieve and maintain interoperability. By the time a war breaks out, alliances are both harder to obtain and (if they are new) militarily less valuable than when they have existed for a sufficient period to accumulate pathways of effective cooperation.

Alliances as Power Projection Tools

A second military gap that alliances help to address for the United States is geographic—the inherent difficulty that America faces in projecting power into the world's major regions. Allies extend the reach of U.S. forces by providing access to bases outside of the Western Hemisphere. This was a central point in Spykman's argument for positioning U.S. power closer to key theaters of Eurasia, where its greatest challengers are most likely to emerge. Averting hostile coalitions means that the United States has to be physically present in these regions, and alliances fill this need by providing politically reliable places from which U.S. ships, troops, and planes can deploy. To this end, the United States has acquired numerous overseas bases to establish points of ingress throughout the rimland regions; at present, it has 598 military bases and 160,000 soldiers abroad—about 12 percent of the total U.S. military.

Maintaining this forward presence on or near the territory of allies offers several strategic advantages to the United States. First, it strengthens America's deterrent against potential opponents. Possessing a powerful military alone is not sufficient to create an effective deterrence. Competitors must be convinced that the United

States has both the political will and the capacity to use that military in defense of its interests.[46] Having allies where U.S. troops are positioned as trip wires provides tangible proof to a potential aggressor that the United States is willing to fight for its interests.[47] It also strengthens perceptions of America's ability to bring power quickly to bear in even far-flung conflicts, signaling to would-be aggressors that they will not be able to achieve a quick and easy victory that has been the sine qua non of revisionist military strategy throughout history. "Regional adversaries typically seek short, cheap wars," as one study found, so "those U.S. military forces that can credibly deny a quick victory will be most impressive to the opponent."[48] Great powers that lack forward presence possess a weaker extended deterrent because their credibility is linked in changeable factors like verbal threats, domestic partisan support, and the ability to cobble together last-minute coalitions. Promises are not the same as presence.

It is cheaper and simpler to deter something that has not yet happened than to try to reverse it after the fact. Deterring is easier than compelling.[49] If a competitor can be convinced to remain peaceful because of the high costs that nearby U.S. bases would impose on aggression, then the United States has saved itself the (likely far greater) expense that would be required to re-contain the aggressor once its effort at military aggrandizement is under way. This is especially important for a power like the United States, given the geographic distances that it must transverse to reach global regions and restore stability once it has been lost. The very factor that acts as a built-in military advantage to the U.S. geopolitical position when the system is stable—remoteness from rivals—becomes a built-in disadvantage when the system turns hostile and America is militarily hemisphere-bound. As Spykman saw, America faces a geostrategic either-or proposition: either it can pay the cost of prevention to deter rivals by being militarily present on *their* side of the ocean, or it can pay the cost of reaction by choosing to keep its military primarily on *its own* side of the ocean. Because the costs of the latter are inevitably higher, it makes sense to invest in a more effective deterrent through forward deployment of forces, and that requires allies.

A second benefit of forward basing is the role that it plays in reassuring allies. In the same way that trip wires deter rivals by showing that the United States is willing and able to repulse aggression, they also comfort allies by making America a physical presence in regional security equations. This is especially important for a maritime power, whose fidelity as a patron to allies in far-flung theaters tends to be more frequently doubted. Without effective offshore military backing, allies could be tempted to pursue more nationalistic or aggressive policies and to search for home-grown forms of reassurance. As will be discussed in the next chapter, this could include conventional military self-help or, in the absence of U.S. extended deterrence, possibly even the development of indigenous nuclear weapons development.[50] A U.S. military presence helps to prevent *allies themselves* from becoming drivers of regional or global instability. It provides the United States with a source of leverage and, to an extent, even control over the decisions of allies, enabling it to discourage states from pursuing aggressive policies that might lead to regional conflict.[51] This restraining function of reassurance represents a major and under-recognized source of American power, without which the United States would lose a major part of its ability to shape global security outcomes.

Third, using allies as forward bases improves the responsiveness of the U.S. military to global crises. Even in the age of long-range weapons technology, the United States needs a forward presence to be able to project power from the confines of North America. Using overseas bases, most of them on or near the territory of allies, the United States can get to potential hotspots faster, with a greater preponderance of force, at less cost, and to greater military effect than if it were to use domestic bases. The combination of forward and en route basing drastically cuts the transit time of U.S. forces, providing airfields and ports for refueling, prepositioned troops, and stocks of ammunition and supplies, and offering the multiple routing options that are critical in wartime. In a study examining nine global crisis scenarios, the RAND Corporation found that use of overseas bases dramatically reduced the reaction time of U.S. forces compared to operating strictly from the territory of the United States (see figure 5.2).[52] Moreover, the use of allied basing also reduces the overall *amount* of force that the United States would have to use in a crisis. Without the airfields, ports, and infrastructure its allies provide, the

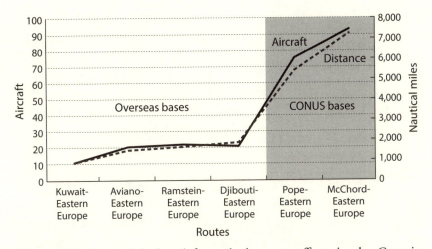

Figure 5.2. Forward-deployed force deployment effects in the Georgia scenario.
Source: RAND Corporation.

United States would need a considerably larger number of planes and ships to deploy units to foreign theaters and keep them supplied and protected once there.[53]

Critics of maintaining U.S. bases on the territory of allies contend that long-range airpower is sufficient to provide for American power projection needs in the twenty-first century without incurring the risk and expense of forward posture.[54] But without access to basing, even sophisticated next-generation airpower is limited in its effectiveness. The bombers that have a range of 6,000 nautical miles and are capable of conducting intercontinental strikes require protection from fighter aircraft with ranges of 1,300–1,800 miles. They must have bases outside of North America to support long-range strikes.[55] Without such bases, the United States would need to either forgo the option of effective engagement in many potential crises or build a considerably larger and longer-range global strike force to produce the same effect. And this would be expensive. B-2 bombers cost $730 million, C-17s cost $236 million, and JDAM missiles (of which the United States used three thousand per month in Afghanistan) cost $14,000 each.[56] The cost of a larger force of such weapons has to be weighed against the approximately $10 billion in annual expenditures required for the maintenance of U.S. forces in overseas installations.[57] Even in the age of advanced technology, distance is a defining constraint for American power; distance is still a "power-gradient."[58] By providing forward stations from which to project power, allies help the United States to overcome distance more cheaply, sustainably, and effectively than any other method yet found.

THE GEO-ECONOMIC BENEFITS OF ALLIANCES

Alliances also benefit the United States in a less dramatic but equally important way that Americans experience on an everyday basis: they allow the modern global economy to function by providing the security necessary for wide-scale investment and growth. The link between trade and allies is not direct; the former occurs on the scale that it does in the current international system because of the stability provided by the latter. Without allies, the United States would be unable to provide the global certainty necessary to make current levels of trade and prosperity possible. Trade would still occur without these alliances, but with greater transaction costs (literally, premiums) imposed to offset for the lack of rules and predictability provided by security. It is cheaper to invest in allies than to pay the premium for higher instability.

It is through the medium of alliances that America has created an international economic system largely modeled on its own image. The post–World War II Bretton Woods agreement locked in a set of rules governing commercial and financial interactions that broadly favored the United States. Most notably, it required heightened coordination of monetary policy (tying currencies to the dollar) and the creation of intermediary institutions to correct imbalances of payments. This system includes the key pillars of the liberal international economic system as we know it today—the International Monetary Fund, World Bank, and International Bank for Reconstruction and Development (IBRD). As with other features of the U.S. alliance system, the central aim was stability: to create a system that would act as a bulwark against the degenerative features of geo-economic competition—autarky, mercantilism, competitive devaluation—that have created the conditions for recurrent patterns of war throughout history.[59] Creating these mechanisms after World War II provided for a successor to the previous British-led global system of open sea-lanes, imperial preferences, and the gold standard. The smooth transition to and functioning of the American system have been possible only because of the voluntary, proactive support of a large number of the world's states—in other words, because of alliances.

The resulting system of global economic management has brought enormous benefits for the United States. It has provided a foundation for U.S. political leadership of international institutions and given America a decades-long and at times disproportionate say in global economic decision making. It has provided open markets for product and capital flows that encourage cooperation and provide a basis for the globalization of American business norms and culture. And, most important, it has acted as a backstop to American power by creating built-in advantages that favor the U.S. economy. The most significant of these is the ability to run large annual deficits that fund outlays on social spending and maintain the dollar as the global reserve currency. At $17.5 trillion, the U.S. public debt has become both a central strength and weakness of the contemporary American economy. The ability to issue debt at low interest rates represents an extraordinary advantage that enables Washington to fund everything from domestic programs and expansions in entitlements to American wars without the constraints that other countries would face. To an even greater degree than was the case for Britain, it gives the United States a commanding presence in international finance that allows it to not worry as much about sustaining a manufacturing base as the sole source of national power.[60] The ability to do so comes down to the ongoing decision of other nations to buy American bonds. American allies are essential to making this possible, accounting for 58.3 percent (some $3.47 trillion) of the $5.95 trillion of U.S. debt that is held by foreign powers.[61] Moreover, given the large amount of the public debt that is held by China, having a major portion in the hands of friendly states acts as a stabilizing mechanism for the U.S. economy.

Another way that allies make the modern economy possible is by helping to keep open the pathways of global trade. An essential precondition of the success of the globalized, U.S.-led economic order is the ability to keep commerce flowing not only in regulatory terms but in literal terms, in the movement of goods and products. An often overlooked characteristic of the modern world economy is that the vast majority of world trade still moves by water: about 75 percent, compared to 16 percent by rail or road, 9 percent by pipeline, and less than 1 percent by air.[62] Measured financially, this represents roughly 60 percent of annual world trade—around $9 trillion. The sea is especially important for global energy flows; altogether, more than half of world oil production (about 87 million barrels per day in 2011) is shipped over water rather than transported over land.[63] "In 1950 the world seaborne trade comprised about 0.5 billion metric tons, whereas today it has expanded to about 9 billion metric tons. Thus seaborne trade has grown about eighteen-fold, while GDP has grown roughly eight- or nine-fold in the same period."[64]

Waterways are important for a maritime power like the United States that relies on imports and exports. In 2012, for example, about 127 million metric tons of material entered the American economy by sea, of which 3.1 trillion barrels of crude oil were imported.[65] A central element of U.S. national security is to ensure that global trade continues in a predictable manner, and this means keeping sea-lanes open. Doing so means having the ability to monitor and secure the handful of global maritime passageways, control over which disproportionately affects the stability of broader trade and energy flows. Measured by volume and value of annual shipping, these include the Strait of Malacca, Strait of Hormuz, Suez Canal, Bosporus Strait, and Bab el-Mandab. These are the major choke points regulating ingress and egress around the peripheries of the Eurasian landmass. Historically, their functioning has had an outsized impact on global geopolitical outcomes. The first two are especially important. The Malacca Strait is the main thoroughfare for energy supplies entering Asia; sixty thousand vessels and 35 percent of all waterborne traded oil pass through the strait each year en route to the countries of the Pacific Rim—around 15 million barrels per day, including 3.3 million bound for Japan alone.[66] Similarly, the Strait of Hormuz is the primary point of exit for Persian Gulf crude to global markets; around 17 million barrels per day and a quarter of the world's annual traded oil.[67]

Disruption of these waterways by a hostile power would impede the supply of goods and energy to a major portion of the world's population, with far-reaching negative effects for the U.S. and global economies. Prolonged blockage of the Malacca Strait would affect about 50 percent of the world's merchant fleet, while interruption of the Strait of Hormuz would have almost overnight effects on international oil prices, which would lead in turn to higher U.S. and global inflation rates. One study found that an interruption of even half of the oil exiting the Strait of Hormuz would lead to an increase of 0.25 percent in aggregate prices in the United States (compared to the highest-ever inflation rate of 0.069 percent in 1946).[68] Another study found that blocking even a fifth of the oil supply moving through the Strait of Hormuz would cost the United States about 1 percent of its annual GDP for every ninety days of interruption, while the Energy Information Administration predicted that a complete disruption to the strait for a month could cost the United States almost $15 billion in GDP.[69]

Given their importance to the global and U.S. economies, it is advantageous for the United States to maintain alliances with the states located close to these resource arteries. In all the world's major choke points, there is at least one U.S. ally within 200 miles, and in most within less than 50 miles. In the cases of the Malacca Strait and the Hormuz Strait, the United States maintains military and political links with small states located directly astride the waterways. Maintaining these alliances near the globe's critical choke points provides tangible strategic benefits to the United States. It allows America to bring power quickly and effectively to bear directly in the places where the international economy is most vulnerable to destabilization. The U.S. Navy, like the Royal Navy before it, is a force designed to patrol the global commons, but to do so it needs secure ports from which to operate. Allies provide these points of access, as well as the facilities from which U.S. air and land forces (and the forces of the ally itself) can radiate outward into the surrounding area. These allies provide cost-effective ways for the United States to sustain global trade and energy flows—in effect, "stents in the arteries" of global commerce through which it keeps markets open and the overall world economy functioning stably without having to deploy a larger navy. They provide for the United States what Britain derived from its maintenance of a strategic presence at Gibraltar, Suez, Aden, and Singapore but without the direct economic costs of empire.

Having standing allies and bases near these choke points also gives the United States important competitive advantages in wartime. They act as a geographic access denial mechanism writ large, curtailing the ability of rivals to use them against the United States. With control of Malacca, for example, China would be able to project naval power deep into the Indian Ocean and exercise a decisive influence over the flow of oil to the rest of Asia. By maintaining nearby allies, the United States ensures its ability to use the strait against hostile states in the event of war. America's ability to conduct a blockade of China or Iran—a critical strategic option in wartime—is a function of its alliances and bases near maritime choke points. With Malacca and the surrounding ports in politically friendly hands, the strait becomes an energy cut-off valve enabling the United States to starve the Chinese mainland of 80 percent of its annual 5.4 million barrels per day supply of oil.[70]

By extension, control of global choke points allows the United States to ensure a stable energy supply to itself and its allies during a conflict. In the past the primary strategic consideration in this regard was keeping oil and gas flowing to North America in the event of a major global crisis. In the future, however, their role may be to keep these resources flowing *from* the United States to its allies. As a result of technological advances in the extraction of natural gas, America is set to become a major energy exporter within the next two years. With a large portion of the world's known natural gas supplies, long coastlines, and abundant deep harbors, the United States has the ability to bring large quantities of waterborne liquefied natural gas (LNG) into the global energy market. Some experts believe this could place the United States and Russia in a long-term geopolitical contest for European and Asian markets, in which low-cost energy comes to replace low-cost labor as the sine qua non of the global economy.[71] Supplying this gas, particularly to allies, will offer the United States an important advantage in regional geopolitics. Doing so in wartime could prove to be a strategic necessity for supporting frontline states in a prolonged military competition. In both cases, the ability to use America's gas as a strategic weapon will be a function of its maintenance of a strategic presence at the key maritime choke points through which these resources must pass to reach global markets. And that comes down to allies.

NET ASSESSMENT

In sum, alliances perform a range of geopolitical, military, and economic functions that directly benefit the United States. They do what neither technology nor geography, nor a faith in a harmonious or self-balancing world, can provide the United States. By providing sustainable entry points of influence into the "World Island," they address America's central strategic problem in a way that other assets at America's disposal—the navy, airpower, nuclear weapons—cannot. Allies at the frontier, while individually small and weak, play a significant strategic role in hindering consolidation of important regions under the control of hostile powers. They also prevent aggregation by those powers of enough resources to pose a direct threat to the United States. Like small powers for centuries, U.S. allies today counterbalance the ambitions of the strong in order to maintain their own independence and, in doing so, provide support for America's effort to create a bulwark against the dangers of interstate rivalry, resource competition, and great-power confrontation that characterized previous eras of geopolitical history. Strategically, they drive up the costs of military aggression and drive down the costs of American global management, providing bases for the U.S. military to reach otherwise inaccessible zones and helping to maintain the predictable flow of commerce and energy that makes the world economy as we know it possible. Without alliances with the United States, it is not clear that they would automatically choose to play these roles.

This runs counter to the picture often painted of alliances as costly structures, the jettisoning of which would yield a windfall of benefits—lower defense spending, fewer disagreements with rivals, greater focus on domestic problems. These projections are based on a lopsided ledger that overemphasizes current costs and fails to account for the benefits that the United States derives from its alliances—or the expenditures that would be required to replace the advantages that allies provide through other means, such as a larger air force. A world without U.S. alliances might be one in which the United States spent less on overseas basing, but it would also be a world in which U.S. extended deterrence breaks down, revisionist powers surge into traditional expansion routes, global energy supplies are subject to frequent interruption, and the United States is no longer able to maintain its favored position as holder of the global reserve currency. These advantages, once lost, will not be cheaply or easily regained. The costs of losing them have to be weighed against the envisioned cost savings that would supposedly result from downgrading alliances in U.S. foreign policy.

The value of alliances to the United States is likely to increase in the years ahead. As the margins of relative power narrow, the weight of even small allies will matter more than it did in the immediate post–Cold War era.[72] A tighter global military balance in which the United States spends less and its rivals more will increase the "force multiplier" value that America derives from even small allies—many of which at the frontier are increasing the funding and sophistication of their militaries. The continued growth of large rivals, especially China, will increase the practical value to the United States of nearby states that keep these powers on the defensive rather than offensive at a critical stage in their growth cycle. The return of resource competition and diminishing size of the U.S. Navy will magnify the strategic importance of ensuring friendly control over the world's principal energy routes. And the proliferation of advanced weapons and nuclear technology will make it more important that the United States have as many states on its side in future military contests as possible. In all these areas, the greatest returns on America's investment in the creation of extensive alliances may come not in the twentieth century but in the twenty-first.

CHAPTER 6

RECOMMENDATIONS

The acquisitive state, inherently unsatisfied, needs to gain victory in order to gain its object—and must therefore court greater risk in the attempt. The conservative state can achieve its object by merely inducing the aggressor to drop his attempt at conquest—by convincing him that "the game is not worth the candle."

—B. H. Liddell Hart, *Strategy*, 1954

It is by leagues, well concerted and strictly observed, that the weak are defended against the strong, that bounds are set to the turbulence of ambition, that the torrent of power is restrained, and empires preserved from those inundations of war that, in former times, laid the world in ruin.

—Sir Robert Walpole, 1741

The alliances that the United States has accumulated over the past seven decades could offer an important competitive advantage against rivals in the geopolitics of the twenty-first century. By any measure—numerical strength, combined wealth, fighting abilities, ideological and cultural affinity—these alliances are stronger than any international relationships that U.S. rivals now possess or are likely to acquire. Whatever other advantages some rising powers may seem to have in the way of economic growth, ideological fervor, or revisionist determination, they have few allies. To the extent that they are able to expand their alliances in the years ahead, it is likely to be by appealing to shaky members of the U.S. alliance system who doubt American strength, perceive some temporary gain from bandwagoning, or simply wish to avoid conflict. The ability to coax America's current allies away from the U.S.-led order would be based not in the inherent attractiveness of their models of government or in the desire of states to see the United States supplanted as the system leader but in a permissive environment U.S. policy has created for such recruitment. These allies would be lost because of their doubt about American power. Alliances, in other words, are America's to lose—if we are denied the advantages of having them, it will largely be because of our own mismanagement.

This would be unfortunate—and dangerous. The United States will need every possible strategic advantage it can get to compete successfully in the twenty-first century. Unlike in the past, America is unlikely to be able to rely on full-spectrum preponderance across the range of power assets that have traditionally composed its national strategic advantage. As the rate of increase in the national debt exceeds economic growth rates, the United States is unlikely to be able to continue to simply grow its way out of fiscal problems, virtually guaranteeing a continuation and possible deepening of reductions in defense spending.[1] Similarly, the U.S. lead in critical technologies and weapons systems, while still significant, is likely to narrow as rival powers expand their military investments. In conditions of contested primacy, America's main geopolitical advantage may lie less in its GDP, technology, or political system—important as these will all continue to be—and more in the historically unique system of alliances that the United States has built. No matter how we may fare in other metrics of power, we still have a striking advantage in alliances.

It is for this reason that revisionist powers have worked so creatively and persistently to weaken American alliance systems. They understand the strategic value of allies to the United States. Where domestic critics of alliances see them as a fiscal burden or strategic encumbrance, U.S. opponents correctly identify them as an important source of American strength, the reduction of which is a precondition to undermining the wider U.S.-led global economic and strategic system. Operating from Sun Tzu's injunction to isolate an enemy from its allies before attempting to wage war against it, they are using probes to chisel away at the mortar of America's alliances—U.S. credibility—until the system breaks because the United States tires of defending it or because allies give up resistance and choose to align with the new regional order. This strategy works only insofar as there are pre-existing fears about American abandonment among allies that revisionist probes can exploit. Defensive alliances are effective as deterrence tools only if the political and economic linkages undergirding them are strong.[2] Conversely, they are most susceptible to erosion from the outside if these linkages are weak. Confident allies make good deterrents and poor targets; unconfident allies make poor deterrents and tempting targets.

COUNTING THE COSTS OF LOSING ALLIES

U.S. policy should therefore seek to restore American credibility and thus the strength of our alliances. A strategy to visibly strengthen alliances would offer the most immediate path to countering rivals' efforts at opportunistic revisionism because it would address probes at their intended source: allied perceptions of American confidence and power. Doing so will not be easy, since U.S. alliances are being tested not only from the outside, by rival powers, but from the inside, by the strains created through our own deprioritization of alliance relationships. But such a strategy would be more cost-effective over the long term than either of the main strategic alternatives: seeking a grand bargain with principal rivals or attempting to reduce the direct costs of U.S. leadership by pursuing a strategy of offshore balancing. While offering potentially lucrative tactical gains in the near term, each of these strategies would require the United States to relinquish built-in advantages that it has amassed over the past several decades in exchange for, at best, temporary improvements to the U.S. power position.

The Pitfalls of Big-Power Bargaining

Seeking grand bargains with rivals is one of the options that powers in America's position have occasionally employed in history to navigate conditions of contested primacy.[3] Though infrequently used in past U.S. foreign policy, this temptation is likely to grow in the years ahead as the economic and strategic burdens of competing with multiple competitors become more apparent. It is especially attractive for a power in America's constrained fiscal position, as a possible means of reducing the external pressures that would necessitate a large defense budget in order to free up scarce resources for outlays on domestic programs. Put differently, cutting a deal with a large power, however authoritarian its political system or antithetical its long-term interests to those of the United States, may seem to future U.S. policy makers like a way to avoid building political consensus at home to reform federal spending and tame the deficit.

But as the experiences of previous great powers show, big-power bargaining can be a slippery slope: once lost, strategic credibility with traditional allies can be difficult to regain while the benefits of alignments with other large states are by definition temporary. British foreign policy of the 1930s provides the most obvious illustration of the damage that can be done to a great power from even short spells of strategic infidelity in prompting unfavorable realignments among states that otherwise would have supported the status quo and reducing the number of available allies when war breaks out. For a power like the United States, the payoff of big-power bargaining would be especially low, given the fundamental and increasingly territorial nature of the demands of rivals for revising the post–Cold War international order. Turn-of-the-century Britain could come to terms with former rivals France and Russia through bilateral concessions and trade-offs in far-flung parts of the world because they possessed a formal empire rather than allies. Colonies are appendages of the great power with no independent foreign policy. Allies are strategic actors in their own right that can adjust their foreign policy on the basis of their assessment of the security guarantees from their protector. It is therefore hard to envision the United States cutting a bilateral deal with, say, China to concede sovereignty over Asian waterways or with Russia to partition Ukraine without generating destabilizing effects among U.S. allies. As the troubled attempt at achieving a U.S. reset with Russia has demonstrated, even temporary efforts at improving relations have a low likelihood of success if the rival power in question nurses historical grievances and is determined to challenge foundational elements of the post–Cold War security order.

The worst possible combination for the United States would be to invest in efforts at détente with rivals at the same time that these states are intensifying their probes of U.S. alliances. Such a combination creates a widespread impression that hardball tactics can be used successfully to force U.S. concessions and pave a path to inexpensive revision of the system. For the United States, this would be the worst of all worlds: paying the price for détente by accommodating the demands of the revisionist while still absorbing the risk of the very aggressive moves that détente was meant to forestall. Moreover, as recent policy experience has shown, the perception of U.S. bargaining inevitably drives up the eventual costs of subsequent efforts to reassure allies, leading to a desire for more tangible demonstrations of U.S. support than would have been required if the United States had maintained credibility from the outset. Allies are already likely to have a greater fear of U.S. abandonment at moments of systemic flux and therefore call for greater U.S. commitments; signs of American outreach to rivals that appear to result from probes will only intensify this abandonment dilemma for the United States.[4]

The Hidden Costs of Offshore Balancing

The option of withdrawing into North America and conducting a strategy of offshore balancing is also likely to become more tempting to the United States over time as a means of alleviating the pressures of geopolitical competition abroad and financial retrenchment at home. Offshore balancing differs from big-power bargaining in that, where the latter acknowledges the general benefit of continued engagement abroad but seeks to shift the focus of that engagement from allies to rivals, the former is inherently skeptical of the strategic value of forward engagement and seeks to shift the burden of managing regional problems to allies. The attractiveness of offshore balancing has grown in recent years as an apparently straightforward means of lessening the direct costs of U.S. regional management by reducing the physical size of our military presence and range of political commitment there. While such an approach might offer temporary advantages, it would come with its own significant, often undercounted strategic costs to the United States in the long term.

First, recent evidence suggests that a policy of U.S. military retrenchment would make major regions less rather than more stable.
For decades advocates of offshore balancing have asserted as an un-
proven dogma that a reduction in American alliance commitments
would lead regional states to automatically balance against threatening powers, replacing the function of containment normally provided by U.S. extended deterrence, and that this would make regions
more stable—all at lower expense to the United States. Recent experience provides a laboratory for testing the validity of these claims.
As discussed in chapter 4, the behavior of U.S. allies over the past few
years has shown that small states do not only balance against threats
as offshore balancing advocates would predict; some also acquiesce in
revisionist behavior through various forms of accommodation. Moreover, while many U.S. allies are investing in greater local military
capabilities, it is not just taking the form of defensive postures; many
are considering offensive or even nuclear capabilities that could contribute to regional destabilization unless accompanied by a U.S. security presence. The deterrent value of defensive alliances and the
benefits of combined U.S. and allied balancing against rivals, once
lost, may not be so easy to replace.

Second, it is not clear that jettisoning alliances would result in the
financial windfall to the United States that many offshore balancing
advocates expect. Losing the advantage of forward positions provided
by allies would impose two new kinds of cost on the United States.
One is the need to increase air and naval power: to achieve a level
of power projection capability similar to what it possesses through
overseas basing, much of which is on the territory of allied states, the
United States would have to develop a significantly larger air force capable of conducting offensive and lift operations mainly from North
America and U.S. territories. It would also have to design and build
large numbers of airplanes capable of crossing large distances into
hostile air zones, a technological feat that is costly and unlikely to be
achieved anytime soon. Similarly, relying on the oceanic moat would
call for a much larger navy capable of maintaining a continuous presence across multiple oceans. Developing such a force would cost the
United States a lot of money—perhaps as much if not more than it
currently spends on overseas installations.[5] A second, longer-term prob-

lem would be strategic in nature: the high costs of achieving reentry into the global rimlands once the United States has lost a forward presence there. The wars of the twentieth century are a reminder of the degree of national economic, military, and human exertion required of a power in America's geographic position to achieve landfall in the Eurasian littorals and mainland once regional balances have been upset. Fortunately, in those eras, U.S. enemies did not develop the capability to deny the United States access to these regions. In the era of rapidly accelerating A2AD warfare technology, it cannot be assumed that America's technological edge would allow it to do so again without enduring prohibitively high costs in U.S. blood and treasure— costs that are likely to be higher than any temporary savings from an ad hoc retrenchment.

A STRATEGY TO STRENGTHEN ALLIANCES

Alliances remain the best-known instrument at America's disposal for guaranteeing its national security and competing effectively against rivals in the new conditions of the twenty-first century. No other current or foreseeable strategic alternative is likely to provide cost-effective replacements to built-in advantages that alliances offer to the United States at as low a cost. And contrary to claims of many critics on both left and right, they are likely to continue to offer a strategic value to the United States under conditions of economic austerity and contested primacy; indeed, they may be even more important to the United States under such conditions than in the immediate post–Cold War period, when America's power was less constrained and its rivals less numerous. In a more competitive landscape, alliances may represent the crucial margin of advantage when our edge in other traditional areas of strength is, at least for a time, less decisive. The costs of losing even a portion of these relationships, whether through defection or through continued slippage due to rival probes and U.S. devaluation, could be high. It could mean a weaker barrier against great-power war, a more permissive environment for the territorial growth of Eurasian competitors, and perhaps someday the need for a larger U.S. military to re-project power in and re-stabilize the system once its balance has been lost—all on the iffy proposition that the United States can achieve similar benefits by bargaining with large rivals or by withdrawing from the complicated affairs of the world's regions entirely.

It is therefore in the strategic interests of the United States to strengthen its alliances. Doing so should be an urgent policy priority at a moment of intensifying probes by U.S. rivals and widespread doubts about American intentions and capabilities in the international system. Already these patterns represent a significant global challenge for the United States; allowed to persist unchecked, they could lead to a general and potentially militarized crisis in the U.S.-led international order, with multiple vulnerable allied frontiers in various stages of advanced geopolitical competition, alliance fragmentation, or even local war. Given the strategic similarities of probing efforts in such hotspots as eastern Ukraine and the South China Sea and the fungible nature of frontline allies' concerns in these regions, the prospects for a multiregional crisis involving American power are higher today than at other any point in the modern era. However, such a crisis has not yet occurred, giving the United States an important and perishable window of opportunity to shore up its alliances as a preventive to further destabilization. A strategy to do so would focus on restoring American strategic credibility and raising the visible costs that aggressive powers would have to pay to revise the system to their favor. It would prioritize those alliances most in need of attention while working systematically to reinforce the central pillars of U.S. extended deterrence that are most in danger of collapse.

The "Rimland Imperative"

Such a strategy would begin by making choices. Globalization has not obviated the need for states to focus on some areas of the world more than others in order to be effective strategically. Despite recent advances in technology, the map of the world still matters, and strategy requires successful powers to pick and choose what is most relevant for security. America's strategic goal should not be to defend some abstract global architecture or global principle but to defend specific states against specific threats. The "where," in other words, matters in strategy as much as the "wherefore"—a rule that is especially true when resources for national defense are tight. For the United States, an effective strategy must therefore be built on a coherent rationale for understanding which states matter most for our survival and prosperity in the competitive landscape of the twenty-first century.

On a broad level, such a strategy would begin with the principle that alliances—their maintenance, retention, and general health—matter more than relationships with non-allies. Not all allies will be of equal importance to the United States in the decades ahead. Those that matter most, from a long-term economic and geopolitical standpoint, are the ones that provide the United States with a presence in the key productive zones of the Eurasian World Island—the so-called rimlands—and, more specifically, those that occupy the dangerous outer edge of the rimlands, in close proximity to the new century's rising and revisionist power centers. The importance of these states is not measured in their physical size, power, or wealth but in the real estate that they occupy. Roughly speaking, they compose a narrow belt that runs from the Baltic Sea to the Black Sea in Europe, through the Levant and Persian Gulf to the Indian Ocean and up through littoral Asia to the Sea of Japan. What happens to these states in coming years will have a disproportionate impact on the shape of the twenty-first century—whether it is stable or unstable, whether the United States and other large powers go to war or remain at peace.

U.S. alliances in this swath of territory mark the furthest reach that U.S. influence achieved the twentieth century into the vastness of Mackinder's World Island. Collectively, they represent the best solution to date to the strategic problem of remoteness from the regions most likely to threaten U.S. national survival. The fate of the rimlands, the degree of geopolitical pluralism they are able to retain amidst the growth of revisionist power centers, and the extent to which the United States can maintain influence there matter far more for U.S. security than what happens elsewhere in the American alliance network. France and Australia are valuable allies, but, unlike Estonia or Taiwan, they do not exist on or near territories that rivals covet as a prerequisite to global competition with the United States. "As go the rimlands," to modify Mackinder's famous expression, "so goes U.S. global power"; if the rimlands are populated by states that are stable and free, then revisionist powers will face an uphill climb to directly challenging the United States. But if they are populated by states that America's continental rivals have co-opted or invaded, then the United States will compete at a disadvantage in geopolitics. To defend everything is to defend nothing, and in an era of scarce resources the United States must defend here first.

Abiding by this principle—what might be called the "rimland imperative"—will be essential for the United States in the twenty-first century. The importance of securing access to and stability of these regions has been an underlying but rarely articulated principle of U.S. strategy for decades. Since the end of the Cold War the quiescence of the rimlands and the saliency of the fight against Islamic terrorism and resulting policy emphasis on the greater Middle East and Central Asia have tended to overshadow this objective in immediacy. But America's ability to maintain a near-exclusive focus on the terrorist threat has been possible only because it had already fulfilled the prior condition of securing the rimlands. Had these regions not been stable, the United States would have found it difficult to divert such attention and resources without jeopardizing its competitive position against other large powers. In the decades ahead, for the first time since the end of the Cold War, the rimlands will once again be at play geopolitically. The central goal of U.S. strategy should be to stabilize these regions by building up and maintaining clusters of states that are politically confident, economically advanced, well-armed, and aligned with U.S. interests.

Maintaining the rimland imperative in the future is far from assured. By virtually any measure—public confidence, elite opinions, and, most important, allied military and diplomatic behavior—American alliances are in a deeper and more prolonged state of disarray than at any point since the Second World War. The decay is greatest precisely in those regions where we have argued the United States needs its alliances to be strongest: the frontline rimland states, where the need for effective U.S. security patronage is greatest, the doubts about its fidelity are deepest, and the exposure to its rivals' probes are most severe. If there is an overriding priority for U.S. foreign policy, it is to restore America's credibility among these states as being an actor that is as able to provide effective security support in conditions of contested primacy as it was in unipolarity and the Cold War—even if that support ultimately takes a different form from what it did in the past. Restoring this baseline credibility offers the most direct path to countering rival probes at their source: allied perceptions of American power. Such a strategy would target policy-making inputs to bolstering the two pillars of U.S. extended deterrence that rival probes and U.S. alliance deprioritization have most deeply eroded: (1) American political will and (2) American military effectiveness.

AMERICAN POLITICAL WILL

Any effort to strengthen U.S. alliances has to begin at the taproot of American credibility: the perception among allies that the United States lacks the political will to honor security commitments in the event that they are attacked. As chapter 2 showed, doubts about this among U.S. allies are widespread and deeply rooted among frontline states. They are driven in part by allies' assessment of the statements and actions of U.S. leaders devaluing alliances and the occasional prioritization in recent U.S. diplomacy of relations with rivals over relations with traditional allies. But they are also driven by the nature of new revisionist threats—probes—that allies worry are below the threshold of state-on-state violence that would be needed to stir American action and trigger automatic security mechanisms in large alliances like NATO. Whatever form subsequent allied coping strategies have taken, whether resistance or accommodation, all stem in one form or another from this same source of a loss of faith in America's will, even more fundamentally than its future ability, to protect them as it has in the past. The process of rebuilding credibility must therefore start with revaluing alliances in U.S. foreign policy.[6]

Convincing allies that the United States has the political will to uphold its security commitments will be hard to do, in part because such credibility, once lost, is difficult to regain when it involves matters of life and death (hence the frenzied efforts at self-armament), and partly because it is inherently challenging to prove to others what a state will do in the future. Moreover, the basic requirements of effective reassurance have been altered by the changed geopolitical conditions. It can no longer take a generic form across or within regions, given the uneven threat perceptions and coping strategies that various allies increasingly possess, even within the rimland zones. Strategic reassurance to Poland or the Philippines, for example, which desire it in almost any form, must be tailored differently from reassurance to Slovakia or Thailand, which do not seem to desire it as acutely. For a similar reason, reassurance can no longer always take the form of a blanket reaffirmation of alliance mechanisms forged in the Cold War, which some allies view as being of dubious reliability in the event of a crisis.

This latter point is worth stressing. Unlike in the past, the United States can no longer assume that large, multilateral defense alliances will remain effective vehicles for reassuring frontline allies. Alliances are artificial constructs that require constant work to maintain because they are temporal, responding to particular and changeable conditions. The main effect of geopolitical changes is that they alter the level of threat perceived by the various members of the alliance. Multilateral alliances in particular are built on uneven risk pools. NATO worked in the Cold War because all the states in the alliance, irrespective of their exact geography, were more or less equally threatened and therefore had a generally similar perception of risk. The Soviet threat was large, total, and, in the worst case, nuclear, affecting all Western states. In such an environment, the distinction between the frontier and the hinterland of an alliance was blurred; West Germany was more exposed than France, but both shared the threat of large Soviet land forces and, ultimately, nuclear annihilation.

America's frontier allies today face a very different situation. They exist in places that revisionist states often desire to possess or control and are not mere highways for armored columns to pass through en route to other parts of the alliance. Estonia and the South China *are* the target. They are not just real estate to cross to reach another territorial goal. By reintroducing limited war techniques such as probing and Crimea-style "creeping" invasions, revisionist powers are able to stoke these differences between allies and further isolate the frontliners. Security arrangements linking Germany and Poland or Australia and Japan may have general value for the exposed state, but the latter will doubt their reliability in a real crisis. More and more, the United States will therefore increasingly find these large, multilateral groupings of limited utility for managing vulnerable frontiers.

With these constraints in mind, the United States needs to develop a revised set of methods for building and maintaining political credibility among frontline states. The overarching aim should be to build up the confidence of allies, both individually and in small groupings, in ways that increase their organic willingness to resist revisionist states in their own region, and to help provide the physical capacity for doing so effectively. The key to a successful U.S. strategy will be intra-regional differentiation. Where Cold War–era U.S. alliancecraft operated on the inductive principle of finding a common denominator among the states of a given region (resistance to Soviet influence) and building community security commitments around that denominator, a revised strategy would start by recognizing that some states (e.g., Poland, Saudi Arabia, Japan) in each frontline region are more inclined to oppose regional revisionism than others. It would use these states as individual points of strength or as hubs from which to radiate influence to other (weaker or less resistant) allies in that region. Such a strategy would translate into a broad set of ranked priorities for U.S. policy that includes:

1. Empowering resisters: providing full U.S. political and military support for the main states in each region that possess the greatest incentive and ability to resist revisionist powers (e.g., Poland, Japan, South Korea);
2. Buttressing the weak: working with resisters to bolster and caucus with regional states that are willing to resist revisionism but lack the size or means to do so effectively (e.g., Baltic states, Philippines, smaller Gulf states);
3. Nudging fence-sitters: to the extent possible, using U.S. diplomacy to stiffen resistance among states that are nominal U.S. allies but tending toward neutral or accommodationist stances (e.g., Bulgaria Oman, Thailand).

Under this approach, the United States would increase its overall efforts at reassurance to frontline states while sizing the objectives of its efforts to the increasingly disparate postures of various allies in these regions. It would work with the momentum of existing small-state coping strategies where possible, providing the highest level of (bilateral) engagement and security support to countries where the will to resist is strongest and already manifested through state-level investments (e.g., increased defense spending). It would encourage regional security caucusing where possible, favoring ad hoc security groupings built on shared risk pools over larger multilateral or symbolic groupings, if necessary devoting U.S. diplomatic capital to helping overcome historical disputes between states within these clusters. And it would seek to re-win lost influence among allies that are tending toward accommodation, using both U.S. diplomacy and improved relations between regional resisters and accommodators to increase the likelihood that the latter would at least not impede and if possible would support the sharper security interests of their more vulnerable neighbors. Details of the strategy would vary by region.

Asia: Tighter Frontline Webs

The U.S.-Japanese bilateral security relationship is the key to future American strategy in Asia. As the most willing and capable resister ally in the region, Japan is valuable to the United States both as an effective counter to China and as a potential organizer of resistance among other smaller states in the region. Like Poland in Europe and Saudi Arabia in the Middle East, it has the most to lose from Chinese military revisionism and the most to contribute in combating it. A U.S. strategy for rimland Asia should focus first and foremost on ensuring that Japan has both the confidence to resist China politically and the means to do so militarily (more on the latter below). In both cases, America's actions are critical in shaping Japanese behavior.

The main credibility gap in U.S.-Japanese relations stems from the ambiguity of U.S. positions in regional territorial disputes. The problem is compounded by Washington's slow and sometimes confusing response to Chinese probes, including most notably its contradictory handling of the air identification zone (AIZ) issue in 2013 and

positioning as a "mediator" in the Senkaku Islands dispute. Such behavior signals vagueness of intention, which dilutes U.S. credibility
and invites further probes. The United States should be firmer about
its support of Japan in regional disputes and more explicit about the
form that such support will take. The United States and Japan should
revise the bilateral security treaty to clarify and amplify its applicabil-
ity to disputes such as the Senkaku Islands while conducting joint
contingency planning for responding to a unilateral Chinese military move against the islands. Going forward, Washington should be
wary of taking middle-ground positions that weaken deterrence and
muddle messages of reassurance to allies.

Building on a strengthened U.S.-Japanese security relationship, the
United States should seek to chaperone the creation of a new regional security framework. The cornerstone should be a thickened
network of bilateral security relationships between weaker regional
states and Japan. Most notably, the United States should encourage
the burgeoning security and diplomatic linkages between Tokyo and
the region's three most exposed states—Taiwan, the Philippines, and
Vietnam. This will be difficult, in part because of historical grievances, but the United States should encourage it nevertheless. Asia
is unique among the rimland regions in possessing a relatively even
degree of risk among the frontline states there. Virtually all the littoral and archipelagic states along the Asian coastline share a high
degree of proximity to Chinese military power; only Indonesia and
Australia enjoy some insulation. This is significant from the standpoint of U.S. strategy because it suggests that, unlike in modern-day
Europe, multilateral security cooperation could function effectively
in Asia. Moreover, China's increasingly assertive behavior may open
possibilities—and demands—for such coordination that did not
exist in the past. Faced with the prospect of growing Chinese military capabilities and aspirations, Asian states may be more inclined
to accept the burdens of collective security. As in Cold War Europe,
it will be up to the United States as the ordering power in the region
to organize and lead such groupings.

Where collective security mechanisms have become an impediment to effective defense in Central and Eastern Europe, their absence in Asia may actually make conflict more likely.[7] Relying on the
combination of the U.S.-Japanese bilateral relationship plus ASEAN

to contain a rising China would be similar to trying to use a U.S.-German bilateral relationship plus Benelux grouping to contain Russia in the early days of the Cold War. The United States should actively encourage Asian states to move toward a collective security grouping involving formal, explicit, and overlapping security pledges. Doing so would blunt the effects of Chinese probes by tying the security of its small-state targets to something larger than just the immediate U.S. reaction and reducing China's ability to single out individual states in future regional crises.

One important component in such a strategy may need to be a revised U.S. approach to how it handles Asian allies who have shown tendencies toward accommodation. To build more effective containment coalitions, it is important that China not be able easily to recruit such states into passive stances in regional disputes—or worse, eventual assistance to Chinese aims. In some cases, guarding against this tendency may require the United States to adjust its traditional approach in policies that isolate such states and increase their receptivity to Chinese courtship. One early test case will be Thailand, whose leadership has drawn closer to China in response to U.S. criticism of its recent military coup. The situation threatens to spill over into U.S.-Vietnamese relations and could affect the cohesiveness of ASEAN in presenting a common front to future maritime disputes. As one Thai leader recently said, "We will remember who gives us support when we need it."[8] The altered security environment suggests that the United States will need to consider the implications of its stances on democracy for regional security goals. While taking these trade-offs on a case-by-case basis, abiding by the rimland imperative may mean that, when in doubt, the United States should favor the latter over the former.

Central Europe: Toughening the Frontier

U.S. strategy toward the European rimlands begins with Poland. Poland combines many of the characteristics of Japan, being the largest and most determined resister in its region, and of South Korea, owing to its extreme geographic exposure and position between two larger powers. As in Japan, damage to U.S. credibility in Poland has revolved primarily around doubts concerning the willingness of the United States to intervene on the country's behalf in the event of a security crisis. To an even greater extent than in Japan, where extensive U.S. installations already exist, the primary policy solution in Poland's case rests in the sphere of military/technological cooperation (see below). For the foreseeable future, the overwhelming focus of U.S. policy in the CEE region should be the deepening of the U.S.-Polish security relationship both diplomatically and militarily. Diplomatically, this is likely to require greater bilateral U.S. engagement with Poland and less through multilateral mechanisms. Militarily, it will require a greater U.S. political willingness to create trip wires with American forces on Polish soil.

In both cases, a central feature of U.S. policy in the years ahead is likely to be the diminished utility of NATO as a tool for securing frontline allies. Unlike in Asia, the risks associated with a nearby revisionist are unevenly spread, not only between CEE and Western European states but within the CEE region itself. From a U.S. strategic perspective, this heightens the potential strategic value of subregional groupings as means of bolstering the ability of states to resist Russian aggression. The United States has a unique role to play as an outside enabler of such groupings, both through its diplomatic approach to the region and in its targeted use of military/technological export and similar incentives to encourage effective defense collaboration.

The biggest cluster of such states involving staunch resister countries is in northern Central Europe, including Poland and its neighbors to the north: the Baltic states, Finland, and Sweden. To a greater extent than possibly any other informal grouping in Europe, these states possess both the will and, in the cases of Poland and the larger Nordic countries, the ability to resist Russian expansion. Surprisingly, compared to its linkages in the more politically divided Visegrád Group, Poland's strategic association with these northern states is underdeveloped.[9] The United States should encourage such linkages as part of a broader strategy aimed at strengthening the frontline security webs throughout the full length of the Baltic-to-Black Sea frontier.

172 • Chapter 6

In the North, one role for the United States could be helping to address political barriers to cooperation such as lingering Polish-Lithuanian bilateral friction. In the South, it can help to promote greater military coordination between Poland and Romania, using the Visegrád Group as a bridging mechanism. The challenge here is more formidable and is rooted in structural divergences in threat perceptions among the less exposed states of Hungary, Slovakia, and the Czech Republic. Much has been made in policy circles of the latent potential for cooperation among the Visegrád states. In reality, the depth of differences in strategic outlook on the nature of the Russian threat suggests a limited role for this grouping from the standpoint of U.S. rimland strategy, at least in the near future.

To the extent that the United States can create incentives for these states to align more with the regional resister camp, it is likely to be mainly through political rather than military means. In the southern CEE states, the approach should be not to offer stronger bilateral security relationships but to reengage in the battle for political influence against growing Russian commercial and subversive inroads in the region. In cases such as the Czech Republic and Slovakia, this can be waged through public diplomacy and use of Visegrád mechanisms to increase policy coordination with Poland. In the case of Hungary, Romania, and Bulgaria, it may mean taking a less publicly critical stance of states underperforming in democratic governance in order to advance pragmatic security cooperation against Russia. Democratic values continue to matter, but security must come first. Here and in Asia, the goal should be to strengthen the frontier; all other policy objectives are secondary. Achieving this will require the United States to improve its credibility as an engaged ally, thereby diminishing Russia's ability to recruit "fence-sitters" into passive or accommodationist stances in future crises.

Middle East: Mending Fences with Saudi Arabia and Israel

As in Europe and Asia, the central focus of U.S. strategy in the Middle East should be to build up those local allies most disposed to and capable of resisting regional revision and use these states as rallying points to organize resistance among wider networks of states.

The two primary regional hubs for such a strategy in the Middle East are Saudi Arabia and Israel. Compared to other regions, the military threat in the Middle East is more mature and immediate to these states, both in a conventional (and potentially nuclear) form from Iran and, increasingly, in the unconventional form of ISIS and similar groups. The latter is significant from the perspective of U.S. rimland strategy in that it has the potential to undermine America's principal regional allies from within and, should it succeed at state capture in Iraq, eventually morph into a more traditional state-level actor threatening to U.S. allies and interests.

From a U.S. strategic perspective, Saudi Arabia and Israel represent the main regional bulwarks against these threats. These are the largest and most capable U.S. allies in the region. As such, both stand to lose disproportionately from the spread of Iranian influence or the success of ISIS radicalism. Conditions of instability elevate the need to prioritize security cooperation in U.S. regional alliances over other considerations, including the nature of the regime in the case of Saudi Arabia or territorial disagreements (e.g., West Bank settlements) in the case of Israel. The key to regional strategy is to increase the capability of both states to resist growing regional threats in cooperation with the United States. As a preliminary to doing so, the United States must repair relations with these states at the political level. Both bilateral relationships have suffered in recent years, primarily as a result of the United States prioritizing something else over the security of these allies—whether it was U.S. policy on Iranian nuclear development, U.S. pressure on Israel in the peace process, or divergences in U.S. and allied policy following the Arab Spring uprisings and handling of the crisis in Syria. Increasingly, these allies and the smaller Gulf states doubt America's willingness to confront threats to regional stability. The near-term concern is ISIS; the longer-term concern is the Iranian nuclear armament program. Allies openly worry that the United States will "sell out" its allies—for example, by passing the buck of containing regional radical groups or by seeking some form of accommodation with Iran—leaving them to manage the regional disorder on their own.

A refocused U.S. rimland strategy for the Middle East must begin by dispelling the perception of U.S. withdrawal. This can be done only by demonstrating an unambiguous prioritization of allied security concerns in U.S. policy, which will require greater trade-offs than it did in the past. Most important, it will require the United States to take stronger diplomatic, economic, and, if necessary, military measures to dissuade Iran from developing nuclear capabilities. In the case of Saudi Arabia, the United States should make greater efforts to consult with it and other regional allies ahead of any future parlays with Iran and take visible military steps (see below) to encourage the development of allied defenses against Iran. Given the rise of ISIS extremism in neighboring Iraq, the United States should be prepared to show greater support for regime stability in Saudi Arabia as a goal in itself, even if it conflicts with other, broader democratic goals in the region. For similar reasons, the United States should be willing to take a less critical stance on Israeli policies in the occupied territories. As in Europe and Asia, a rimland strategy will require the United States to prioritize security relations with these allies over other aims, however important they may seem politically.

AMERICAN AND ALLIED MILITARY CAPABILITIES

But the United States must do more than strengthen its political commitment to alliances; it must also strengthen the physical military capabilities supporting these commitments. It is in this area that the insecurity produced in the rimland regions by the assertive forays of revisionist rivals and a shrunken credibility of U.S.-backed security guarantees is also an opportunity for the United States. The most exposed U.S. allies are increasingly afraid for their own security and geopolitical independence, which until now American power and quiescent revisionist states had solidly guaranteed. This fear spurs allies in all three regions, to varying degrees, to invest more in their own security, thereby reducing the "free-riding" problem that has plagued U.S. alliances and been a central focus of the critics of American alliances for most of the post–Cold War era. Such investment in national defenses is still in the very early stages; in many cases it is tentative and, in some cases, still futuristic. But the signs from the most exposed allies are that there is political will to mobilize domestic support behind an increase in defense spending. If this materializes, it would allow Washington to make more efficient use of its own reduced defense investments and focus with greater effect on the most pressing region of the day.

The opportunity can, however, be wasted if American leadership does not encourage and manage it. The rearming of the rimlands will not occur, or may occur in an inchoate and destabilizing way, without the continued presence of the United States, despite what offshore balancing advocates may postulate. There is nothing natural and axiomatic about stable regional balances of power; they have to be willed, led, and managed by a strong patron (the United States) on overwatch.

Three risks in particular are worth considering. First, with the exception of the most exposed and security-conscious rimland allies (e.g., the Baltic states and Poland in Central Europe, Saudi Arabia and Israel in the Middle East, and Japan in East Asia), not all U.S. allies are eager to take the steps necessary to rearm. In the case of some countries that are more distant from the frontier with the revisionist power, the threat is not considered to be urgent or even real. Combined with the fiscal woes facing many liberal states, rearmament is unlikely to occur, confronting the United States with a stark choice: to keep defending them or not. Still other allies are cautious and undecided in their security attitudes. The continued reassurance provided by the United States is likely to be decisive because it could have a staunching effect—convincing hesitant allies that it is worthwhile to invest in their own defense rather than seek an accommodation with the nearby regional predator. This was the effect that Britain's patronage produced in many small continental European states in the eighteenth and nineteenth centuries. It may also buy them the time to develop under-nurtured national defense programs, a process that will be especially important over the next generation as small powers close the gap in regional military balances.[10] As we pointed out in chapter 4, the absence of a credible American security presence does not automatically lead to allies stepping up to defend themselves and maintain the stability of the regional (and global) order. They may choose to accommodate the revisionist power in their region, hiding behind the ideological conceit that geopolitical competition is not what it used to be in past centuries and that political and economic life will continue more or less unchanged, even if regional or even global power relationships are altered. A renewed and reasserted American security commitment to such countries is therefore necessary if we want to use the opportunity of this moment to spur some of our allies to spend more on their own defense. As in previous centuries, allies—especially small states—are most likely to fight to sustain the status quo if they see a reasonable chance of success, and the United States is indispensable to providing this.

The second risk is that U.S. allies, perceiving American retrenchment, will pursue a rearming strategy that it is not effective. This could occur in several ways. One is through the pursuit of *tous azimuts* defense policies, seeking equal protection from all neighbors rather than focusing on the principal regional revisionist. This would result in a kind of geopolitical autarky in which allies attempt to hold the line on their state borders against everybody else in the region, including both real and imagined threats. Under such conditions, attempts to establish regional cooperation or alliances to counter the local revisionist power will be much more difficult and are unlikely to succeed in forming effective counterbalancing fronts. Fear of abandonment by the offshore American security patron can, in other words, lead to allies retreating into a defensive shell, watching with suspicion all their neighbors. One role of the United States is therefore to reassure its allies that they are not alone and should not mistrust all other states in the region; it is trust building because its presence serves as a geopolitical glue, calming the worst fears of an "all against all" regional order. The threat alone of the revisionist power does not suffice to guarantee the rise of an effective regional counterbalancing alliance.

The risk of an omnidirectional defense posture is associated with another risk: that U.S. allies will develop overly offensive doctrines. It is reasonable to expect that allies that want to oppose a revisionist neighbor but that also perceive themselves as abandoned by their security patron are likely to seek ways of imposing the highest possible degree of unacceptable costs on the potential aggressor. The temptation is to develop plans and capabilities for cost-imposing actions, ranging from preventive war to deep strikes on military (counterforce) and economic (counter-value) targets. In the most extreme case, the ally may pursue the path of nuclear weapons development, with some (e.g., Japan) being more credible than others (e.g., Poland) because of their pre-existing technical know-how and working nuclear power plants. But conventional weapons can escalate a conflict in ways that are highly destabilizing and dangerous. With modern missile technology, for instance, even a small state can inflict damage deep inside enemy territory, hitting command-and-control centers, radar installations, or logistical and staging bases, effectively threatening to blind and cut off the hostile forces. While there are benefits (mentioned below) of such a posture, an ally that fears abandonment may see few options but to increase its offensive capabilities and strike sooner rather than later.

Another risk is that the ally, fearing strategic loneliness, will attempt to mimic the spectrum of U.S. capabilities, reputed to be the most successful in deterring and waging war. With considerably smaller resources, such an approach would mean acquiring and developing "a little bit of everything," ranging from most advanced airpower to missile defense and, in the extreme case, nuclear weapons. Several factors would drive such an approach. Many U.S. allies, in Europe in particular but also in Asia and less so in the Middle East, have in past years essentially outsourced their security to the United States. The outsourcing was both material, in the sense that these allies chose not to spend resources to maintain and develop their own military capabilities in a competitive fashion, and conceptual, as most allies did not have to devote deep thought to their surrounding strategic environment. Hence, now that some of them may experience a reawakened interest in investing in their own security, the intellectual framework will take time to develop. It is easier therefore to simply attempt to import the capabilities and strategic thinking of the most successful power, the United States, in toto, even though obviously this would be done on a much smaller scale.

Another factor that drives allies to mimic U.S. capabilities, and in particular seek the acquisition of high-end platforms, is the appeal that such a course of action holds domestically. New F16s landing at a local airport make for good headlines and augment the domestic prestige and public support for political leaders—more so, of course, in an age of heightened security worries. Relatedly, some allies may seek capabilities deemed useful by American leaders in "out-of-area operations." This requires them to follow the lead of the United States in focusing on theaters far from their immediate regions, and to train and acquire distinctive (but narrow) technologies for those conflicts. Local defensive capabilities were less useful for this purpose and took second place behind power-projection capacities, air campaigns, anti-piracy operations, counterinsurgency skills, or desert warfare—all helpful for assisting the United States in the management of the global order but less so in protecting their own territories and regions from local revisionists. This last factor was more a consequence of the allies' (in particular, those in CEE) desire to be close to the United States, seeking to build goodwill in Washington to be cashed in at some distant future. But in the current security landscape, the fear that goodwill is not sufficient does not necessarily translate into a development of different defense tools and thinking, and allies may aspire to continue a policy of aping U.S. capabilities.[11]

The desire of allies to invest again in their own security is an opportunity, in that it represents a window for addressing military free riding, but one that without continued and credible U.S. security guarantees and political leadership can easily degenerate into undesirable outcomes. Allies' mimicking of U.S. military power, combined with a more offensive mind-set, are not necessarily appropriate to the threat created by regional revisionists and may lead to highly unstable regional interactions. More important, the challenge posed by the revisionist states requires the cooperation of the vulnerable states on the frontier and the distant but powerful security patron, the United States. Alone, neither the frontier allies nor the United States can maintain the status quo and repel the probes of the regional revisionists. They need one another much more than during the Cold War, a bipolar confrontation in which the two superpowers had an overwhelming advantage that dwarfed anything that allies could bring to the field. The geopolitical map now is different: the United States has to compete with several hostile powers in different regions for local stakes but with global repercussions. Even though the superiority of American power continues to be large according to most metrics, it is clearly being challenged by the aggressive behavior of all, and the growth of some (notably China), rivals. And the fact that these rivals create crises in their own respective regions (Central and Eastern Europe for Russia, the Middle East for Iran, and East Asia for China) spreads American attention and resources thin. The mere geographic extent of the competition elevates the role of U.S. allies, the local first responders.

Most important, even if the United States were much more powerful than it is, the nature of the threat presented by the revisionists makes frontline allies, and their ability to provide local defense, indispensable. As we have argued, the revisionist powers are conducting a series of local probes, in some cases even escalating into limited wars, but they are always careful not to reach the threshold of all-out war. To deter and, when needed, react to such a threat, there is no alternative but to form a robust local defense.[12] And to achieve this, frontier allies need the United States. It is unlikely that a country much weaker than the attacking power, like any of the neighboring countries of Russia or the littoral states around China, would be able to defend itself alone in a crisis. The security guarantees the United States provides continue to be vital as local defenses serve only as a complement to—not a replacement for—this extended deterrence. But at the same time, the credibility and effectiveness of the American security guarantee are weak without strong local defenses, which can be provided only on a standing basis by the frontier ally. Without local defensive capabilities, extended deterrence is fragile, in particular in the case of a limited offensive war; without an extended deterrent, local defense by small states facing more powerful neighbors is sacrificial.

Creating stronger local defense capabilities among frontier allies is therefore imperative. Placing greater emphasis on local defense achieves several things. It drives up the costs of military aggression: the more difficult it is for the revisionist state to achieve the political objective sought by probing and limited war, the more force the aggressor will have to employ and the higher the risk of a stronger response by external forces. This defeats the very purpose of probing—low-cost, low-risk revision—from the outset. The role of local defense is to force the aggressor to escalate the level of violence, which adds both military and political costs. A probe that aims to achieve a small but quick fait accompli—whether a territorial adjustment, a change in the boundaries of exclusive economic zones (EEZs), or an incursion of an individual plan—is below the threshold of extended deterrence. The problem facing vulnerable states is that the United States is unlikely to respond to such a low-intensity test. It may be either unwilling, because of the risk of escalation, or incapable, because of the limited nature of the rival's action. Only the immediately targeted state can provide the deterrent and (failing that) the capacity to defend against this type of revisionist behavior.

In the event that the aggressor does attack, an effective local defense buys time for the target state, increasing the likelihood that external reinforcements will arrive before the offensive has succeeded. In a limited-war scenario, space cannot be traded for time, but time can be bought by local defensive actions. The longer it takes for the aggressor to achieve its limited territorial objectives, the greater the opportunity for external military aid to buttress the targeted country. This also applies to probing in general. A foray of "civilian" Chinese vessels into Japanese waters or a Russian train on its way to Kaliningrad stopping suddenly in Lithuania is best dealt with by local forces that are both more cognizant of the local features of such an action (the topography, the most likely targets and vulnerabilities, the assets immediately available for a quick response) and more credible in their response as their country is directly affected. But a local defensive response must occur under a strong, extended deterrent provided by the United States. In fact, as noted earlier, without a firm trust in the American security guarantee, the frontier ally may choose not to respond to a revisionist probe at all.

Finally, local defensive forces permit the revisionist probing and the resulting conflict to remain limited, an outcome that is manifestly in the interest of all parties. As William Kaufmann wrote in 1956, "To the extent, therefore, that a conflict starts with local forces clashing over local issues, to that extent will the chances of limiting it be improved."[13] This, paradoxically, increases the likelihood of external support for the targeted party. The security patron of a targeted small country has no interest in, and very little ability to generate domestic support for, a large-scale conflict in defense of a distant ally. If the extended deterrent is predicated on a massive military response, it is less credible in the event of a limited attack and certainly in the case of low-range probing. The ability of the frontier ally to be the first responder to a local foray by the revisionist power limits the clash, thereby increasing the willingness of the distant security guarantor to support the ally in such a localized confrontation and to back it in case it escalates to a larger conflagration.

Another way to put this need to emphasize local defensive capabilities is by presenting it as a necessary but missing step in the escalatory ladder. Without local defenses, there is no credible response to low-intensity probing and local limited wars, and the next step available to the frontier ally and its security protector is a full-out confrontation. But such a threat is not credible for the reasons discussed earlier. It is also ineffective and prohibitively costly, as the United States cannot afford to hold the line in three regions at all times. Moreover, revisionist powers are modifying the geopolitical status quo gradually, through small local steps, and cautiously, avoiding a confrontation with the United States. Local defensive capabilities force the revisionist state to face the decision whether it wants to escalate to a direct, higher-intensity clash with the United States. They add the missing step between no response and a direct confrontation, neither of which is a deterrent to a probing revisionist power.

The next question, then, is how to make local defenses credible and effective. In the first and necessary place, such local defense has to occur under the umbrella of U.S. extended deterrence. To be deterred, revisionist powers must know that, were they inclined to escalate and respond with greater assertiveness against the defensive moves of the local state, the United States will be there—period. This is an element that has been increasingly missing in the glue of American-provided global stability. But the second and also necessary step is to make frontier allies capable of offering effective opposition to the revisionists. They need to be made prickly and indigestible to the aspirations of a revisionist power. The broad goal for the United States should be to create well-armed frontier regions in Central Europe, the Middle East, and East and Southeast Asia that will be able to deter and hinder the expansion of revisionist powers. The presence of militarily capable ally states in close proximity to the three main revisionists— Russia, Iran, and China—will give the United States the opportunity to move its attention and resources to different sections of the global

U.S.-backed *limes* as needed and avoid the problem of having to be strong everywhere simultaneously that undermined great powers of the past.

The United States should encourage and enable frontline allies to arm themselves in two related ways: by making them more impervious to a revisionist's attack and by making them more capable to independently strike the enemy. The first facet of rearming allies stems from the nature of geopolitical competition: the revisionist powers are the ones who are interested in altering the status quo and thus are the aggressive actors. They have to go on the offensive, even if it takes the form of low-intensity probing. This creates an inherent strategic advantage for the United States and its allies as they have to defend themselves, their territories, and their sphere of influence and do not have to project power into hostile areas. Allies, therefore, have to develop capabilities to hinder the projection of power of the revisionist powers. In defense lingo, they should invest in their own A2AD capabilities, making them resilient to an attack by increasing the costs to the revisionist power. The technical details of how this can be achieved must, of course, vary from region to region because, on a most basic level, denying access to an enemy on land (Russia in Central Europe) is different from doing so on the sea (China in East Asia). In one case the focus must be, for instance, anti-tank and anti-personnel capabilities, while in the other, anti-ship and anti-submarine warfare. But the broad principle is similar: to increase the revisionist power's costs of operating outside of its territory.[14]

Furthermore, an effective preclusive defense that can force the revisionist to rein in its aspirations should incorporate both a "wall" and an "insurgency" approach. The "wall" is to deter an attack, from a probe to limited war; the "insurgency" is to compel the retreat of the revisionist power. A wall approach comprises technologies and operational doctrines that aim to stop the revisionist state's offensives at the border or, more broadly, that inflict costs on the hostile projection of power. Missile defense is one such asset that is particularly important to develop given the rapid and prolific development of missile technologies among the revisionist powers. Anti-air defenses are another, parallel and to a degree overlapping, set of capabilities that hinder the mobility and the air operations of the enemy. The insurgency approach is a backup of sorts, were the initial defense to fail. It aims to make conquest, or whatever form the extension of the revisionist's influence takes, costly and untenable in the long term. Again, the technical specifics will vary depending on the theater in question, but the underlying concept is similar: even if the revisionist power managed to extend its control or influence over a new piece of real estate (air, land, or sea), the frontier allies should be able to inflict low-intensity but persistent costs. In the case of extension of influence or control over land, this may involve the pre-placement of weapons, portable anti-tank weapons, anti-personnel mines, guided mortar munitions, as well as training in small-unit tactics and guerilla warfare, all geared to inflict costs on the occupying forces and cut their logistical lines. On the sea, an analogous set of capabilities would involve the ability to interdict navigation between the bases of the revisionist power and the newly acquired maritime spaces (or islands and above-the-sea rocks, as the case may be) through a combination of different assets and tactics, such as submarine warfare, mines, anti-ship missiles.[15]

In a nutshell, the first set of capabilities hinders the ability of the revisionist to achieve a low-cost, quick fait accompli; the second aims to make that fait accompli difficult to hold. Politically, it appears to be easier to convince allies of the benefits of the first approach. For instance, the idea of theater missile defense is appealing to most frontier allies, from Central Europe to Japan. The opposition to it is driven in part by fiscal concerns (the costs of shooting down an incoming missile favor the offense) and in part by fears that it may weaken the relationship of deterrence (making oneself less vulnerable to an attack may make one more inclined to pursue an aggressive policy). But these tend to be discussions among policy experts; politically, it is relatively easy to argue that a state ought to expend resources to defend itself from missiles of a hostile power. It is more difficult to sell the second approach, which involves an admission that the initial foray of the neighboring revisionist power may succeed and a contingency plan needs to be developed. Pursuing an insurgency against a revisionist power, with the goal of expelling it from the space over which it had successfully extended its influence, is risky and requires patience and great sacrifices. Compelling tends to be more arduous than deterring because it must alter the existing situation, the fait accompli of the revisionist, by exercising some form of punishment. As Henry Kissinger put it:

> A *fait accompli* changes the attempt to *prevent* a given event, which is the basis of deterrence, to an effort to *compel* a certain course of action. Once a *fait accompli* exists, the purpose of strategy is no longer to induce a potential aggressor to refrain from attacking. It must force him to withdraw.... Once the aggressor is in possession of his prize ... the psychological burden shifts in his favor. The defender must now assume the risk of the first move. The aggressor can confine himself to outwaiting the opponent. The aggressor becomes more committed to his prize the longer he is in possession of it, while his opponent's incentive to preserve is diminished with every day that the *fait accompli* endures.[16]

Because it is more difficult and lengthy to evict an aggressor, it is also more problematic to convince domestic publics that it is worth investing in the defensive capabilities required for this. The easy and appealing counterargument is that, if the neighboring power has already achieved some sort of geopolitical revision, maps should be redrawn to reflect the new status quo. Such an accommodationist temptation is perhaps even more pronounced among commentators and political leaders in the capital of the distant security patron—in this case, the United States—because the revision is far away and affects its interests only tangentially: Crimea and the Donbas are remote to the United States, and the Senkaku Islands attract little attention among the American public. American allies and friends therefore have a greater incentive to develop insurgency postures, but they are also unlikely to expend domestic political capital to do so if they consider that option as a "last-stand" heroic act with few chances of American support. Hence we go back again to American credibility and resolve in backing allies.

Another part of an effective local defense resides in the ability of frontier allies to have some offensive capabilities to strike inside the regional revisionists. These are still defensive assets in the strategic sense because they would be used in case of an aggression or a more forceful probing by revisionists. But they are not merely tools of interdiction or of territorial defense. They include but are not limited to medium-range cruise missiles, long-range artillery, air-delivered precision guided munitions, long-range UAVs, and an array of targeting capabilities. Such a set of assets would be expressly acquired and developed in order to have the capacity to threaten targets inside the territories of the revisionist states. Three reasons in particular speak to the need to develop such capabilities. The first is operational— namely, it is difficult to consider an effective preclusive defense simply by holding the line on the border. It is much more effective to defend the frontier allies through a variety of tools that can blind and disorganize the enemy by hitting its command-and-control centers, can downgrade the enemy's force by cutting its logistical lines and staging areas, and above all can threaten greater escalation. The assumption, derived by observing the current revisionist behavior, is that these aspirant powers do not want a large-scale and prolonged war because they are likely to lose it. Hence the ability of frontier states to threaten escalation, and in the end draw in American power, is a powerful deterrent.

The second reason why frontline allies should develop limited offensive capabilities is that their own territories are gradually falling, if they have not already done so, under the A2AD capabilities of revisionist states. The ability of American power to back them up is predicated on being able to gain rapid and predictable access to the territory of the frontier allies in order to deliver supplies, personnel, air cover, and so on. But such access is no longer unfettered as the rival powers, from Russia to China to Iran, have invested in considerable capabilities to attack U.S. forward bases, close airspace to U.S. airplanes, and push U.S. naval forces away from the littoral or the seas near frontier allies. Most of the attention has been devoted to China's A2AD capabilities, but the other revisionist powers, Iran and Russia, have also developed their own version to match their geographic conditions and political strengths. Iran, for instance, is likely to use proxy forces, such as Hezbollah, to strike at U.S. bases and allies, while "swarming" U.S. ships in the Persian Gulf and the Strait of Hormuz.[17] Similarly, Russia's anti-air cover extends well over the Baltic states and large portions of Poland, all NATO members, while its medium-range missiles can strike bases inside these countries. To make extended deterrence credible, it is necessary to reopen the space over frontline allies. And this should be a task not only of the United States but also of the allies themselves.[18] Allies have a much stronger incentive than the United States has to keep their air, sea, and land space accessible to American forces. To do so, it is necessary for them to have offensive capacity to strike inside the revisionists' territories, at the radar installations, ports, and missile control centers that are part of the revisionists' networks of assets aimed at hindering access to the frontier regions.

The third and final reason is related to the previous one. If the capacity to oppose the enemy's A2AD is left only to the United States, frontier allies will fear abandonment. To put it another way, the vulnerable allies on the frontier of American power do not want to be passive speed bumps on the path of revisionist states. One of the greatest fears that allies in such geopolitically dangerous locations share is that they will be sacrificial targets, areas that ought to slow down the advances of revisionist states to give time to the United States to prepare a defensive line farther off, at some other point in time and space. If they develop and acquire more offensive capabilities that could inflict greater costs on the revisionists, threaten to escalate the conflict, and begin to reopen access to American power, these frontline allies may also have greater trust in the stability of the U.S.-backed order.

The United States therefore has a strong interest in encouraging a vigorous rearming of its frontier allies. To do so, it needs to alter its mind-set and become an aider and abettor of a more capable, well-armed, and strategically serious web of global alliances.[19] This requires four sets of interrelated and mutually reinforcing approaches. First, the United States has to engage in targeted proliferation by, for instance, easing export controls for advanced weapons to frontier allies and in particular to resisters. This also involves speeding up the process of selling such weapons to allies.

Second, it should pursue technological research and development in conjunction with frontline allies, in particular to be able to assess their peculiar security needs and help them to develop the appropriate technical solutions. Much of U.S. military development is in high-end, expensive platforms that take decades to design and produce and that carry a price tag that is prohibitive to most of our allies. These are less useful to frontline allies as they prepare for local, low-intensity wars. They have a much greater need for abundant, affordable, and thus expendable weapons that can function in a hostile environment and can degrade through sheer quantity revisionists' offensive assets.

Third, the United States should encourage frontline allies to develop territorial defense rather than skills and assets for out-of-area operations. Most of the frontline allies were eager to join various "coalitions of the willing" in the past two decades in regions far from their own, but for the express desire to build up goodwill in American eyes and to be able to ask for stronger demonstration of U.S. security guarantees. Washington should insist less on allies providing help outside of their regions and more on allies defending their own. Hence, for example, frontline allies need less training in counterinsurgency operations and more in insurgency; less in power projection and more in local defense.

Finally, the United States should be willing to share intelligence with allies about revisionists' vulnerabilities, operational doctrines and capabilities, and potential targets. One way to allow allies to be more resilient to the revisionists' probing and low-intensity advances is by giving them greater operational "vision."

These are broad principles of policies rather than specific technical recommendations, and their objective is to steel the space adjacent to the revisionist powers, from Russia to Iran to China.

On a larger political level, but with important operational consequences, it is time to recognize that the Cold War alliance structures are not a perfect match to the new geopolitical map. It is not a question of jettisoning old alliance treaties or collective security arrangements such as NATO, arguably one of the most successful alliances in history. Rather, it is a case of adapting these structures to new circumstances. This implies a move toward stronger bilateral relationships with allies and friends—the vulnerable frontline states—with whom the United States has stronger common interests in managing regional stability. They are the ones more interested in maintaining the geopolitical status quo, and thus they are the ones most eager to enhance and deepen a relationship with the United States. The four points mentioned above are therefore most appropriate to these states, rather than a blanket set of approaches to be followed with all allies equally. This is the age of small states, after all.[20] The proliferation of lethality that so far has benefited more American rivals by empowering them in ways that are disproportionate to their economic welfare and political vitality can be turned to the U.S., and Western, advantage. Precision-guided munitions, UAVs, cruise and ballistic missiles, and anti-tank and anti-ship weapons are some of the tools in the growing portfolio of affordable technologies that can transform small and weaker states into resilient and hard-to-overcome targets. It is the task of the United States to strengthen these states, allies, and friends by making these capabilities readily available to them.

CONCLUSION

The United States is in the midst of a robust competition with its rivals, spread in three key regions of Eurasia. Russia, Iran, and China are eager to revise the order established over the past six decades on the basis of Western political and economic principles and supported by American power. This competition is, at time of writing in summer 2015, still below the horizon of formal war. But it is fast becoming military in nature. Limited wars fought by Russia, proxy conflicts fueled by Iran, and increasingly forceful Chinese forays into the Pacific theater are no longer merely rhetorical challenges to the Western order. All these actions are characterized by clear caution on the part of revisionist powers, eager to avoid at this point a direct clash with the United States. The prize of the current competition is the allies America has gathered over the past century. The competition is for allies—in particular those at the frontier, nearest to the revisionist powers. With these allies on its side, the United States can maintain the geopolitical status quo, thereby frustrating the aspirations of revisionists; without them, without their active and enhanced cooperation, it is unlikely to be able to muster the resources necessary to face the combined challenges presented by the world's revisionist states.

There are many reasons why the United States and its allies ought to oppose vigorously the probes and the increasingly assertive behavior of today's revisionist powers. Russia, Iran, and China have a warped vision of the role of the state in relation to the human person, with very limited built-in modes of political improvement, if any at all. They are motivated by a skewed understanding of reality that they themselves built through propaganda, placing, for example, a fantastic level of blame on the United States or more broadly on the West for frustrations often rooted in the failings of their own social and economic models. But there is also a simple geopolitical reason to oppose them: they aspire to destroy an international order, built and maintained by the United States, that is the most stable in history and provides benefits to a wide majority of the world's people—including the citizens of revisionist states.

These same powers do not offer an alternate order that can be as stable and as prosperous as the current one; they seek only to destroy. They can wreck the present order without supplying anything comparable. This is partly due to the ideological limitations of their systems. But it is also partly due to their view of alliances, which can be deduced by their behavior. Theirs is a view that considers allies—independent, sovereign states cooperating in the maintenance of security and stability of a mutually beneficial political and economic order—as burdens and not as sources of mutual advantage and benefit.

The revisionists' bet is that alliances are a burden to the United States, and consequently they expect the United States to fear entrapment more than abandonment. Lacking extensive alliances themselves, they are wagering that these structures will become a source of competitive disadvantage to the United States. The behavior of revisionists points to such a view: they target the Western, U.S.-built and -led structure of alliances, at the same time fearful of the strength that such a system bestows on the United States and perhaps disdainful of the American ability and willingness to maintain it. Their probing is based on this dual vision: they want to weaken and ultimately tear apart the alliances America possesses in their respective regions by eroding gradually the credibility of, and belief in, the U.S. extended deterrent—and they pursue this by betting that America is afraid of getting involved in conflicts that are regional and relatively small but with a high escalatory possibility more than it fears strategic solitude. This is not an altogether unreasonable bet, as voices from

Washington, as well as from some populist political leaders from the left and right, have expressed disdain for allies and more broadly for American active involvement in the Eurasian balance of power.

Our goal is to suggest that for the United States abandonment of, or by, allies is more dangerous in the long run to our health, happiness, and prosperity as a nation than any supposed entrapment to protect states whose existential interest in the perpetuation of a stable and prosperous world order is the same as—and, if anything, greater than—our own. America fought for seven decades to build the globe-girdling array of allies that now guard its international strategic frontier. It should fight to maintain them.

NOTES

CHAPTER 1

1. See Christopher Preble, "Revisiting the Flawed Assumptions That Guide U.S. Foreign Policy," presented in American Grand Strategy and Seapower, conference report, November 2011; Justin Logan, "Asia's Free Riders," *Foreign Policy*, November 9, 2011; Ted Galen Carpenter, "U.S. China Hawks Perpetuate East Asian Free Riding," *National Interest*, September 7, 2011; and Ted Carpenter, "Taiwan and Other Security Clients Are Not Valuable Allies," *National Interest*, August 3, 2011.

2. Notable examples of research that acknowledged or expanded on probing and similarities in allied regions include Walter Russell Mead, "The End of History Ends," *American Interest*, December 3, 2014; Ian Bremmer, "Three Troubled Allies, One Superpower," *Wall Street Journal*, January 11, 2013; Zbigniew Brzezinski, "Eight Geopolitically Endangered Species," *Foreign Policy*, January 3, 2012; and Jim Thomas, "From Protectorates to Partnerships," *American Interest*, May 1, 2011.

CHAPTER 2

1. The focus on insularity is tied with the desire to establish a unique polity that would not need to devote resources to armaments and thus a large government. As Alfred Vagts writes, "The geographic situation of the isolated country has been such as to approximate an 'insular' character, allowing the isolated country among other things a high degree of autarchy. The ideal state, which is also the safest state, the State of 'Christian Security,' like More's *Utopia*, Campanella's *Sun State*, Johann Valentin Andreae's *Christianopolis*, Cabet's *Icarie*, is almost typically situated on an island in order to make 'isolation' possible, that isolation which is largely the flight from the competition in point of power. Where power need not be competed for or with, the means for this—the army and navy—seem not to be called for." Alfred Vagts, "The United States and the Balance of Power," *Journal of Politics* 3, no. 4 (November 1941): 404.

2. On the "age of free security," see C. Vann Woodward, "The Age of Reinterpretation," *American Historical Review* 66, no. 1 (October 1969): 1–19.

3. Robert Art, "The United States, the Balance of Power, and World War II: Was Spykman Right?" *Security Studies* 14, no. 3 (July–September 2005): 387. Others have also argued that the United States did not need to intervene in the war, and some go as far as to posit that American participation in it (as well as British commitment to Poland and thus its entry into a war against Germany) was a mistake. For the former, see Bruce Russett, *No Clear and Present Danger: A Skeptical View of the United States Entry into World War II* (New York: Harper and Row, 1972). For the latter, see Patrick Buchanan, *Churchill, Hitler, and the Unnecessary War* (New York: Crown, 2008).

4. Michael Howard has challenged the idea that Britain was able to successfully rely on

this combination without the use of continental allies. See Michael E. Howard, *Continental Commitment: The Dilemma of British Defence Policy in the Era of the Two World Wars* (London: Maurice Temple Smith, 1972). In the current context some propose a similar approach of imposing a maritime blockade on China, were the competition with the United States to turn more heated. The argument is that a blockade may be less escalatory and does not require the immediate defense of U.S. allies (Japan, Taiwan, Philippines). But the effectiveness of maritime blockades is highly doubtful: they take time to impose serious costs on the rival, can lead to escalation, and risk alienating the most exposed allies. See Aaron Friedberg, *Beyond Air-Sea Battle: The Debate over U.S. Military Strategy in Asia* (London: Adelphi Books, 2014), 105–10.

5.   See Pericles's speech in Thucydides, *The Landmark Thucydides: A Comprehensive Guide to the Peloponnesian War*, ed. Robert B. Strassler, trans. Richard Crawley (New York: Free Press, 1996), 1:140–45.

6.   Nicholas J. Spykman, *America's Strategy in World Politics* (New York: Harcourt, Brace, 1942), 448.

7.   Robert Jervis, "Cooperation under the Security Dilemma," *World Politics* 30, no. 2 (January 1978): 195.

8.   U.S. Senate, 76th Congress, 3rd Session, Report no. 1615, cited in Vagts, "The United States and the Balance of Power," 444. For how the U.S. Navy dealt with the changing geopolitical landscape during and after World War II, see also Jeffrey G. Barlow, *From Hot War to Cold* (Stanford: Stanford University Press, 2009).

9.   Walter Lippmann, *U.S. Foreign Policy: Shield of the Republic* (Boston: Little, Brown, 1943), 93, 94.

10.   Bernard Brodie, *A Guide to Naval Strategy* (Princeton: Princeton University Press, 1944), 4; Lippmann, *U.S. Foreign Policy*, 113.

11.   Melvyn P. Leffler, "The American Conception of National Security and the Beginnings of the Cold War, 1945–48," *American Historical Review* 89, no. 2 (April 1984): 351.

12.   Ibid., 353; Elliott V. Converse III, *Circling the Earth: United States Plans for a Postwar Overseas Military Base System, 1942–1948* (Maxwell Air Force Base, AL: Air University Press, 2005).

13.   Kent Calder, *Embattled Garrisons: Comparative Base Politics and American Globalism* (Princeton: Princeton University Press, 2008), 4–35.

14.   Spykman, *America's Strategy*, 467–68.

15.   Colin S. Gray, "Ocean and Continent in Global Strategy," *Comparative Strategy* 7, no. 4 (1988): 440.

16.   Philip Gordon, "Charles de Gaulle and the Nuclear Revolution," *Security Studies* 5, no. 1 (Autumn 1995): 118–48.

17.   Cited in Bruno Tertrais, "Destruction Assurée: The Origins and Development of French Nuclear Strategy, 1945–81," in *Getting Mad: Nuclear Mutual Assured Destruction, Its Origins and Practice*, ed. Henry Sokolski (Carlisle, PA: Strategic Studies Institute, 2004), 58. See also Pierre Gallois, "French and European Security in a Defense-Oriented Environment: An Interview with General Pierre Gallois," *Fletcher Forum* (Winter 1986): 43–49.

18.   Hans Morgenthau, "The Crisis in the Western Alliance," *Commentary*, March 1, 1963.

19.   C. E. Zoppo, *France as a Nuclear Power* (Santa Monica: RAND Corporation, 1962).

20.   Albert Wohlstetter, "Nuclear Sharing: NATO and the N+1 Country," in *Nuclear Heuristics*, ed. R. Zarate and H. Sokolski (Carlisle, PA: Strategic Studies Institute, 2009), 279.

21.   John Mearsheimer, "Why We Will Soon Miss the Cold War," *Atlantic* (August 1990). See also Kenneth Waltz, "The Spread of Nuclear Weapons: More May Better," *Adelphi Papers*, no. 171 (London: International Institute for Strategic Studies, 1981).

22.   John Mearsheimer, "The Case for a Ukrainian Nuclear Deterrent," *Foreign Affairs* (Summer 1993); John Mearsheimer, "Getting Ukraine Wrong," *New York Times*, March 13, 2014

23.   H. J. Mackinder, *Britain and the British Seas* (New York: Appleton, 1902), 358.

24.   Spykman, *America's Strategy*, 31.

25.   Felix Gilbert, *To the Farewell Address* (Princeton: Princeton University Press, 1970), 75.

26. Vagts, "The United States and the Balance of Power," 404.

27. Frederick S. Dunn et al., *A Security Policy for Postwar America* (Washington, DC: Naval Historical Center, Strategic Plans Division, 1945).

28. Lippmann, *U.S. Foreign Policy*, 49.

29. Hillary Clinton, speech at the Council on Foreign Relations, September 8, 2010. For a longer exposition of this argument, see also Hillary Clinton, *The First Quadrennial Diplomacy and Development Review QDDR: Leading through Civilian Power* (Washington, DC: U.S. Department of State, 2010).

30. Barack Obama, remarks to the United Nations General Assembly, September 23, 2009.

31. Hillary Clinton, speech at the Council on Foreign Relations, Washington, DC, July 15, 2009.

32. Stephen M. Walt, *Taming American Power* (New York: Norton, 2005).

33. Art, "The United States, the Balance of Power, and World War II."

34. According to Christopher Layne, there are three tools of American defense: its own military capabilities, sheer distance, and regional power balances. Christopher Layne, *The Peace of Illusions* (Ithaca: Cornell University Press, 2006), 181.

35. Ron Paul writes that the "return to the traditional U.S. foreign policy of active private engagement but government noninterventionism is the only alternative that can restore our moral and fiscal health." Ron Paul, "A Tea Party Foreign Policy," *Foreign Policy*, August 27, 2010.

36. Warren Cohen, *Empire without Tears: America's Foreign Relations, 1921–1933* (New York: McGraw-Hill, 1987).

37. John Lewis Gaddis, *We Now Know: Rethinking Cold War History* (New York: Oxford University Press, 1997), 34–35.

38. Chicago Council on Global Affairs, *Survey of American Public Opinion and U.S. Foreign Policy*, (Chicago: Chicago Council on Global Affairs, 2012).

39. Ibid., 16.

40. George W. Bush, "The 2000 Campaign; 2nd Presidential Debate between Gov. Bush and Vice President Gore," Winston-Salem, NC, October 11, 2000.

41. Barack Obama, remarks to the troops at Fort Bliss, TX, August 31, 2012.

42. Richard N. Haass, *Foreign Policy Begins at Home* (New York: Basic Books, 2013).

43. Rajan Menon, *The End of Alliances* (New York: Oxford University Press, 2007), 182.

44. Robert M. Gates, "The Security and Defense Agenda (Future of NATO)," speech in Brussels, Belgium, June 10, 2011.

45. Steven Erlanger, "Panetta Urges Europe to Spend More on NATO or Risk a Hollowed-Out Alliance," *New York Times*, October 5, 2011.

46. Arnold Wolfers, "Alliances as a Means of Defense," *Naval War College Review* 7, no. 8 (April 1955): 6.

47. See T. R. Reid, *The United States of Europe: The New Superpower and the End of American Supremacy* (New York: Penguin Press, 2004); Charles A. Kupchan, *No One's World: The West, the Rising Rest, and the Coming Global Turn* (Oxford: Oxford University Press, 2012).

48. Paul Stevens, *The 'Shale Gas Revolution': Development and Changes* (London: Chatham House Royal Institute of International Affairs, 2012), 7.

49. Edward L. Morse et al., "Energy 2020: Independence Day," *Citi GPS* (February 2013).

50. Alan Riley, "The Shale Revolution's Shifting Geopolitics," *New York Times*, December 25, 2012.

51. Taniguchi Tomohiko, "Japan and the Geopolitics of the Shale Revolution," *Nippon*, December 27, 2012.

52. Were the United States to adopt an isolationist, or offshore balancing, posture, the navy would in fact be the preeminent guardian of U.S. security. It is not surprising, therefore, that after a decade of wars that have seen the army and air force as the key actors for American force projection, the navy seeks a policy that would augment its standing. See, for instance, Admiral Gary Roughead's remarks at the University of Chicago Conference on Terrorism & Strategy, October 12, 2010.

53. Jackson Diehl, "Where Are Obama's Foreign Confidants?" *Washington Post*, March 8, 2010.

54. Colin Dueck, *The Obama Doctrine* (New York: Oxford University Press, 2015).

55. Kelley Currie, "The Doctrine of 'Strategic Reassurance,'" *Wall Street Journal*, October 22, 2009.

56. Hillary Clinton, speech at the Council on Foreign Relations, Washington, DC, July 15, 2009.

57. "The Obama Doctrine," *Economist*, December 1, 2012.

58. Benjamin Miller, *States, Nations, and the Great Powers: The Sources of Regional War and Peace* (New York: Cambridge University Press, 2007), 218.

59. For a defense of the Russian "reset," arguing exactly that it had lowered the costs for solving some problems such as a START Treaty or logistical help in Afghanistan, see Hillary Clinton's interview on *Newsnight*, BBC, June 12, 2014.

60. Walter Pincus, "Poland Won't Lobby Obama on Missile Defense," *Washington Post*, November 20, 2008. For a detailed analysis, see also U.S. Library of Congress, Congressional Research Services, *Long-Range Ballistic Missile Defense in Europe* by Steven Hildreth and Carl Ek (Washington, DC: Office of Congressional Information and Publishing, September 23, 2009).

61. Aleksandr Vondra, speech at the Atlantic Council, May 25, 2010.

62. See, for example, Michael Doran, "The Silent Partnership," *Mosaic*, October 15, 2014.

63. Mark Landler, "Obama Finds a Pen Pal in Iran," *New York Times*, September 19, 2013.

64. White House press secretary Jay Carney, cited in "White House: Obama Tells Rouhani He Sees Way to Resolve Iran Nuclear Issue," *Reuters*, September 18, 2013.

65. Barrack Obama, "Message to the Iranian People on Nowruz," U.S. Department of State, March 20, 2013.

66. Barrack Obama, in David Remnick, "Going the Distance," *New Yorker*, January 27, 2014. See also Michael Doran, "What Was He Thinking?" *Mosaic*, August 6, 2014.

67. Zvi Bar'el, "Reconciliation with the U.S. Could Bolster Iran's Regional Power, Global Standing," *Haaretz*, September 28, 2013.

68. See, for example, comments by Israeli prime minister Benjamin Netanyahu to the U.S. Congress, "The Complete Transcript of Netanyahu's Address to Congress," *Washington Post*, March 3, 2015, http://www.washingtonpost.com/blogs/post-politics/wp/2015/03/03/full-text-netanyahus-address-to-congress/.

69. Ray Takeyh, "The U.S. Needs a Deal with Iran, Not Détente," *Washington Post*, January 12, 2014.

70. Robert Pape, *Bombing to Win: Air Power and Coercion in War* (Ithaca: Cornell University Press, 1996).

71. For a critique of drones, see Audrey Cronin, "Why Drones Fail," *Foreign Affairs* (July/August 2013); and Sarah Kreps and Micah Zenko, "The Next Drone Wars," *Foreign Affairs* (March/April 2014).

72. Nadia Schadlow, "Peace and War: The Space Between," *War on the Rocks*, August 18, 2014.

73. Michael Mandelbaum, *The Nuclear Revolution: International Politics before and after Hiroshima* (New York: Cambridge University Press, 1981), 151–52; Glenn H. Snyder, "The Security Dilemma in Alliance Politics," *World Politics* 36, no. 4 (July 1984): 461–95; Glenn H. Snyder, *Alliance Politics* (Ithaca: Cornell University Press, 2007), 186–92.

74. After the murder of Franz Ferdinand, the German chancellor expressed a similar fear: "If we encourage [the Austrians], they say we pushed them into it. If we discourage them, they say we left them in the lurch." Kurt Riezler, personal assistant to the chancellor, in Konrad H. Jarausch, "The Illusion of Limited War: Chancellor Bethmann Hollweg's Calculated Risk, July 1914," *Central European History* 2, no. 1 (1969): 62.

75. Victor D. Cha, "Powerplay Origins of the U.S. Alliance System in Asia," *International Security* 34, no. 3 (Winter 2009/2010): 163–64.

76. Dov Waxman, "The Real Problem in U.S.-Israeli Relations," *Washington Quarterly* 35, no. 2 (Spring 2012): 79–80.

77. Snyder, "The Security Dilemma in Alliance Politics," 471.

CHAPTER 3

1. See Aaron Friedberg, *The Weary Titan* (Princeton: Princeton University Press, 1988); William C. Wohlforth, "The Perception of Power: Russia in the Pre-1914 Balance," *World Politics* 39, no. 3 (April 1987): 353–81.

2. A sample of those who argue that the United States is in decline for a variety of reasons includes Andrew Bacevich, *The Limits of Power* (New York: Metropolitan Books, 2009); and Robert A. Pape, "Empire Falls," *National Interest* (January–February 2009). A counter-list of those who disagree includes Robert Lieber, *Power and Willpower in the American Future* (New York: Cambridge University Press, 2012); Josef Joffe, *The Myth of America's Decline* (New York: Liveright, 2014); Eric Edelman, *Understanding America's Contested Primacy* (Center for Strategic and Budgetary Assessments: 2010); Robert Kagan, *The World America Made* (New York: Vintage, 2013); and Michael Beckley, "China's Century? Why America's Edge Will Endure," *International Security* 36, no. 3 (Winter 2011/12): 41–78.

3. Charles F. Doran, *Systems in Crisis: New Imperatives of High Politics at Century's End* (Cambridge: Cambridge University Press, 1991).

4. Emily Goldman, *Power in Uncertain Times: Strategy in the Fog of Peace* (Stanford: Stanford University Press, 2011).

5. Geoffrey Blainey, *The Causes of War* (New York: Free Press, 1973), 114.

6. A.J.P. Taylor, *The Struggle for Mastery in Europe, 1848–1918* (Oxford: Oxford University Press, 1954), xxiv.

7. William C. Fuller, Jr., *Strategy and Power in Russia* (New York: Free Press, 1992), 265–73; David Schimmelpenninck Van der Oye, "Russian Foreign Policy, 1815–1917," in *The Cambridge History of Russia*, ed. Dominic Lieven (Cambridge: Cambridge University Press, 2006), 2:560–61. Aleksandr Gorchakov, Russia's foreign minister after the Crimean War and author of the *recueillement* policy, has seen an impressive resurgence in interest in recent years in Russia, in large measure because of his policy of seeking a pause in the conflicts with the other great powers and of using the time to strengthen the empire for long-term competition. See Flemming Splidsboel-Hansen, "Past and Future Meet: Aleksandr Gorchakov and Russian Foreign Policy," *Europe-Asia Studies* 54, no. 3 (2002): 377–96.

8. Thomas Schelling writes that war "is a confused and uncertain activity, highly unpredictable, depending on decisions made by fallible human beings organized into imperfect governments, depending on fallible communications and warning systems and on the untested performance of people and equipment." Schelling, *Arms and Influence*, 93.

9. Robert Haddick, "The Civilianization of War," *National Interest*, April 11, 2014.

10. Julian Corbett, *Sir Francis Drake* (London: Macmillan, 1890), 88–89, 112.

11. Mark Thompson, "The 600 Years of History behind Those Ukrainian Masks," *Time*, April 17, 2014; Andrew Higgins, Michael Gordon and Andrew Kramer, "Photos Links Masked Men in East Ukraine to Russia," *New York Times*, April 20, 2014;

12. Lyle Goldstein, "Strategic Implications of Chinese Fisheries Development," *Jamestown Foundation China Brief* 9, no. 16 (August 5, 2009).

13. Jens Kastner, "China's Fishermen Charge Enemy Lines," *Asia Times*, May 16, 2012.

14. Authors' conversations with Japanese officials, November 2012.

15. The "loss of strength gradient," the fact that distance diminishes the effectiveness and availability of power, continues to hold in both material and political terms. Projecting power is costly, and distance augments the costs and thus the quantity of power that can be delivered. Consequently the credibility of a state is also affected by distance; political influence is directly related to distance. Hence the opposite is true too. The closer a state attempts to extend influence, the greater the chance of its success. See Kenneth E. Boulding, *Conflict and Defense: A General Theory* (New York: Harper, 1962).

16. Thucydides, 4.108.

17. Although more pronounced, this "frontier problem" is not limited to a global maritime empire. A land power, such as Russia, also can face the curse of the long frontier or periphery. In the second half of the nineteenth century, in fact, Russia "could not be sure of whom or where it might have to fight next." Russia's frontiers were too long for the manpower available and for the limited power projection capabilities. Fuller, *Strategy and Power in Russia*, 276.

18. Direct, formal control becomes necessary when the periphery of the empire is politically fragile and difficult to engage in diplomatic relations. The Roman Empire faced this situation on its northern frontier along the Rhine and Danube, where tribal groupings made conquest more feasible than indirect influence. As Michael Doyle writes, the "weakness of the periphery . . . allows it to be conquered and indeed encourages aggression from the metropole." Michael Doyle, *Empires* (Ithaca: Cornell University Press, 1986), 131.

19. Schelling, *Arms and Influence*, 47.

20. Margaret MacMillan, *The War That Ended Peace* (New York: Random House, 2014), 402.

21. Friedberg, *Beyond Air-Sea Battle*, 11.

22. Alexander L. George and Richard Smoke, *Deterrence in American Foreign Policy: Theory and Practice* (New York: Columbia University Press, 1974), 59.

23. On entrapment (fear of being drawn into a local war by an ally) and abandonment (fear of being abandoned by an ally), see Michael Mandelbaum, *The Nuclear Question* (New York: Cambridge University Press, 1981), 151–52; Snyder, *Alliance Politics*, 187–88. For a critical look at entrapment, see Tongfi Kim, "Why Alliances Entangle but Seldom Entrap States," *Security Studies* 20, no. 3 (2011), 350–70.

24. Taylor, *Mastery in Europe*, 458.

25. Lippmann, *U.S. Foreign Policy*, 107.

26. Niccolo Machiavelli, *Discourses*, trans. H. Mansfield and N. Tarcov (Chicago: University of Chicago Press, 1998), 2:9, 146.

27. Fuller, *Strategy and Power in Russia*, 270.

28. See also Gregory D. Miller, *The Shadow of the Past* (Ithaca: Cornell University Press, 2012).

29. Ted Hopf, *Peripheral Visions* (Ann Arbor: University of Michigan Press, 1995).

30. Robert E. Osgood, "The Reappraisal of Limited War," *Adelphi Papers* 9, no. 54 (1969): 53.

31. Schelling, *Arms and Influence*, 55.

32. See, for instance, Jonathan Mercer, *Reputation and International Politics* (Ithaca: Cornell University Press, 1996); Dale Copeland, "Do Reputations Matter?," *Security Studies* 7, no. 1 (1997): 33–71; and Daryl Press, *Calculating Credibility: How Leaders Assess Military Threats* (Ithaca: Cornell University Press, 2005).

33. Shiping Tang, "Reputation, Cult of Reputation, and International Conflict," *Security Studies* 14, no. 1 (October 2005): 34–62.

34. See, for instance, Josef Joffe, "A Letter from the Prince to Putin," *Wall Street Journal*, March 6, 2014.

35. Authors' conversations with CEE officials.

36. Nicholas Spykman, *The Geography of Peace* (New York: Harcourt, Brace, 1944), 45.

37. Lyle Goldstein, "What Does China Really Think about the Ukraine Crisis?" *National Interest*, September 4, 2014.

38. "Chinese General: U.S. Foreign Policy Has 'Erectile Dysfunction,'" *Washington Post*, June 3, 2014. See also Eric Edelman, "Confronting Putin's Invasion," *Weekly Standard*, March 17, 2014.

39. "The Decline of Deterrence: America Is No Longer as Alarming to Its Foes or Reassuring to Its Friends," *Economist*, May 3, 2014, http://www.economist.com/news/united -states/21601538-america-no-longer-alarming-its-foes-or-reassuring-its-friends-decline.

40. Authors' conversations with Polish and Japanese officials. See also, for example, Tomasz Smura and Bartosz Wiśniewski, "Japan-U.S. Security Cooperation: A Litmus Test for America's Commitment to Alliances?," Bulletin No. 48 (501), Polish Institute of International Affairs, May 9, 2013, http://www.pism.pl/files/?id_plik=13570; and Łukasz Kulesa, "U.S. Extended Deterrence Weakened? Lessons Learned from the North Korea Crisis," Bulletin no. 57 (510), Polish Institute of International Affairs, May 28, 2013, http://www.pism.pl/files/?id_plik=13749.

41. Guy Taylor and Rowan Scarborough, "Ominous Warning: Admiral Concedes U.S. Losing Dominance to China," *Washington Times*, January 16, 2014.

42. Statement by the president on Ukraine, Washington, DC, February 28, 2014.

43. On top of the growing structural weaknesses, Moscow has reverted to a form of autocracy ruled by a megalomaniacal tyrant. And, as Stephen Rosen observes, tyrants tend to have "shorter time horizons within which strategic costs and benefits are calculated . . . [and] they severely discount costs and benefits that present themselves far in the future relative to the time of decision." Stephen P. Rosen, *War and Human Nature* (Princeton: Princeton University Press, 2005), 135–36.

44. Schelling, *Arms and Influence*, 68.

45. Macmillan, *The War That Ended Peace*, 379; Christopher Clark, *The Sleepwalkers* (New York: Harper Collins, 2013), 156–57; Robert Massie, *Dreadnought* (New York: Random House, 1991), 363.

46. Brendan Simms, *Europe: The Struggle for Supremacy* (New York: Basic Books, 2014), 277.

47. MacMillan, *The War That Ended Peace*, 382.

48. Massie, *Dreadnought*, 367.

49. Taylor, *Mastery in Europe*, 438.

50. MacMillan, *The War That Ended Peace*, 396; Taylor, *Mastery in Europe* 482.

51. The policy of "calculated risk" in July 1914, albeit no longer a probe by our definition, had similarly unwanted effects in that Germany supported a limited war in the Balkans with the hope of splitting the Franco-Russian alliance but ended with a world war. Berlin's goal was to keep the conflict local: "Among the probable outcomes of the crisis Bethmann clearly preferred local war, was willing to gamble on continental war, but he abhorred world war. Believing that he had no alternative, the Chancellor decided on a 'leap into the dark.'" And yet, as was the case in the summer 1914, it is often difficult to limit the escalation of conflict. Jarausch, "The Illusion of Limited War," 75.

52. Thucydides, 4.108.

53. Ibid.

54. This is akin to what political scientist Richard Smoke called the "inherent upward tendency" in war. See Richard Smoke, *War: Controlling Escalation* (Cambridge, MA: Harvard University Press, 1977), 34.

55. Taylor, *Mastery in Europe*, 364.

56. Richard Smoke, "Theories of Escalation," in *Diplomacy: New Approaches in History, Theory, and Policy*, ed. Paul Gordon Lauren (New York: Free Press, 1979), 172–73.

57. Polybius, *The Rise of the Roman Empire* (New York: Penguin, 1979), 61 (1:20).

58. Arthur Eckstein, *Mediterranean Anarchy, Interstate War, and the Rise of Rome* (Berkeley: University of California Press, 2006), 164–65.

59. Ludwig Dehio, *The Precarious Balance: Four Centuries of the European Power Struggle*, trans. Charles Fullman (New York: Knopf, 1962), 194.

60. Bohlen quoted in Walter Isaacson and Evan Thomas, *The Wise Men: Six Friends and the World They Made* (New York: Simon & Schuster, 1986), 453.

61. George and Smoke, *Deterrence in American Foreign Policy*, 117.

62. Paul Bracken, *The Second Nuclear Age: Strategy, Danger and the New Power Politics* (New York: Times Books, 2012), 52.

63. Plutarch, *Plutarch's Lives*, vol. 1: *Aristides*, trans. John Dryden (New York: Modern Library, 2001), 453.

64. On Russia's "information warfare" that is part of this larger subversive strategy, see Jolanta Darczewska, *Anatomia Rosyjskiej Wojny Informacyjnej: Operacja Krymska* (Warsaw: Centre for Eastern Studies, May 2014).

65. Quoted in MacMillan, *The War That Ended Peace*, 113.

66. Winston Churchill, *The World Crisis*, vol. 1: *1911–1914* (London: Butterworth, 1927), 115.

67. On how "pattern-breaking" behavior can help understand the rival, see Zachary Shore, *A Sense of the Enemy* (New York: Oxford University Press, 2014).

68. Howard, *Continental Commitment*, 90.

69. Goldman, *Power in Uncertain Times*, 17.

CHAPTER 4

1. Robert Rothstein, *Alliances and Small Powers* (New York: Columbia University Press, 1968), 187.

2. Ibid., 195.

3. For an alternate view, see David Kang, "A Looming Arms Race in East Asia?" *National Interest*, May 14, 2014.

4. Sam Perlo-Freeman and Carina Solmirano, "Trends in World Military Expenditure, 2013," SIPRI Fact Sheet, Stockholm International Peace Research Institute, 2013.

5. Andrew F. Krepinevich, Simon Chin, and Todd Harrison, *Strategy in Austerity*, CSBA, June 21, 2012, http://www.csbaonline.org/publications/2012/06/strategy-in-austerity/.

6. Joachim Hofbauer, Priscilla Hermann, and Sneha Raghavan, *Asian Defense Spending 2000–2011* (Washington, DC: CSIS, October 2012), http://csis.org/files/publication/121005_Berteau_AsianDefenseSpending_Web.pdf.

7. International Institute for Strategic Studies (IISS), *The Military Balance, 2014* (London: ISIS, 2014).

8. Jason Miks, "Vietnam Eyes China 'Threat,'" for The Diplomat *Diplomat*, March 28, 2011.

9. Dhara Ranasinghe, "Singapore, the Tiny State with Military Clout," *CNBC*, February 9, 2014; Richard Weitz, "Global Insights: China's Military Buildup Stokes Regional Arms Race," *World Politics Review*, March 16, 2010.

10. Paul Kallender-Umezu, "Big-Ticket Buys Could Hurt Japan," *Defense News*, April 13, 2014.

11. "Taiwan's Force Modernization: The American Side," *Defense Industry Daily*, June 4, 2014, http://www.defenseindustrydaily.com/taiwans-unstalled-force-modernization-04250/.

12. "The Decline of Deterrence."

13. Hagel quoted in "Hagel in Israel to Discuss Missile Defenses," *i24 News*, May 15, 2014, http://www.i24news.tv/app.php/en/news/israel/diplomacy-defense/140515-hagel-lands-in-israel-to-talk-defense-security.

14. Nawaf Obaid, *A Saudi Arabian Defense Doctrine: Mapping the Expanded Force Structure the Kingdom Needs To Lead the Arab World, Stabilize the Region, and Meet Its Global Responsibilities* (Cambridge, MA: Belfer Center for Science and International Affairs, Harvard University, May 2014).

15. "Iran Plans 127 Percent Defense Budget Increase," *Agence France-Presse*, February 2, 2012.

16. "Gulf States—Dangerous Arms Race," *South World*, July 2013, http://www.south world.net/newtest/index.php/component/k2/item/457-gulf-states-dangerous-arms-race.

17. Ariel Ben Solomon, "4 out of 5 Fastest-Growing Defense Budgets Are in Mideast," *Jerusalem Post*, February 4, 2014, http://www.jpost.com/Defense/4-out-of-5-fastest-growing -defense-budgets-are-in-Mideast-340283.

18. Moti Bassok, "Israel Shells Out Almost a Fifth of National Budget on Defense, Figures Show," *Haaretz*, February 14, 2013, http://www.haaretz.com/business/israel-shells-out-almost -a-fifth-of-national-budget-on-defense-figures-show.premium-1.503527.

19. "Gulf States Requesting ABM-Capable Systems," *Defense Industry Daily*, July 15, 2014, http://www.defenseindustrydaily.com/gulf-states-requesting-abm-capable-systems-04390/.

20. Kenneth Pollack, *Unthinkable: Iran, the Bomb, and American Strategy* (New York: Simon & Schuster, 2013), 341.

21. "Hagel in Israel to Discuss Missile Defenses," *i24 News*, May 15, 2014, http://www .i24news.tv/app.php/en/news/israel/diplomacy-defense/140515-hagel-lands-in-israel-to-talk -defense-security.

22. Polish Ministry of National Defense, "Money for New Military Equipment Guaranteed," September 18, 2013, http://web.archive.org/web/20140323233451/http://archiwalny.mon .gov.pl/en/artykul/14701; Tomasz Szatkowski, "Polish Defense Modernization in the Era of U.S. Strategic Rebalancing," Center for European Policy Analysis, March 1, 2013, http://www .cepa.org/content/polish-defense-modernization-era-us-strategic-rebalancing.

23. Leon Mangasarian, "Putin Emboldened on Instability Arc by EU Defense Divide," Bloomberg News, May 15, 2014, http://www.bloomberg.com/news/2014-05-14/eu-east-west -defense-divide-emboldens-putin-s-arc-of-inst.html.

24. "Parengtas 2015–2017 metų krašto apsaugos biudžeto projektas," www.alkas.lt, July 3, 2014, http://alkas.lt/category/naujienos.

25. "Romania to Boost Military Spending over Ukraine Crisis," *Agence France-Presse*, April 28, 2014, http://www.defensenews.com/article/20140428/DEFREG01/304280018/Romania -Boost-Military-Spending-Over-Ukraine-Crisis.

26. Jaroslaw Adamowski, "Russian, NATO Arms Race Takes Shape," *Defense News*, June 7, 2014, http://www.defensenews.com/article/20140607/DEFREG01/306070013/Russian-NATO -Arms-Race-Takes-Shape.

27. Steven Erlanger, "Europe Begins to Rethink Cuts to Military Spending," *New York Times*, March 26, 2014, http://www.nytimes.com/2014/03/27/world/europe/europe-begins-to -rethink-cuts.html?_r=0.

28. *National Security Concept of the Republic of Estonia (2004)* and *National Security Concept of the Republic of Estonia (2011)*, http://www.libertysecurity.org/IMG/pdf/National_Security _Concept_2004.pdf and http://www.kaitseministeerium.ee/files/kmin/img/files/KM_riigikaitse _strateegia_eng(2).pdf.

29. Dominik P. Jankowski, "Issue Brief No. 132: Beyond Air and Missile Defense: Modernization of the Polish Armed Forces," Center for European Policy Analysis, September 5, 2013.

30. See Andrew F. Krepinevich et al., *Meeting the Anti-Access and Area Denial Challenge* (Washington, DC: CSBA, 2003), ii.

31. For an analysis of A2AD as it applies to allies, see Thomas, "From Protectorates to Partnerships."

32. Peter D. Stachura, *Poland, 1918–1945: An Interpretive and Documentary History of the Second Republic* (New York: Routledge, 2004), 121.

33. Or Honig, "The End of Israeli Military Restraint: Out with the New, in with the Old," *Middle East Quarterly* 14, no. 1 (Winter 2007): 63–74.

34. Gabi Siboni, "Disproportionate Force: Israel's Concept of Response in Light of the Second Lebanon War," *INSS Insight* no. 74, Institute for National Security Studies, October 2, 2008.

35. Study referenced in Jarmo Huhtanen and Aleksi Teivainen, "Finland Aborts Missile Acquisition from United States," *Helsinki Times*, March 29, 2014. See, for example, http://www.helsinkitimes.fi/finland/finland-news/domestic/10016-finland-aborts-missile-acquisition-from-united-states.html.

36. Trefor Moss, "Japan's New (Defensive) Attack Force," *Diplomat*, for The Diplomat-November 3, 2013, http://thediplomat.com/2013/11/japans-new-defensive-attack-force/; Yuka Hayashi, "Japan Builds Amphibious Force Modeled on U.S. Marines," *Wall Street Journal*, July 18, 2014, http://online.wsj.com/articles/japan-builds-amphibious-force-modeled-on-us-marines-14055 97172.

37. Paul Kallender-Umezu, "Japan Plans More Aggressive Defense," *Defense News*, May 26, 2013, http://www.defensenews.com/article/20130526/DEFREG03/305260004/Japan-Plans-More-Aggressive-Defense.

38. Obaid, *A Saudi Arabian Defense Doctrine*, 14.

39. See Ethan Meick, "China's Reported Ballistic Missile Sale to Saudi Arabia: Background and Potential Implications," U.S.-China Economic and Security Review Commission Staff Report, June 16, 2014; "US to Sell $10.8B in Missiles, Bombs to Saudis, UAE," *Agence France-Presse*, October 17, 2013, http://www.defensenews.com/article/20131017/DEFREG02/310170014/US-Sell-10–8B-Missiles-Bombs-Saudis-UAE.

40. Jankowski, "Issue Brief No. 132."

41. "Nuclear Arms Card for Japan," *Japan Times*, April 29 2013, http://www.japantimes.co.jp/opinion/2013/04/29/commentary/japan-commentary/nuclear-arms-card-for-japan/#.U80o Qk3Qc6Y; Jay Solomon and Miho Inada, "Japan's Nuclear Plan Unsettles U.S.," *Wall Street Journal*, May 1, 2013, http://online.wsj.com/news/articles/SB100014241278873245820045784 56943867189804.

42. "Prince Hints Saudi Arabia May Join Nuclear Arms Race," *New York Times*, December 6, 2011, http://www.nytimes.com/2011/12/07/world/middleeast/saudi-arabia-may-seek-nuclear-weapons-prince-says.html?_r=1&.

43. Obaid, *A Saudi Arabian Defense Doctrine*, 24.

44. Stewart M. Patrick, "Will the United States Set up a NATO-Like Pacific Treaty Organization in Asia?" Council on Foreign Relations, June 3, 2013, http://www.cfr.org/international-organizations-and-alliances/united-states-set-up-nato-like-pacific-treaty-organization-asia-if-so-/p30828; Zachary Keck, "Is an Asian NATO Possible?" *Diplomat*, April 18, 2014. http://the diplomat.com/2014/04/is-an-asian-nato-possible.

45. Richard Sokolsky, Angel Rabasa, and C. Richard Neu, *The Role of Southeast Asia in U.S. Strategy toward China* (Santa Monica: RAND Corporation, 2001), 43, 44.

46. Martin Fackler, "Japan Offers Support to Nations in Disputes with China," *New York Times*, June 2, 2014, http://cn.nytimes.com/asia-pacific/20140602/c02japan/dual/.

47. Shannon Tiezzi, "To Counter Beijing, Japan Moves Closer to Taiwan," *Diplomat*, February 20, 2014, http://thediplomat.com/2014/02/to-counter-beijing-japan-moves-closer-to-taiwan/; Zachary Keck, "Taiwan and Japan's Collective Self-Defense," *Diplomat*, for The Diplomat July 2, 2014, http://thediplomat.com/2014/07/taiwan-and-japans-collective-self-defense/.

48. Sanchita Basu Das, "ASEAN: A United Front to Tackle the South China Sea Issue," *East Asia Forum*, May 13, 2012, http://www.eastasiaforum.org/2012/05/13/asean-a-united-front-to-tackle-the-south-china-sea-issue/.

49. Yoel Guzansky "Tacit Allies: Israel and the Arab Gulf States," *Israel Journal of Foreign Affairs* 5, no. 1 (2011): 9–17.

50. Obaid, *A Saudi Arabian Defense Doctrine*, 30–31.

51. "The Decline of Deterrence."

52. Marcu Niculescu, "How Crimea Pushed Romania and Poland Closer Together," *International Policy Digest*, June 12, 2014; Jaroslaw Adamowski, "Airliner Strike Intensifies Urgency for E. European Procurement, Cooperation, *Defense News*, July 20, 2014, http://www.defensenews.com/article/20140720/DEFREG01/307200012/Airliner-Strike-Intensifies-Urgency-E-European-Procurement-Cooperation.

53. Juha Saarinen, Mikko Patokallio, and Tomas Wallenius, "Tentative Steps toward Deepening Defense Cooperation in the Baltic Region," *Eurasia Daily Monitor* 10, no. 15, January 28, 2013, http://www.jamestown.org/single/?no_cache=1&tx_ttnews%5Btt_news%5D=40378&tx_ttnews%5BbackPid%5D=620#.U85fvk3Qc6Y.

54. Tomasz Szatkowski, "After Ukraine: Developing Central European Defense Capabilities," Center for European Policy Analysis, June 10, 2014, http://www.cepa.org/content/after-ukraine-developing-central-european-defense-capabilities; "Swedish Defense Commission Says Russian Aggression in Ukraine Has Increased Risk in Nordic and Baltic Region," Mission of Sweden to NATO, May 16, 2014, http://www.atlanticcouncil.org/blogs/natosource/swedish-defense-commission-says-russian-aggression-in-ukraine-has-increased-risk-in-nordic-and-baltic-region. Category: Eurasia Daily Monitor, Home Page, Military/Security, Europe, Baltics

55. Randall L. Schweller, "Bandwagoning for Profit: Bringing the Revisionist State Back In," *International Security* 19, no. 1 (Summer 1994): 72–107.

56. Rothstein, *Alliances and Small Powers*, 194.

57. See, for example, David Owen Kieft, *Belgium's Return to Neutrality: An Essay in the Frustrations of Small-Power Diplomacy* (Oxford: Oxford University Press, 1972).

58. See, for example, Michael Yahuda, "The Evolving Asian Order: The Accommodation of Rising Chinese Power," in *Power Shift: China and Asia's New Dynamics*, ed. David Shambaugh, 347–62 (Berkeley: University of California Press, 2005); Robert Ross, "Balance of Power Politics and the Rise of China: Accommodation and Balancing in East Asia," *Security Studies* 15, no. 3 (July–September 2006): 355–95.

59. Lam Peng Er, Narayanan Ganesan, and Colin Dürkop, eds., *East Asia's Relations with a Rising China* (Berlin: Konrad Adenauer Stiftung, May 10, 2010), http://www.kas.de/wf/doc/kas_19560–1522–2-30.pdf?110608104027, p. 19.

60. Evan S. Medeiros et al., *Pacific Currents: The Responses of U.S. Allies and Security Partners in East Asia to China's Rise* (Santa Monica: RAND Corporation, 2008), xv, http://www.rand.org/content/dam/rand/pubs/monographs/2008/RAND_MG736.sum.pdf.

61. Ibid., xx.

62. Kavi Chongkittavorn, "Thailand Walks a Tightrope on South China Sea," *Nation*, May 7, 2012, http://www.nationmultimedia.com/opinion/Thailand-walks-a-tightrope-on-South-China-Sea-30181423.html.

63. Martin Wagener, "Reliable Kingdom? The USA, Thailand, and the Logic of Bandwagoning," *Journal of Current Southeast Asian Affairs* 28, no. 3 (2009): 40.

64. Eric Yep and Simon Hall, "Malaysia, China Keep Low Profile on Conflicting Sea Claims," *Wall Street Journal*, June 24, 2014, http://online.wsj.com/articles/malaysia-china-keep-low-profile-on-1403622597.

65. Shahriman Lockman, "Why Malaysia Isn't Afraid of China (for Now)," *Strategist*, April 24, 2013, http://www.aspistrategist.org.au/why-malaysia-isnt-afraid-of-china-for-now/.

66. See, for example, John J. Mearsheimer, "Say Goodbye to Taiwan," *National Interest*, February 26, 2014, http://nationalinterest.org/article/say-goodbye-taiwan-9931; Vance Chang, Hans Mouritzen, and Bruce Gilley, "To the Finland Station: Is Taiwan Selling Out to China?" *Foreign Affairs* (May/June 2010), http://www.foreignaffairs.com/articles/66403/vance-chang-hans-mouritzen-and-bruce-gilley/to-the-finland-station; and Bruce Gilley, "Not So Dire Straits: How the Finlandization of Taiwan Benefits U.S. Security," *Foreign Affairs* (January/February 2010), http://www.foreignaffairs.com/articles/65901/bruce-gilley/not-so-dire-straits.

67. Lam, Ganesan, and Dürkop, *East Asia's Relations with a Rising China*, 19.

68. "Chinese General Says U.S. Foreign Policy Has 'Erectile Dysfunction' Problems," *Wall Street Journal*, June 2, 2014, http://blogs.wsj.com/chinarealtime/2014/06/02/chinese-general-says-u-s-foreign-policy-has-erectile-dysfunction-problems/.

69. James Reynolds, "Iran Takes Charm Offensive to the Gulf," *BBC*, December 5, 2013, http://www.bbc.com/news/world-middle-east-25239869.

70. Bilal Y. Saab, "Why the Persian Gulf Isn't Ready for Joint Security," *Defense One*, June 19, 2014, http://www.defenseone.com/ideas/2014/06/why-persian-gulf-isnt-ready-joint-security/86800/; Daniel Wagner and Giorgio Cafiero, "Can Oman and Iran's 'Special' Relationship Last?" Institute for Near East & Gulf Military Analysis, July 29, 2013, http://gulfstateanalytics.com/archives/work/can-iran-and-omans-special-relationship-last.

71. Saab, "Why the Persian Gulf Isn't Ready for Joint Security."

72. Kevin Cosgriff, speech at Atlantic Council event "Defense Cooperation in the Arabian Gulf," *C-Span*, May 28, 2014, http://www.c-span.org/video/?319609-3/defense-cooperation-arabian-gulf.

73. Joshua Teitelbaum, "Saudi-Israeli Relations: Balancing Legitimacy and Security," Begin-Sadat Center for Strategic Studies, December 17, 2013, http://besacenter.org/perspectives-papers/saudi-israeli-relations-balancing-legitimacy-security/.

74. Ibid.

75. Saab, "Why the Persian Gulf Isn't Ready for Joint Security."

76. Wagner and Cafiero, "Can Oman and Iran's 'Special' Relationship Last?"

77. Awad Mustafa, "Source: UAE, Iran Reach Accord on Disputed Hormuz Islands," *Defense News*, January 15, 2014, http://www.defensenews.com/article/20140115/DEFREG04/301150034/Source-UAE-Iran-Reach-Accord-Disputed-Hormuz-Islands.

78. Pollack, *Unthinkable*, 341–42.

79. Ambassador Yousef al-Otaiba, quoted in Jeffrey Goldberg, "The Point of No Return," *Atlantic* (September 2010).

80. See Mark Leonard and Nicu Popescu, "A Power Audit of EU-Russia Relations," European Council on Foreign Relations, November 7, 2007.

81. Hungarian prime minister's chief of staff Janos Lazar, quoted in Zoltan Simon, "Putin $14 Billion Nuclear Deal Wins Orban Alliance," *Bloomberg News*, January 15, 2014, http://www.bloomberg.com/news/2014-01-14/putin-14-billion-nuclear-deal-wins-orban-alliance.html; Mark Varga, "Hungary Turns East as Europe Fades," *National Interest*, February 14, 2014, http://nationalinterest.org/commentary/hungary-turns-east-europe-fades-9878.

82. Authors' conversations with CEE officials.

83. See Leonard and Popescu, "A Power Audit of EU-Russia Relations."

84. V4 Prime Ministers' Panel, Globsec Conference, Bratislava, May 15, 2014; Margit Feher, "Hungary Not Part of Russia-Ukraine Conflict, Premier Orban Says," *Wall Street Journal*, March 3, 2014, http://blogs.wsj.com/emergingeurope/2014/03/03/hungary-not-part-of-russia-ukraine-conflict-premier-orban-says/.

85. "Rozhodujúci duel kandidátov," *TA3* (Slovak TV), March 23, 2014, http://www.ta3.com/clanok/1037180/rozhodujuci-duel-kandidatov.html; Authors' conversations with Czech officials; Joe Parkinson, "Bulgaria's Western Allies Worry about Eastward Tilt," *Wall Street Journal*, May 30, 2014, http://online.wsj.com/articles/bulgarias-western-allies-worry-about-east ward-tilt-1401477681; John R. Haines, "Kárpátalja: Europe's Next Crimea?" Foreign Policy Research Institute (April 2014), http://www.fpri.org/articles/2014/04/karpatalja-europes-next-crimea#note49; Adam Withnall, "Crimea Crisis: Putin Adviser Proposes Division of Ukraine along Nazi-Soviet Lines," *Independent*, March 24, 2014, http://www.independent.co.uk/news/world/europe/crimea-crisis-putin-adviser-proposes-division-of-ukraine-along-nazisoviet-lines-and-says-its-never-too-late-to-correct-historical-errors-9212925.html; Margit Feher, "Hungary Not Part of Russia-Ukraine Conflict, Premier Orban Says," *Wall Street Journal*, March 3, 2014,

http://blogs.wsj.com/emergingeurope/2014/03/03/hungary-not-part-of-russia-ukraine-conflict-premier-orban-says/.

86. "Rozhodujúci duel kandidátov."
87. Parkinson, "Bulgaria's Western Allies Worry about Eastward Tilt."
88. Haines, "Kárpátalja: Europe's Next Crimea?"
89. Withnall, "Crimea Crisis."
90. Waltz, "The Spread of Nuclear Weapons."

CHAPTER 5

1. William E. Odom and Robert Dujarric, *America's Inadvertent Empire* (New Haven: Yale University Press, 2005).

2. Edward Luttwak, *The Grand Strategy of the Roman Empire: From the First Century A.D. to the Third* (Baltimore: Johns Hopkins University Press, 1976), 24.

3. See, for example, Paul Kennedy, *Strategy and Diplomacy 1970–1945* (New York: Harper Collins, 1989).

4. Spykman, *The Geography of the Peace*, 40.

5. Mearsheimer, *The Tragedy of Great Power Politics*, 156.

6. Inis L. Claude, Jr., "The Balance of Power Revisited," *Review of International Studies* 15, no. 2 (January 1989): 80. Authors arguing that alliances cause war include Thomas J. Christensen and Jack Snyder, "Chain Gangs and Passed Bucks: Predicting Alliance Patterns in Multipolarity," *International Organization* 44, no. 2 (Spring 1990): 137–68; and Randolph M. Siverson and Harvey Starr, *The Diffusion of War: A Study of Opportunity and Willingness* (Ann Arbor: University of Michigan Press, 1991).

7. For example, see Scott D. Sagan, "1914 Revisited: Allies, Offense, and Instability," *International Security* 11, no. 2 (Fall 1986): 151–75; Bernadotte Everly Schmitt, *The Origins of the First World War* (Washington, DC: Historical Association, 1968); James Joll and Gordon Martel, *The Origins of the First World War* (New York: Longman, 1992); and Margaret MacMillan, *The Rhyme of History: Lessons of the Great War* (Washington, DC: Brookings Institution, December 14, 2013).

8. Rothstein, *Alliances and Small Powers*, 198. Other authors writing about the deterrent value of alliances include Edward V. Gulick, *Europe's Classical Balance of Power* (New York: Norton, 1955); and Hans Morgenthau, *Politics among Nations: The Struggle for Power and Peace* (New York: Knopf, 1967).

9. Spykman, *America's Strategy*, 24.

10. Brett Ashley Leeds, "Do Alliances Deter Aggression? The Influence of Military Alliances on the Initiation of Militarized Interstate Disputes," *American Journal of Political Science* 47, no. 3 (July 2003): 430.

11. Paul Huth and Bruce Russett, "What Makes Deterrence Work? Cases from 1900 to 1980," *World Politics* 36, no. 4 (July 1984): 518, 516.

12. Charles W. Kegley, Jr., and Gregory Raymond, *A Multipolar Peace? Great-Power Politics in the Twenty-First Century* (New York: St. Martin's Press, 1994), 94.

13. Elbridge Colby and Ely Ratner, "Roiling the Waters," *Foreign Policy*, January 22, 2014.

14. Michael Eisenstadt and David Pollock, "Friends with Benefits: Why the U.S.-Israeli Alliance Is Good for America," *Foreign Affairs*, November 7, 2012.

15. Stephen M. Walt, "Alliances in a Unipolar World," *World Politics* 61, no. 1 (October 2008): 113.

16. Dehio, *Precarious Balance*, 145.

17. Paul W. Schroeder, "Austria and the Danubian Principalities, 1853–1856," *Central European History* 2, no. 3 (September 1969): 218–19; Rothstein, *Alliances and Small Powers*, 174.

18. Dehio, *Precarious Balance*, 126.

19. Fuller, *Strategy and Power in Russia*, 91.

20. Piotr Stefan Wandycz, *France and Her Eastern Allies, 1919–1925: French-Czechoslovak-Polish Relations from the Paris Peace Conference to Locarno* (Minneapolis: University of Minnesota Press, 1962).

21. John Erikson, "'Russia Will Not Be Trifled With': Geopolitical Facts and Fantasies," in *Geopolitics, Geography and Strategy*, ed. Colin S. Gray and Geoffrey Sloan (Abingdon: Routledge, 2013), 246.

22. "China's Military Rise: The Dragon's New Teeth: A Rare Look Inside the World's Biggest Military Expansion," *Economist*, April 7, 2012.

23. For a detailed description of the strategic utility of the Asian coastline from a Chinese perspective, see Robert Kaplan, "Geography of Chinese Power," *Foreign Affairs* (May/June 2010).

24. Geoff Dyer, "US vs. China: Is This the New Cold War?" *Financial Times*, February 20, 2014.

25. George Friedman, *The Next Decade: Empire and Republic in a Changing World* (New York: Anchor Books, 2012), 170.

26. See, for example, Reva Bhalla, *Iran's World: Breaking Out of the Mountain Fortress* (Austin: Stratfor, 2011).

27. Spykman, *America's Strategy*, 19

28. Edward Luttwak, *Grand Strategy of the Byzantine Empire* (Cambridge, MA: Harvard University Press, 2009), 101.

29. Ibid., 138.

30. G. P. Gooch and J.H.B. Masterman, *A Century of British Foreign Policy* (London: Allen and Unwin, 1917), 23.

31. See, for example, Belgian interwar behavior, discussed in David Owen Kieft, *Belgium's Return to Neutrality: An Essay in the Frustrations of Small-Power Diplomacy* (Oxford: Oxford University Press, 1972).

32. Rothstein, *Alliances and Small Powers*, 188.

33. Paul W. Schroeder, "The Lost Intermediaries: The Impact of 1870 on the European System," in *Systems, Stability and Statecraft: Essays on the International History of Modern Europe*, ed. David Wetzel, Robert Jervis, and Jack S. Levy (New York: Palgrave Macmillan, 2004), 83.

34. "One predicts a strong tendency toward balance in the system. The expectation is not that a balance once achieved will be maintained, but that a balance once disrupted will be restored in one way or another. Balances of power recurrently form." Kenneth Waltz, *Theory of International Politics* (New York: McGraw-Hill, 1979), 128.

35. Paul W. Schroeder, "A.J.P. Taylor's International System," *International History Review* 23, no. 1 (March 2001): 17.

36. Wolfers, "Alliances as a Means of Defense," 6.

37. Sam Perlo-Freeman and Carina Solmirano, "Trends in World Military Expenditure, 2013," Stockholm International Peace Research Institute, 2013.

38. *The Military Balance* 114, no. 1 (2014), International Institute for Strategic Studies. Figures based on 2013.

39. All figures calculated from Global Fire Power.

40. Malin Rising, "Russia Boosts Military, Global Arms Spending Fall," *Associated Press*, April 13, 2014.

41. "The Dragon's New Teeth," *Economist*, April 7, 2012, http://www.economist.com/node/21552193.

42. Thucydides, *The Landmark Thucydides* 1:50, 31.

43. Ted Galen Carpenter, "U.S. Allies Bring Little to Table in Iraq, Afghanistan," *Chicago Sun-Times*, February 11, 2016.

44. http://icasualties.org/oef/.

45. A. Wess Mitchell and Jakub J. Grygiel, "Limited War Is Back," *National Interest*, August 18, 2014; Peter Pomerantsev, "How Putin Is Reinventing Warfare," *Foreign Policy*, May 5, 2014.

46. Michael J. Lostumbo et al., *Overseas Basing of U.S. Military Forces: An Assessment of Relative Costs and Strategic Benefits* (Santa Monica: RAND Corporation, 2013), 74.

47. Calder, *Embattled Garrisons*, 219.

48. Kenneth Watman et al., *U.S. Regional Deterrence Strategies* (Santa Monica: RAND Corporation, 1995), xii.

49. Schelling, *Arms and Influence*.

50. Mearsheimer, *Tragedy of Great Power Politics*, 394–95.

51. Wolfers, "Alliances as a Means of Defense," 13–14.

52. Lostumbo et al., *Overseas Basing of U.S. Military Forces*, 109.

53. Ibid., 117. "Without a robust en route infrastructure [i.e., bases], rapid global response is not possible."

54. See this argument discussed in Calder, *Embattled Garrisons*, 214–16.

55. Ibid., 218–19.

56. Ibid., 214.

57. Report of the Senate Armed Services Committee, "Inquiry into U.S. Costs and Allied Contributions to Support the U.S. Military Presence Overseas," April 2013, 1.

58. Boulding, *Conflict and Defense*, 262.

59. Niall Ferguson, *The Ascent of Money: A Financial History of the World* (New York: Penguin Books, 2009), 306–7.

60. John Darwin, *The Empire Project: The Rise and Fall of the British World-System, 1830–1970* (New York: Cambridge University Press, 2009), 275.

61. U.S. Department of the Treasury, "Major Foreign Holders of Treasury Securities," August 2014, http://www.treasury.gov/ticdata/Publish/mfh.txt.

62. Hans Oust Heiberg, "The Merchant Fleet: A Facilitator of World Trade," in *The Global Enabling Trade Report 2012* ed. Robert Z. Lawrence, Margareta Drzeniek Hanouz, and Sean Doherty (Geneva: World Economic Forum, 2012), 85.

63. U.S. Energy Information Administration, "World Oil Transit Chokepoints," August 22, 2012, 1.

64. Heiberg, "The Merchant Fleet," 85.

65. U.S. Department of Transportation, Maritime Administration, "U.S. Waterborne Foreign Container Trade by Trading Partners," November 21, 2014.

66. U.S. Energy Information Administration, "World Oil Transit Chokepoints"; Bill Tarrant "Malacca Strait Is a Strategic 'Chokepoint,'" *Reuters*, March 4, 2010.

67. U.S. Energy Information Administration, "World Oil Transit Chokepoints,"4.

68. Robert Ebel et al, *After an Attack on Iraq: The Economic Consequences* (Washington, DC: Center for Strategic and International Studies, 2002).

69. William Komiss and LaVar Huntzinger, *The Economic Implications of Disruptions to Maritime Oil Chokepoints* (Alexandria, VA: Center for Naval Analyses, 2011), 38; U.S. Energy Information Administration, "World Oil Transit Chokepoints."

70. Komiss and Huntzinger, *Economic Implications of Disruptions*, 12.

71. Vali R. Nasr, "A New Map, Defined by Gas," *New York Times*, June 10, 2014.

72. Rothstein, *Alliances and Small Powers*, 187.

CHAPTER 6

1. Andrew F. Krepinevich, Simon Chin, and Todd Harrison, *Strategy in Austerity* (Washington, DC: Center for Strategic and Budgetary Assessments, 2012).

2. Paul Huth and Bruce Russett, "What Makes Deterrence Work? Cases from 1900 to 1980," *World Politics* 36, no. 4 (July 1984): 518.

3. Krepinevich, Chin, and Harrison, *Strategy in Austerity*.

4. Glenn H. Snyder, *Alliance Politics*, rev. ed. (Ithaca: Cornell University Press, 2007).

5. For a discussion of the costs of stand-off air capabilities, see Calder, *Embattled Garrisons*, 214–15.

6. See also Eliot Cohen, "The 'Kind of Thing' Crisis," *American Interest* 10, no. 3 (December 2014).

7. Aaron Friedberg, "Will Europe's Past Be Asia's Future," *Survival* 42, no. 3 (Autumn 2000): 147–59.

8. Quoted in James Hookway, Newley Purnell, and Nopparat Chaichalearmmongkol, "Thailand's Army Bristles at U.S. Criticism of Coup," *Wall Street Journal*, June 6, 2014.

9. See, for example, Edward Lucas, *The Coming Storm: Baltic Sea Security Report*, Center for European Policy Analysis, June 15, 2015.

10. Stephen P. Rosen, "How America Can Balance China's Rising Power in Asia," *Wall Street Journal*, June 1, 2015.

11. On the dangers of copying the doctrine of another state, in this case applied to the relationship between Syria, Iraq, and Egypt and the Soviet Union, see Michael Eisenstadt and Kenneth Pollack, "Armies of Snow and Armies of Sand: The Impact of Soviet Military Doctrine on Arab Militaries," *Middle East Journal* 55, no. 4 (Autumn 2001): 549–78.

12. See Grygiel and Mitchell, "Limited War Is Back."

13. William Kaufmann, "Limited Warfare," in *Military Policy and National Security*, ed. William W. Kaufmann (Princeton: Princeton University Press, 1956), 115.

14. According to Robert Osgood, "The existence within indigenous regimes of a minimum internal cohesion and stability and a minimum ability to satisfy social and economic demands to prevent Communist ideological and political penetration. . . . The existence of indigenous military establishments capable of combating local insurrection and guerilla activity. . . . The ability of indigenous troops, acting as nuclei of resistance in conjunction with American forces and American military and economic assistance, to defeat larger military incursions on a local basis." Robert Osgood, *Limited War* (Chicago: University of Chicago Press, 1957), 269.

15. This insight was developed through a series of conversations between one of the authors and Jan van Tol. See Jan van Tol, "A2/AD—What Is It and How Would It Work in Central Europe?," *CEPA Deterrence Papers* no. 2, December 10, 2014.

16. Henry Kissinger, *The Necessity of Choice* (Garden City, NY: Doubleday, 1962), 75.

17. Mark Gunzinger with Christopher Dougherty, *Outside-In: Operating from Range to Defeat Iran's Anti-Access and Area-Denial Threats* (Washington, DC: Center for Strategic and Budgetary Assessments, 2011)

18. The technical difficulty, created by the rival's A2AD capabilities, of an American "reentry" into the contested spaces on the frontier leaves the United States with two broad options. One is a large, permanent presence in the most exposed frontier allies à la Germany in the Cold War or South Korea. But such a posture is increasingly difficult in large measure because of the defense drawdown that is resulting in cuts in American forces. There simply will not be sufficient American forces to keep large frontier garrisons, especially because it involves three distant regions. The second option is that of a reentry in case of crisis. But this has its own costs, mentioned here, namely, that the rivals can inflict large losses on American forces, effectively deterring them from coming to the aid of allies. This is why it is necessary to consider options for reopening the access to the areas where rivals are extending their A2AD umbrellas.

19. Thomas, "From Protectorates to Partnerships."

20. Thérèse Delpech, *Nuclear Deterrence in the 21st Century* (Santa Monica: RAND Corporation, 2012).

SELECTED BIBLIOGRAPHY

Adamowski, Jaroslaw. "Airliner Strike Intensifies Urgency for E. European Procurement, Cooperation." *Defense News*, July 20, 2014.

———. "Russian, NATO Arms Race Takes Shape." *Defense News*, June 7, 2014.

Art, Robert J. "The United States, the Balance of Power, and World War II: Was Spykman Right?" *Security Studies* 14, no. 3 (July–September 2005): 365–406.

Bacevich, Andrew. *The Limits of Power*. New York: Metropolitan Books, 2009.

Bar'el, Zvi. "Reconciliation with the U.S. Could Bolster Iran's Regional Power, Global Standing." *Haaretz*, September 28, 2013.

Barlow, Jeffrey G. *From Hot War to Cold*. Stanford: Stanford University Press, 2009.

Bassok, Moti. "Israel Shells Out Almost a Fifth of National Budget on Defense, Figures Show." *Haaretz*, February 14, 2013.

Basu Das, Sanchita. "ASEAN: A United Front to Tackle the South China Sea Issue." *East Asia Forum*, May 13, 2012.

Beckhusen, Robert. "Don't Mess with Poland." *War Is Boring*, March 28, 2014.

Beckley, Michael. "China's Century? Why America's Edge Will Endure." *International Security* 36, no. 3 (Winter 2011/12): 41–78.

Bhalla, Reva. *Iran's World: Breaking Out of the Mountain Fortress*. Austin: Stratfor, 2011.

Blainey, Geoffrey. *The Causes of War*. New York: Free Press, 1973.

Boulding, Kenneth E. *Conflict and Defense: A General Theory*. New York: Harper, 1962.

Bracken, Paul. *The Second Nuclear Age: Strategy, Danger and the New Power Politics*. New York: Times Books, 2012.

Brodie, Bernard. *A Guide to Naval Strategy*. Princeton: Princeton University Press, 1944.

Buchanan, Patrick. *Churchill, Hitler, and the Unnecessary War*. New York: Crown, 2008.

Bush, George W. "The 2000 Campaign; 2nd Presidential Debate between Gov. Bush and Vice President Gore." Winston-Salem, NC, October 11, 2000.

Calder, Kent E. *Embattled Garrisons: Comparative Base Politics and American Globalism*. Princeton: Princeton University Press, 2008.

Carpenter, Ted Galen. *A Search for Enemies: America's Alliances after the Cold War*. Washington, DC: Cato Institute, 1992.

———. "U.S. Allies Bring Little to Table in Iraq, Afghanistan." *Chicago Sun-Times*, February 11, 2016.

Carpenter, Ted Galen, and Marian L. Tupy. "U.S. Defense Spending Subsidizes European Free-Riding Welfare States." *Daily Caller*, July 12, 2010.

Cha, Victor D. "Powerplay Origins of the U.S. Alliance System in Asia." *International Security* 34, no. 3 (Winter 2009/2010): 158–96.

Chang, Vance, Hans Mouritzen, and Bruce Gilley. "To the Finland Station: Is Taiwan Selling Out to China?" *Foreign Affairs* (May/June 2010).

Chicago Council on Global Affairs. *Survey of American Public Opinion and U.S. Foreign Policy*. Chicago: Chicago Council on Global Affairs, 2012.

"China's Military Rise: The Dragon's New Teeth: A Rare Look Inside the World's Biggest Military Expansion." *Economist*, April 7, 2012.

Chongkittavorn, Kavi. "Thailand Walks a Tightrope on South China Sea." *Nation*, May 7, 2012.

Christensen, Thomas J., and Jack Snyder. "Chain Gangs and Passed Bucks: Predicting Alliance Patterns in Multipolarity." *International Organization* 44, no. 2 (Spring 1990): 137–68.

Churchill, Winston S. *The Second World War*, vol. 1: *The Gathering Storm*. Boston: Houghton Mifflin, 1948.

———. *The World Crisis*, vol. 1: *1911–1914*. London: Butterworth, 1927.

Clark, Christopher. *The Sleepwalkers*. New York: Harper Collins 2013.

Claude, Inis L., Jr. "The Balance of Power Revisited." *Review of International Studies* 15, no. 2 (January 1989): 77–85.

Clinton, Hillary. *The First Quadrennial Diplomacy and Development Review QDDR: Leading through Civilian Power*. Washington, DC: U.S. Department of State, 2010.

———. Interview with Hillary Clinton. *Newsnight*, BBC, June 12, 2014.

———. Speech at the Council on Foreign Relations, Washington, DC, July 15, 2009.

———. Speech at the Council on Foreign Relations, Washington, DC, September 8, 2010.

Cohen, Warren. *Empire without Tears: America's Foreign Relations, 1921–1933*. New York: McGraw-Hill, 1987.

Colby, Elbridge, and Ely Ratner. "Roiling the Waters." *Foreign Policy*, January 22, 2014.

Conry, Barbara. *Cato Institute Policy Analysis No. 239: The Western European Union as NATO's Successor*. Washington, DC: Cato Institute, 1995.

Converse, Elliott V., III. *Circling the Earth: United States Plans for a Postwar Overseas Military Base System, 1942–1948*. Maxwell Air Force Base, AL: Air University Press, 2005.

Copeland, Dale. "Do Reputations Matter?" *Security Studies* 7, no. 1 (1997): 33–71.

Corbett, Julian. *Sir Francis Drake*. London: Macmillan, 1890.

Cosgriff, Kevin. Speech at Atlantic Council event "Defense Cooperation in the Arabian Gulf." *C-Span*, May 28, 2014.

Cronin, Audrey. "Why Drones Fail." *Foreign Affairs* (July/August 2013).

Currie, Kelley. "The Doctrine of 'Strategic Reassurance.'" *Wall Street Journal*, October 22, 2009.

Darczewska, Jolanta. *Anatomia Rosyjskiej Wojny Informacyjnej: Operacja Krymska*. Warsaw: Centre for Eastern Studies, May 2014.

Darwin, John. *The Empire Project: The Rise and Fall of the British World-System, 1830–1970*. New York: Cambridge University Press, 2009.

Davis, Paul K., and Robert D. Howe. *Planning for Long-Term Security in Central Europe*. Santa Monica: RAND Corporation, August 1990.

"The Decline of Deterrence: America Is No Longer as Alarming to Its Foes or Reassuring to Its Friends." *Economist*, May 3, 2014.

Dehio, Ludwig. *The Precarious Balance: Four Centuries of the European Power Struggle*. Translated by Charles Fullman. New York: Knopf, 1962.

Diehl, Jackson. "Where Are Obama's Foreign Confidants?" *Washington Post*, March 8, 2010.

Doran, Charles F. *Systems in Crisis: New Imperatives of High Politics at Century's End*. Cambridge: Cambridge University Press, 1991.

Doran, Michael. "The Silent Partnership." *Mosaic*, October 15, 2014.

———. "What Was He Thinking?" *Mosaic*, August 6, 2014.

Doyle, Michael. *Empires*. Ithaca: Cornell University Press, 1986.

Dueck, Colin. "The Accommodator: Obama's Foreign Policy." *Policy Review*, no. 169 (October 2011): 13–28.

———. *The Obama Doctrine*. New York: Oxford University Press, 2015.

Dunn, Frederick S., Edward M. Earle, William T. R. Fox, Grayson L. Kirk, David N. Rowe, Harold Sprout, and Arnold Wolfers. *A Security Policy for Postwar America*. Washington, DC: Naval Historical Center, Strategic Plans Division, 1945.

Dyer, Geoff. "US vs. China: Is This the New Cold War?" *Financial Times*, February 20, 2014.

Ebel, Robert, Herman Franssen, Larry Goldstein, and Adam Sieminski. *After an Attack on Iraq: The Economic Consequences*. Washington, DC: Center for Strategic and International Studies, 2002.

Eckstein, Arthur. *Mediterranean Anarchy, Interstate War, and the Rise of Rome*. Berkeley: University of California Press, 2006.

Edelman, Eric. "Confronting Putin's Invasion." *Weekly Standard*, March 17, 2014.

———. *Understanding America's Contested Primacy*. Washington, DC: Center for Strategic and Budgetary Assessment, 2010.

Eisenstadt, Michael, and David Pollock. "Friends with Benefits: Why the U.S.-Israeli Alliance Is Good for America." *Foreign Affairs*, November 7, 2012.

Erikson, John. "'Russia Will Not Be Trifled With': Geopolitical Facts and Fantasies." In *Geopolitics, Geography and Strategy*. Edited by Colin S. Gray and Geoffrey Sloan, 242–68. Abingdon: Routledge, 2013.

Erlanger, Steven. "Europe Begins to Rethink Cuts to Military Spending." *New York Times*, March 26, 2014.

———. "Panetta Urges Europe to Spend More on NATO or Risk a Hollowed-Out Alliance." *New York Times*, October 5, 2011.

Fackler, Martin. "Japan Offers Support to Nations in Disputes with China." *New York Times*, June 2, 2014.

Feffer, John. "World Cuts Back Military Spending, but Not Asia." *Inter-Press Service*, April 14, 2014.

Feher, Margit. "Hungary Not Part of Russia-Ukraine Conflict, Premier Orban Says." *Wall Street Journal*, March 3, 2014.

Ferguson, Niall. *The Ascent of Money: A Financial History of the World*. New York: Penguin Books, 2009.

Friedberg, Aaron. *Beyond Air-Sea Battle: The Debate over US Military Strategy in Asia*. London: Adelphi Books, 2014.

———. *The Weary Titan*. Princeton: Princeton University Press, 1988.

Friedman, George. *The Next Decade: Empire and Republic in a Changing World*. New York: Anchor Books, 2012.

Fuller, William C., Jr. *Strategy and Power in Russia, 1600–1914*. New York: Free Press, 1992.

Gaddis, John Lewis. *We Now Know: Rethinking Cold War History*. New York: Oxford University Press, 1997.

Gallois, Pierre. "French and European Security in a Defense-Oriented Environment: An Interview with General Pierre Gallois." *Fletcher Forum* (Winter 1986): 43–49.

Gates, Robert M. "The Security and Defense Agenda (Future of NATO)." Speech in Brussels, Belgium, June 10, 2011.

George, Alexander L., and Richard Smoke. *Deterrence in American Foreign Policy: Theory and Practice*. New York: Columbia University Press, 1974.

Gilbert, Felix. *To the Farewell Address*. Princeton: Princeton University Press, 1970.

Gilley, Bruce. "Not So Dire Straits: How the Finlandization of Taiwan Benefits U.S. Security." *Foreign Affairs* (January/February 2010).

Goldberg, Jeffrey. "The Point of No Return." *Atlantic* (September 2010).

Goldman, Emily. *Power in Uncertain Times: Strategy in the Fog of Peace*. Stanford: Stanford University Press, 2011.

Goldstein, Lyle. "Strategic Implications of Chinese Fisheries Development." *Jamestown Foundation China Brief* 9, no. 16 (August 5, 2009).

Gooch, G. P., and J.H.B. Masterman. *A Century of British Foreign Policy*. London: Allen and Unwin, 1917.

Gordon, Philip. "Charles de Gaulle and the Nuclear Revolution." *Security Studies* 5, no. 1, (Autumn 1995): 118–48.

Gray, Colin S. *Modern Strategy*. Oxford: Oxford University Press, 1999.

———. "Ocean and Continent in Global Strategy." *Comparative Strategy* 7, no. 4 (1988): 439–44.

"Gulf States—Dangerous Arms Race." *South World* (July 2013).

"Gulf States Requesting ABM-Capable Systems." *Defense Industry Daily*, July 15, 2014.

Gulick, Edward V. *Europe's Classical Balance of Power*. New York: Norton, 1955.

Guzansky, Yoel. "Tacit Allies: Israel and the Arab Gulf States." *Israel Journal of Foreign Affairs* 5, no. 1 (2011): 9–17.

Haass, Richard N. *Foreign Policy Begins at Home*. New York: Basic Books, 2013.

Haddick, Robert. "The Civilianization of War." *National Interest*, April 11, 2014.

"Hagel in Israel to Discuss Missile Defenses." *i24 News*, May 15, 2014.

Haines, John R. "Kárpátalja: Europe's Next Crimea?" Foreign Policy Research Institute, April 2014.

Hayashi, Yuka. "Japan Builds Amphibious Force Modeled on U.S. Marines." *Wall Street Journal*, July 18, 2014.

Heiberg, Hans Oust. "The Merchant Fleet: A Facilitator of World Trade" In *The Global Enabling Trade Report 2012*. Edited by Robert Z. Lawrence, Margareta Drzeniek Hanouz, and Sean Doherty, 85–90. Zurich: World Economic Forum, 2012.

Higgins, Andrew, Michael Gordon, and Andrew Kramer. "Photos Links Masked Men in East Ukraine to Russia." *New York Times*, April 20, 2014.

Hofbauer, Joachim, Priscilla Hermann, and Sneha Raghavan. *Asian Defense Spending 2000–2011*. Washington, DC: CSIS, October 2012.

Honig, Or. "The End of Israeli Military Restraint: Out with the New, in with the Old." *Middle East Quarterly* 14, no. 1 (Winter 2007): 63–74.

Hopf, Ted. *Peripheral Visions*. Ann Arbor: University of Michigan Press, 1995.

Howard, Michael E. *Continental Commitment: The Dilemma of British Defence Policy in the Era of the Two World Wars*. London: Maurice Temple Smith, 1972.

Huhtanen, Jarmo, and Aleksi Teivainen. "Finland Aborts Missile Acquisition from United States." *Helsinki Times*, March 29, 2014.

Huth, Paul, and Bruce Russett. "What Makes Deterrence Work? Cases from 1900 to 1980." *World Politics* 36, no. 4 (1984): 496–526.

"Iran Plans 127 Percent Defense Budget Increase." *Agence France-Presse*, February 2, 2012.

Isaacson, Walter, and Evan Thomas. *The Wise Men: Six Friends and the World They Made*. New York: Simon & Schuster, 1986.

Jankowski, Dominik P. "Issue Brief No. 132: Beyond Air and Missile Defense: Modernization of the Polish Armed Forces." *Center for European Policy Analysis*, September 5, 2013.

Jarausch, Konrad H. "The Illusion of Limited War: Chancellor Bethmann Hollweg's Calculated Risk, July 1914." *Central European History* 2, no. 1 (1969): 48–76.

Jervis, Robert. "Cooperation under the Security Dilemma." *World Politics* 30, no. 2 (January 1978): 167–214.

Joffe, Josef. "A Letter from the Prince to Putin." *Wall Street Journal*, March 6, 2014.

———. *The Myth of America's Decline*. New York: Liveright, 2014.

Joll, James, and Gordon Martel. *The Origins of the First World War*. New York: Longman, 1992.

Kagan, Robert. *The World America Made*. New York: Vintage, 2013.

Kallender-Umezu, Paul. "Big-Ticket Buys Could Hurt Japan." *Defense News*, April 13, 2014.

———. "Japan Plans More Aggressive Defense." *Defense News*, May 26, 2013.

Kaplan, Robert. "Geography of Chinese Power." *Foreign Affairs* (May/June 2010).

Kastner, Jens. "China's Fishermen Charge Enemy Lines." *Asia Times*, May 16, 2012.

Kazer, William. "Chinese General Says U.S. Foreign Policy Has 'Erectile Dysfunction' Problems." *Wall Street Journal*, June 2, 2014.

Keck, Zachary. "Is an Asian NATO Possible?" *Diplomat*, April 18, 2014.

———. "Taiwan and Japan's Collective Self-Defense." *Diplomat*, July 2, 2014.

Kegley, Charles W., Jr., and Gregory Raymond. *A Multipolar Peace? Great-Power Politics in the Twenty-First Century*. New York: St. Martin's Press, 1994.

Kieft, David Owen. *Belgium's Return to Neutrality: An Essay in the Frustrations of Small-Power Diplomacy*. Oxford: Oxford University Press, 1972.

Kim, Tongfi. "Why Alliances Entangle but Seldom Entrap States." *Security Studies* 20, no. 3 (2011): 350–77.

Komiss, William, and LaVar Huntzinger. *The Economic Implications of Disruptions to Maritime Oil Chokepoints*. Alexandria, VA: Center for Naval Analyses, 2011.

Krepinevich, Andrew F., et al. *Meeting the Anti-Access and Area Denial Challenge*. Washington, DC: CSBA, 2003.

Kreps, Sarah, and Micah Zenko. "The Next Drone Wars." *Foreign Affairs* (March/April 2014).

Kupchan, Charles A. *No One's World: The West, the Rising Rest, and the Coming Global Turn*. Oxford: Oxford University Press, 2012.

Lam Peng Er, Narayanan Ganesan, and Colin Dürkop, eds. *East Asia's Relations with a Rising China*. Berlin: Konrad Adenauer Stiftung, 2010.

Landler, Mark. "Obama Finds a Pen Pal in Iran." *New York Times*, September 19, 2013.

Layne, Christopher. *The Peace of Illusions*. Ithaca: Cornell University Press, 2006.

Leeds, Brett Ashley. "Do Alliances Deter Aggression? The Influence of Military Alliances on the Initiation of Militarized Interstate Disputes." *American Journal of Political Science* 47, no. 3 (July 2003): 427–39.

Leffler, Melvyn P. "The American Conception of National Security and the Beginnings of the Cold War, 1945–48." *American Historical Review* 89, no. 2 (April 1984): 346–81.

Leonard, Mark, and Nicu Popescu. "A Power Audit of EU-Russia Relations." European Council on Foreign Relations, November 7, 2007.

Lieber, Robert. *Power and Willpower in the American Future*. New York: Cambridge University Press, 2012.

Lippmann, Walter. *U.S. Foreign Policy: Shield of the Republic*. Boston: Little, Brown, 1943.

Lockman, Shahriman. "Why Malaysia Isn't Afraid of China (for Now)." *Strategist*, April 24, 2013.

Logan, Justin. "Asia's Free-Riders." *Foreign Policy*, November 9, 2011.

Lostumbo, Michael J., Michael J. McNerney, Eric Peltz, Derek Eaton, David R. Frelinger, Victoria A. Greenfield, John Halliday, Patrick Mills, Bruce R. Nardulli, Stacie L. Pettyjohn, Jerry M. Sollinger, and Stephen M. Worman. *Overseas Basing of U.S. Military Forces: An Assessment of Relative Costs and Strategic Benefits*. Santa Monica: RAND Corporation, 2013.

Luttwak, Edward. *The Grand Strategy of the Byzantine Empire*. Cambridge, MA: Harvard University Press, 2009.

———. *The Grand Strategy of the Roman Empire: From the First Century A.D. to the Third*. Baltimore: Johns Hopkins University Press, 1976.

Machiavelli, Niccolo. *Discourses* Translated by H. Mansfield and N. Tarcov. Chicago: University of Chicago Press, 1998.

Mackinder, H. J. *Britain and the British Seas*. New York: Appleton, 1902.

MacMillan, Margaret. *The Rhyme of History: Lessons of the Great War*. Washington, DC: Brookings Institution, December 14, 2013.

———. *The War That Ended Peace*. New York: Random House, 2014.

Mandelbaum, Michael. *The Nuclear Question*. New York: Cambridge University Press, 1981.

———. *The Nuclear Revolution: International Politics before and after Hiroshima*. New York: Cambridge University Press, 1981.

Mangasarian, Leon. "Putin Emboldened on Instability Arc by EU Defense Divide." *Bloomberg News*, May 15, 2014.

Massie, Robert. *Dreadnought*. New York: Random House, 1991.

Mearsheimer, John. "The Case for a Ukrainian Nuclear Deterrent." *Foreign Affairs* (Summer 1993).

———. "Getting Ukraine Wrong." *New York Times*, March 13, 2014.

———. "Say Goodbye to Taiwan." *National Interest*, February 26, 2014.

———. *The Tragedy of Great Power Politics*. New York: Norton, 2001.

———. "Why We Will Soon Miss the Cold War." *Atlantic* (August 1990).

Medeiros, Evan S., Keith Crane, Eric Heginbotham, Norman D. Levin, Julia F. Lowell, Angel Rabasa, and Somi Seong. *Pacific Currents: The Responses of U.S. Allies and Security Partners in East Asia to China's Rise*. Santa Monica: RAND Corporation, 2008.

Menon, Rajan. *The End of Alliances*. New York: Oxford University Press, 2007.

Mercer, Jonathan. *Reputation and International Politics*. Ithaca: Cornell University Press, 1996.

Miho Inada. "Japan's Nuclear Plan Unsettles U.S." *Wall Street Journal*, May 1, 2013.

Miks, Jason. "Vietnam Eyes China 'Threat.'" for The Diplomat *Diplomat*, March 28, 2011.

Miller, Benjamin. *States, Nations, and the Great Powers: The Sources of Regional War and Peace*. New York: Cambridge University Press, 2007.

Miller, Gregory D. *The Shadow of the Past*. Ithaca: Cornell University Press, 2012.

Mitchell, A. Wess, and Jakub J. Grygiel. "Limited War Is Back." *National Interest*, August 28, 2014.

Morgenthau, Hans. "The Crisis in the Western Alliance." *Commentary*, March 1, 1963.

———. *Politics among Nations: The Struggle for Power and Peace*. New York: Knopf, 1967.

Morse, Edward L., Eric G. Lee, Kingsmill Bond, Tina M. Mordham, Deane M. Dray, and Stan Fediuk. "Energy 2020: Independence Day." *Citi GPS* (February 2013).

Moss, Trefor. "Japan's New (Defensive) Attack Force." *Diplomat*, for The Diplomat November 3, 2013.

Mustafa, Awad. "Source: UAE, Iran Reach Accord on Disputed Hormuz Islands." *Defense News*, January 15, 2014.

Nasr, Vali R. "A New Map, Defined by Gas." *New York Times*, June 10, 2014.

Niculescu, Marcu. "How Crimea Pushed Romania and Poland Closer Together." *International Policy Digest*, June 12, 2014.

"Nuclear Arms Card for Japan." *Japan Times*, April 29, 2013.

Nussey, Sam. "Tension Fuels Arms Race in East Asia." *Nikkei Asian Review*, February 13, 2014.

Obaid, Nawaf. *A Saudi Arabian Defense Doctrine: Mapping the Expanded Force Structure the Kingdom Needs to Lead the Arab World, Stabilize the Region, and Meet Its Global Responsibilities*. Cambridge, MA: Belfer Center for Science and International Affairs, Harvard University, May 2014.

Obama, Barack. "Message to the Iranian People on Nowruz." Washington, DC: U.S. Department of State, March 20, 2013.

———. Remarks to the Troops at Fort Bliss, TX, August 31, 2012.

———. Remarks to the United Nations General Assembly, September 23, 2009.

———. Statement on Ukraine. Washington, DC, February 28, 2014.

"The Obama Doctrine." *Economist*, December 1, 2012.

Odom, William E., and Robert Dujarric. *America's Inadvertent Empire*. New Haven: Yale University Press, 2005.

Osgood, Robert E. "The Reappraisal of Limited War." *Adelphi Papers* 9, no. 54 (1969): 41–54.

Pape, Robert. *Bombing to Win: Air Power and Coercion in War*. Ithaca: Cornell University Press, 1996.

———. "Empire Falls." *National Interest* (January–February 2009).

"Parengtas 2015–2017 metų krašto apsaugos biudžeto projektas." *Alkas*, July 3, 2014.

Parkinson, Joe. "Bulgaria's Western Allies Worry about Eastward Tilt." *Wall Street Journal*, May 30, 2014.

Patrick, Stewart M. "Will the United States Set up a NATO-Like Pacific Treaty Organization in Asia?" Council on Foreign Relations, June 3, 2013.

Paul, Ron. "A Tea Party Foreign Policy." *Foreign Policy*, August 27, 2010.

Perlo-Freeman, Sam, and Carina Solmirano, "Trends in World Military Expenditure, 2013," SIPRI Fact Sheet, Stockholm International Peace Research Institute, 2013.

Pincus, Walter. "Poland Won't Lobby Obama on Missile Defense." *Washington Post*, November 20, 2008.

Plutarch. *Plutarch's Lives*. Translated by John Dryden. New York: Modern Library, 2001.

Pollack, Kenneth. *Unthinkable: Iran, the Bomb, and American Strategy*. New York: Simon & Schuster, 2013.

Polybius. *The Rise of the Roman Empire*. New York: Penguin, 1979.

Pomerantsev, Peter. "How Putin Is Reinventing Warfare." *Foreign Policy*, May 5, 2014.

Posen, Barry R. "Pull Back: The Case of a Less Activist Foreign Policy." *Foreign Affairs* (January/February 2013).

Preble, Christopher A. "What Some Call 'Isolationism,' Others Call Common Sense." *U.S. News*. May 2, 2013.

Press, Daryl. *Calculating Credibility: How Leaders Assess Military Threats*. Ithaca: Cornell University Press, 2005.

"Prince Hints Saudi Arabia May Join Nuclear Arms Race." *New York Times*, December 6, 2011.

Ranasinghe, Dhara. "Singapore, the Tiny State with Military Clout." *CNBC*, February 9, 2014.

Reid, T. R. *The United States of Europe: The New Superpower and the End of American Supremacy*. New York: Penguin Press, 2004.

Remnick, David. "Going the Distance." *New Yorker*, January 27, 2014.

Republic of Estonia. *National Security Concept of the Republic of Estonia (2004)*.

———. *National Security Concept of the Republic of Estonia (2011)*.

Reynolds, James. "Iran Takes Charm Offensive to the Gulf." *BBC*, December 5, 2013.

Riezler, Kurt. "The Illusion of Limited War: Chancellor Bethmann Hollweg's Calculated Risk, July 1914." *Central European History* 2, no. 1 (1969): 48–76.

Riley, Alan. "The Shale Revolution's Shifting Geopolitics." *New York Times*, December 25, 2012.

Rising, Malin. "Russia Boosts Military, Global Arms Spending Fall." *Associated Press*, April 13, 2014.

"Romania to Boost Military Spending over Ukraine Crisis." *Agence France-Presse*, April 28, 2014.

Rose, Thomas. "Gulf States Break with Qatar over Its Support for Islamists and Iran." *Breitbart News*, March 7, 2014.

Rosen, Stephen P. *War and Human Nature*. Princeton: Princeton University Press, 2005.

Ross, Robert. "Balance of Power Politics and the Rise of China: Accommodation and Balancing in East Asia." *Security Studies* 15, no. 3 (July–September 2006): 355–95.

Rothstein, Robert L. *Alliances and Small Powers*. New York: Columbia University Press, 1968.

Roughead, Gary. Remarks at the University of Chicago Conference on Terrorism & Strategy, Chicago, October 12, 2010.

Russett, Bruce. *No Clear and Present Danger: A Skeptical View of the United States Entry into World War II*. New York: Harper and Row, 1972.

Saab, Bilal Y. "Why the Persian Gulf Isn't Ready for Joint Security." *Defense One*, June 19, 2014.

Saarinen, Juha, Mikko Patokallio, and Tomas Wallenius. "Tentative Steps toward Deepening Defense Cooperation in the Baltic Region." *Eurasia Daily Monitor* 10, no. 15, January 28, 2013.

Sagan, Scott D. "1914 Revisited: Allies, Offense, and Instability." *International Security* 11, no. 2 (Fall 1986): 151–75.

Schadlow, Nadia. "Peace and War: The Space Between." *War on the Rocks*, August 18, 2014.

Schelling, Thomas C. *Arms and Influence*. New Haven: Yale University Press, 1966.

Schmitt, Bernadotte Everly. *The Origins of the First World War*. Washington, DC: Historical Association, 1968.

Schroeder, Paul W. "Austria and the Danubian Principalities, 1853–1856." *Central European History* 2, no. 3 (September 1969): 216–36.

———. "The Lost Intermediaries: The Impact of 1870 on the European System." In *Systems, Stability and Statecraft: Essays on the International History of Modern Europe.* Edited by David Wetzel, Robert Jervis, and Jack S. Levy, 77–95. New York: Palgrave Macmillan, 2004.

Schwarz, Benjamin, and Christopher Layne, "NATO: At 50, It's Time to Quit." *Nation,* May 10, 1999.

Schweller, Randall L. "Bandwagoning for Profit: Bringing the Revisionist State Back In." *International Security* 19, no. 1 (Summer 1994): 72–107.

Shore, Zachary. *A Sense of the Enemy.* New York: Oxford University Press, 2014.

Simms, Brendan. *Europe: The Struggle for Supremacy.* New York: Basic Books, 2014.

Simon, Zoltan. "Putin $14 Billion Nuclear Deal Wins Orban Alliance." *Bloomberg News,* January 15, 2014.

Siverson, Randolph M., and Harvey Starr. *The Diffusion of War: A Study of Opportunity and Willingness.* Ann Arbor: University of Michigan Press, 1991.

Smoke, Richard. "Theories of Escalation." In *Diplomacy: New Approaches in History, Theory, and Policy.* Edited by Paul Gordon Lauren, 162–83. New York: Free Press, 1979.

———. *War: Controlling Escalation.* Cambridge, MA: Harvard University Press, 1977.

Snyder, Glenn H. *Alliance Politics.* Revised edition. Ithaca: Cornell University Press, 2007.

———. "The Security Dilemma in Alliance Politics." *World Politics* 36, no. 4 (July 1984): 461–95.

Sokolsky, Richard, Angel Rabasa, and C. Richard Neu. *The Role of Southeast Asia in U.S. Strategy toward China.* Santa Monica: RAND Corporation, 2001.

Solomon, Ariel Ben. "4 Out of 5 Fastest-Growing Defense Budgets Are in Mideast." *Jerusalem Post,* February 4, 2014.

Solomon, Jay, and Peter D. Stachura. *Poland, 1918–1945: An Interpretive and Documentary History of the Second Republic.* New York: Routledge, 2004.

Splidsboel-Hansen, Flemming. "Past and Future Meet: Aleksandr Gorchakov and Russian Foreign Policy." *Europe-Asia Studies* 54, no. 3 (2002): 377–96.

Spykman, Nicholas J. *America's Strategy in World Politics.* New York: Harcourt, Brace, 1942.

———. *The Geography of Peace.* New York: Harcourt, Brace, 1944.

Stachura, Peter D. *Poland, 1918–1945: An Interpretive and Documentary History of the Second Republic.* New York: Routledge, 2004.

Stevens, Paul. *The 'Shale Gas Revolution': Development and Changes.* London: Chatham House Royal Institute of International Affairs, 2012.

"Swedish Defense Commission Says Russian Aggression in Ukraine Has Increased Risk in Nordic and Baltic Region." Mission of Sweden to NATO, May 16, 2014.

Szatkowski, Tomasz. "After Ukraine: Developing Central European Defense Capabilities." Center for European Policy Analysis, June 10, 2014.

"Taiwan's Force Modernization: The American Side." *Defense Industry Daily,* June 4, 2014.

Takeyh, Ray. "The U.S. Needs a Deal with Iran, Not Détente." *Washington Post,* January 12, 2014.

Tang, Shiping. "Reputation, Cult of Reputation, and International Conflict." *Security Studies* 14, no. 1 (October 2005): 34–62.

Tarrant, Bill. "Malacca Strait Is a Strategic 'Chokepoint.'" *Reuters,* March 4, 2010.

Taylor, A.J.P. *The Struggle for Mastery in Europe, 1848–1918.* Oxford: Oxford University Press, 1954.

Taylor, Guy, and Rowan Scarborough, "Ominous Warning: Admiral Concedes U.S. Losing Dominance to China." *Washington Times,* January 16, 2014.

Tebin, Prokhor. "South China Sea: A New Geopolitical Node." *Asia Times,* October 14, 2011.

Teitelbaum, Joshua. "Saudi-Israeli Relations: Balancing Legitimacy and Security." Begin-Sadat Center for Strategic Studies, December 17, 2013.

Tertrais, Bruno. "Destruction Assurée: The Origins and Development of French Nuclear Strategy, 1945–81." In *Getting Mad: Nuclear Mutual Assured Destruction, Its Origins and Practice*. Edited by Henry Sokolski, 51–122. Carlisle, PA: Strategic Studies Institute, 2004.

Thompson, Mark. "The 600 Years of History behind Those Ukrainian Masks." *Time*, April 17, 2014.

Thucydides. *The Landmark Thucydides: A Comprehensive Guide to the Peloponnesian War.* Edited by Robert B. Strassler, translated by Richard Crawley. New York: Free Press, 1996.

Tiezzi, Shannon. "To Counter Beijing, Japan Moves Closer to Taiwan." *Diplomat*, February 20, 2014.

Tomohiko, Taniguchi. "Japan and the Geopolitics of the Shale Revolution." *Nippon*, December 27, 2012.

U.S. Department of the Treasury. "Major Foreign Holders of Treasury Securities." August 2014.

U.S. Energy Information Administration, U.S. Department of Energy. "World Oil Transit Chokepoints." August 22, 2012.

U.S. Library of Congress, Congressional Research Services. *Long-Range Ballistic Missile Defense in Europe*, by Steven Hildreth and Carl Ek. Washington, DC: Office of Congressional Information and Publishing, September 23, 2009.

"US to Sell $10.8B in Missiles, Bombs to Saudis, UAE." *Agence France-Presse*, October 17, 2013.

Vagts, Alfred. "The United States and the Balance of Power." *Journal of Politics* 3, no. 4 (November 1941): 401–49.

Van der Oye, David Schimmelpenninck. "Russian Foreign Policy, 1815–1917." In *The Cambridge History of Russia*. Vol. 2. Edited by Dominic Lieven. Cambridge: Cambridge University Press, 2006.

Varga, Mark. "Hungary Turns East as Europe Fades." *National Interest*, February 14, 2014.

Vondra, Aleksandr. Speech at the Atlantic Council, Washington, DC, May 25, 2010.

Wagener, Martin. "Reliable Kingdom? The USA, Thailand, and the Logic of Bandwagoning." *Journal of Current Southeast Asian Affairs* 28, no. 3 (2009): 39–80.

Wagner, Daniel, and Giorgio Cafiero. "Can Oman and Iran's 'Special' Relationship Last?" Institute for Near East & Gulf Military Analysis, July 29, 2013.

Walt, Stephen M. "Alliances in a Unipolar World." *World Politics* 61, no. 1 (October 2008): 86–120.

———. *Taming American Power*. New York: Norton, 2005.

Waltz, Kenneth. "The Spread of Nuclear Weapons: More May Better." *Adelphi Papers*, no. 171. London: International Institute for Strategic Studies, 1981.

Wandycz, Piotr Stefan. *France and Her Eastern Allies, 1919–1925: French-Czechoslovak-Polish Relations from the Paris Peace Conference to Locarno*. Minneapolis: University of Minnesota Press, 1962.

Watman, Kenneth, Dean Wilkening, Brian Nichiporuk, and John Arquilla. *U.S. Regional Deterrence Strategies*. Santa Monica: RAND Corporation, 1995.

Waxman, Dov. "The Real Problem in U.S.-Israeli Relations." *Washington Quarterly* 35, no. 2 (Spring 2012): 71–87.

Weitz, Richard. "Global Insights: China's Military Buildup Stokes Regional Arms Race." *World Politics Review*, March 16, 2010.

"White House: Obama Tells Rouhani He Sees Way to Resolve Iran Nuclear Issue." *Reuters*, September 18, 2013.

Withnall, Adam. "Crimea Crisis: Putin Adviser Proposes Division of Ukraine along Nazi-Soviet Lines." *Independent*, March 24, 2014.

Wohlforth, William C. "The Perception of Power: Russia in the Pre-1914 Balance." *World Politics* 39, no. 3 (April 1987): 353–81.

Wohlstetter, Albert. "Nuclear Sharing: NATO and the N+1 Country." In *Nuclear Heuristics: Selected Writings of Albert and Roberta Wohlstetter.* Edited by R. Zarate and H. Sokolski, 268–300. Carlisle, PA: Strategic Studies Institute, 2009.

Wolfers, Arnold. "Alliances as a Means of Defense." *Naval War College Review* 7, no. 8 (April 1955): 1–21.

Woodward, C. Vann. "The Age of Reinterpretation." *American Historical Review* 66, no. 1 (October 1969): 1–19.

Wyllie, James H. "NATO's Bleak Future." *Parameters* 28, no. 4 (1998–1999): 113–23.

Yahuda, Michael. "The Evolving Asian Order: The Accommodation of Rising Chinese Power." In *Power Shift: China and Asia's New Dynamics.* Edited by David Shambaugh, 347–62. Berkeley: University of California Press, 2005.

Yep, Eric, and Simon Hall. "Malaysia, China Keep Low Profile on Conflicting Sea Claims." *Wall Street Journal,* June 24, 2014.

Zoppo, C. E. *France as a Nuclear Power.* Santa Monica: RAND Corporation, 1962.

INDEX

Dahiya Doctrine, 92, 95
Dalberg-Acton, John (Lord Acton), 1
de Gaulle, Charles, 23
"defense in depth," 5
Denmark, 100
deterrence, extended, 86; decline/weakening
    of, 23, 78–80, 81, 89; diminishing utility of
    to smaller U.S. allies, 80
Discourses (Machia velli), 55
Donbas, the, 184
Doyle, Michael, 196n18
Drake, Francis, 48–49
drones, 39

East Asia, 5, 41, 62, 97, 181, 182; littoral East
    Asia, 10; self-defeating probes of China in,
    103–6. *See also* United States, similar char-
    acteristics of its frontier allies in East Asia,
    East-Central Europe, and the Middle East
East China Sea, 129, 130
East-Central Europe, 5; Russia's influence
    in Europe's eastern "borderlands," 44. *See
    also* United States, similar characteristics
    of its frontier allies in East Asia, East-
    Central Europe, and the Middle East
Egypt, 98, 107
Elizabeth I (queen of England), 48–49; raid-
    ing probes of Spain during her reign, 50–51
entrapment, 196n23; fear of entrapment by
    stronger allies of the United States, 40–41;
    management by alliances of the twin fears
    of entrapment and abandonment, 54;
    probes arising from a view that entrap-
    ment is the congenital flaw of alliances,
    69–70
"equidistancing," 102
escalation, 69–70, 71, 74
Estonia, 1, 3, 95, 100, 163; increase in defense
    spending of, 87
Estonian National Security Concept (2004),
    90
Eurasia, 18, 23, 119, 144, 188; and the bal-
    ance of power with the United States,
    22; equilibrium of, 27; presence of the
    United States in Eurasian littorals, 5. *See
    also* Spykman, Nicholas: argument of
    for positioning U.S. power closer to key
    theaters of Eurasia
Europe, 18, 31, 44, 58, 65. *See also* Central
    and Eastern Europe (CEE); Central Eu-
    rope; East-Central Europe

"European Balance of Power," 67–68, 70
European Union (EU), 5, 8, 65, 66, 99
exclusive economic zones (EEZs), 180

Ferdinand, Franz, 194n74
Fico, Robert, 110
Finland, 94, 95, 100, 114, 171; attempts to
    obtain long-range strike weapons such as
    JASSM and ATACM tactical missiles, 93;
    offensive military posture and capabilities
    of, 93; possession of F-18 Hornet fighters
    by, 93; universal male conscription in, 93
Foch, Ferdinand, 53
"fog of peace," 75
France, 20, 45, 52, 53, 64, 68, 126, 158; the
    French Fourth Republic, 127; quest of
    to acquire nuclear weapons (the "French
    nuclear temptation"), 22–23, 24; and
    rapprochement with Germany, 67; as a
    valuable ally of the United States, 163–64
Franco-British Entente Cordiale, 67
French Fifth Republic, 22
"frontier problem," the, 52, 196nn17–18

Gaddafi, Muammar, 39
Gallipoli, 141
Gallois, Pierre, 23
Gates, Robert, 30
Gaza, 107
geopolitics, 8; the dangerous contempo-
    rary moment in global geopolitics, 13;
    geopolitical payoffs at the lowest possible
    strategic cost (low-cost revision), 9; geo-
    political pluralism, 21, 126, 127, 163;
    transition in, 42–43
Georgia, war of with Russia, 50, 60, 61, 87, 100
Germany, 4, 8, 10, 14, 64, 67, 102, 126, 128;
    French campaign against (1914), 140;
    imperial Germany's probes of the Anglo-
    French alliance, 51; Nazi Germany, 27; and
    the problem of facing a two-front war, 52;
    the question of U.S. bases in, 29; strategy
    of in the decade prior to World War I, 55;
    view of Great Britain's global influence
    and the "artichoke" policy, 74. *See also*
    Churchill, Winston, on Germany in the
    years prior to World War I; West Germany
Gibraltar, 51, 152
Gilbert, Felix, 25
global powers, and the "periphery or frontier
    problem," 52

wars, 58; and abstractions, 76; danger of
engaging in, 46, 195n8; desire to avoid,
48–49; global war, 61; outcomes of, 45
West Germany, 73
Wohlstetter, Albert, 23
Wolfers, Arnold, 31
World Bank, 148
World War I, 46, 55, 121; "calculated risk"
strategy during, 197n51; French campaign
against Germany during (1914), 140

World War II, 21; argument that U.S. involvement in was unnecessary, 18, 191n3

Yemen, 98
Yom Kippur War (1973), 92
Yugoslavia, 95, 100

Zeman, Milos, 110
Zhengmu Reef incident, 104–5
Zhu Chenghu, 42